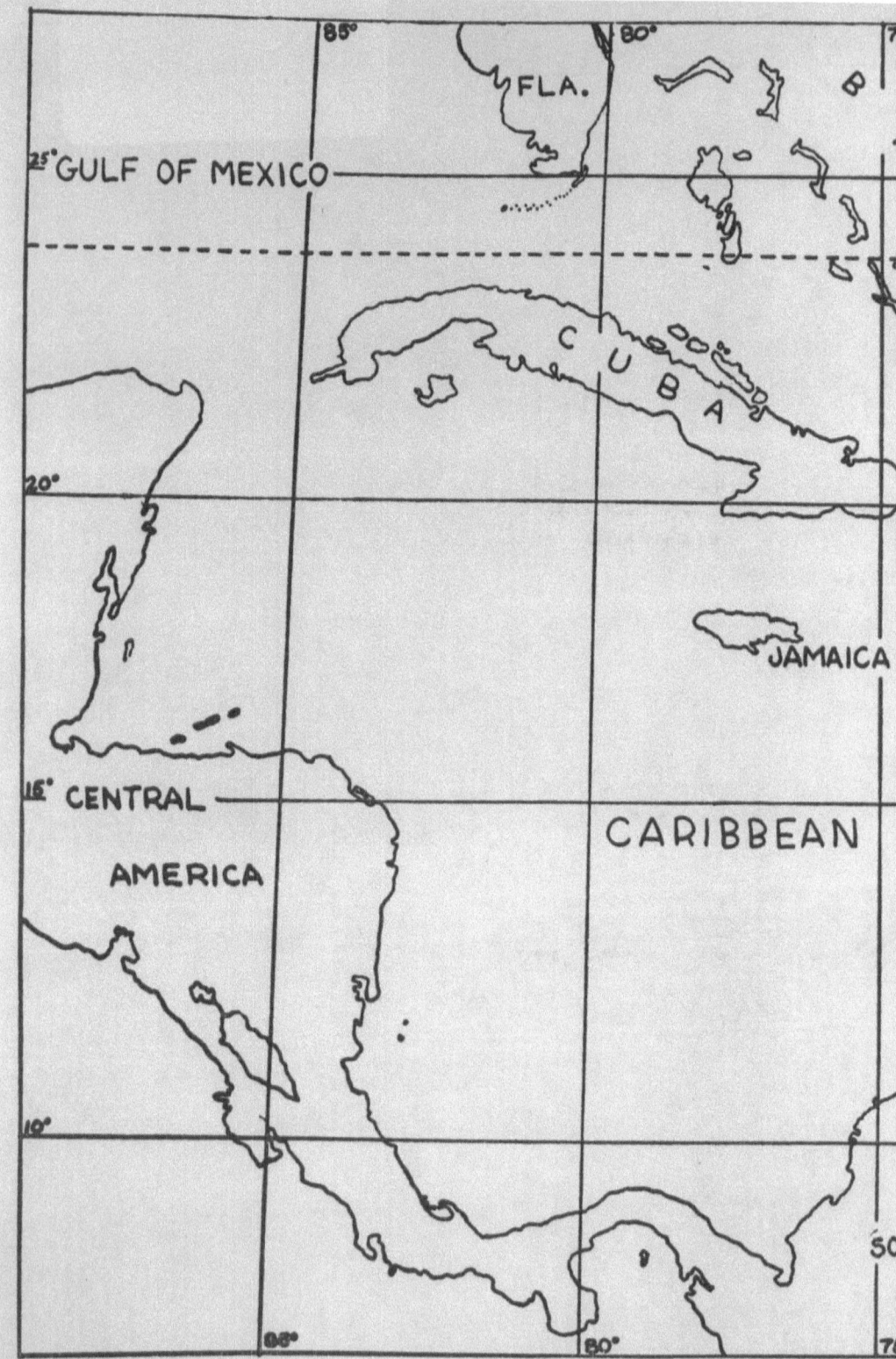

THE LANDS OF THE CARIBBEAN

HISPANIOLA

PUERTO RICO ST. EUSTATIUS ANTIGUA

GUADELOUPE
DOMINICA

MARTINIQUE

BARBADOS

GRENADA

AMERICA

The Campaign for the
Sugar Islands, 1759

The Institute of Early American History and Culture is sponsored jointly by the College of William and Mary and Colonial Williamsburg, Incorporated.

THE CAMPAIGN FOR THE SUGAR ISLANDS, 1759

A Study of Amphibious Warfare

BY MARSHALL SMELSER

FOREWORD BY
SAMUEL ELIOT MORISON

PUBLISHED FOR
The Institute of Early American History and Culture
AT WILLIAMSBURG, VIRGINIA
BY

The University of North Carolina Press · Chapel Hill
1955

COPYRIGHT, 1955
THE UNIVERSITY OF NORTH CAROLINA PRESS

MANUFACTURED IN THE UNITED STATES OF AMERICA
BY THE SEEMAN PRINTERY, INC., DURHAM, N. C.

THIS BOOK WAS DIGITALLY PRINTED.

Foreword

The amphibious is the oldest form of aggressive warfare known to civilized man. Owing to the fiasco at Gallipoli in World War I, amphibious warfare received a bad name; but owing largely to the efforts of the United States Navy and Marine Corps, it was revived, streamlined, and modernized for World War II. And as all of us are now familiar with one or more of the colossal "landings" in North Africa, Sicily, Normandy, the Gilberts, Marshalls, New Guinea, the Philippines and Okinawa, it is interesting to see how such things were done in the eighteenth century.

Dr. Smelser has written a lively account of what is perhaps the most successful amphibious landing in history, between King Agamemnon's at Troy and General Eisenhower's in Normandy. The year 1759, England's *Annus Mirabilis,* was marked by a series of brilliant campaigns in different parts of the world; so many that, as Horace Walpole wrote, "The very bells of London were worn threadbare pealing out victories." Consequently the British operation against Martinique and Guadeloupe has been overlooked.

One is astonished to find that almost all the elements of a modern amphibious operation were there in 1759, although in a primitive or attenuated form. There was naval gunfire support, here rather ineffective against shore batteries; underwater obstacles of up-ended palm logs; flatbottomed landing craft (the LCP of the era) holding sixty-three men, propelled by twelve oars, and requiring about three hours to debark the troops from sailing transports; other landing craft (LCM), constructed on the catamaran principle, for lightering the field artillery ashore; and of course a horrible foul-up on the landing beaches. No D-day could be set, owing to the uncertainties of sailing navigation; the expedition departed from England about three weeks late (Mr. Pitt writing daily to General Hopson inquiring why he had not got off, and the General always wanting a few more men and supplies); and it took the fleet seven weeks and three days to reach its staging point at Barbados.

After an initial check at Martinique, Captain Moore and General Hopson withdrew their troops in good order and took a whack at Guadeloupe. There they established a beachhead very quickly but were thwarted for three months by the local French defenders retiring to the jungle and the mountains. General Hopson and many hundreds of British soldiers and sailors died of tropical fever; and the next in command, General John Barrington, was beginning to consider the painful alternatives of losing his entire force to disease, or retreating altogether, when the inhabitants of Guadeloupe came to his rescue by surrendering the island. A few days later, a relief French naval force showed up and landed reinforcements, much to the embarrassment of the defeated and dispirited inhabitants. Such was amphibious warfare in the days of slow communications and incompetent physicians.

Altogether, this was one of the gayest and most gallant operations of a war which brought England glory, territory—and a colonial revolution.

Samuel Eliot Morison

Cambridge, Massachusetts

Acknowledgments

It is common knowledge that a great debate developed in the Anglo-American world during the latter part of the Seven Years' War on the question whether to keep Canada or Guadeloupe when the peace treaty was written. It is commonly known how the British acquired Canada. But almost no one knows the details of the acquisition of Guadeloupe, nor even the purpose of the campaign, nor the price paid in treasure, blood, and energy, for the place. Standard historians have been almost silent on the subject, except for Lawrence H. Gipson's *The British Empire before the American Revolution,* Volume VIII: *The Great War for the Empire—The Culmination,* recently published. It is the purpose of the present study to make known the details of the campaign among the islands in 1759.

To the foregoing remarks on the obscurity of the campaign one important exception must be made. It is difficult to believe that any better introduction to the history of the time and place and circumstances could be written than has been written by Richard Pares in his *War and Trade in the West Indies, 1739-1763* (Oxford, 1936). He has painted a grand panorama of which this monograph is only a magnified detail; any reader who is also acquainted with Mr. Pares's excellent study will quickly see what a great debt this work owes to his.

This specific campaign has been separately (and briefly) described in English by a military historian and by a naval historian, each emphasizing his special interest. The present essay explains it as an amphibious operation, in as much detail as complete understanding demands. French scholars have presented it as a combined and naval operation but never in more than a few pages. These facts seem to justify offering a relatively long story of a little war. Guadeloupe, a relatively unimportant place in our age (except in strategic considerations) seemed to many men of the eighteenth century equally important with Canada, and they governed their politics accordingly. I think their attitude, and the events it caused, are worth studying for their own sake.

A word on emphasis and methodology might be useful to the reader. The most difficult problem of methodology I met was posed by the voluminous French court-martial record—about forty thousand words—in the Archives Nationales, Marine et Colonies, B⁴ 92. French process admitted hearsay to the record apparently without exception—"ouï dire" occurring on almost every folio page. Cross examination was not practiced. Every deponent was naturally anxious to record his own good conduct and superior judgment and to pin any guilt for the defeat elsewhere. Rather than a trial or inquest in the Anglo-American sense, the inquiry was a duel of reputation versus reputation, using sworn depositions as weapons, at a distance of twelve months. Although the resulting accumulation of unverified (and perhaps spiteful) hearsay may have been of use to the responsible ministers in Paris in a way not obvious to the historian, they are plainly not so weighty by the historian's criteria as the less self-conscious documents on the British side. Hence the narrative that follows is a narrative of events as seen, in most cases, through British eyes, and the French records appear as details incidental to what French witnesses were trying to prove, or as facts where agreement approached unanimity.

Librarians have been very good to me. I wish to mention especially the staffs of the Library of Congress, the Huntington Library, the Widener Library, the University of California Library, the University of Chicago Library, the St. Louis University Library, the Washington University Library, and the University of Notre Dame Library. The archivists of the Public Record Office, the British Museum, the Wisconsin State Historical Society, and the Archives Nationales, were very helpful.

ACKNOWLEDGMENTS

Anna P. Smelser, my wife, has been helpful in too many ways to mention. Majie Padberg Sullivan has searched the Huntington Library for me, with good results. Professor Frank Sullivan, of Loyola University at Los Angeles, was generous with linguistic, geographical, and other assistance. Herbert Coulson, of Ottawa, Canada, assisted me with his first hand knowledge of British military and naval organization. Walter Muir Whitehill, as editor of *The American Neptune* in which preliminary studies appeared, gave encouragement to finish the work. Professor James Corbett of the University of Notre Dame gave technical help when much needed. The Reverend Thomas T. McAvoy, C.S.C., Head of the Department of History, University of Notre Dame, secured a leave of absence for me in the final stages of the work. Professor Samuel Eliot Morison, of Harvard University, was of greatest help in matters bibliographical, geographical, nautical, and historical; at the beginning of the study he provided stimulus and advice. Publication has been made possible by a subvention from the University of Notre Dame, to whom I am profoundly grateful, for payment of a portion of the manufacturing cost.

For permission to quote from *John Brown's Body*, Rinehart & Company, Copyright, 1927, 1928, by Stephen Vincent Benét, I am indebted to Mrs. Benét and Brandt & Brandt of New York City.

MARSHALL SMELSER

South Bend, Indiana, October 1954.

Contents

	PAGE
FOREWORD BY SAMUEL ELIOT MORISON	v
ACKNOWLEDGMENTS	vii

I. THE CONTENTIOUS EMPIRES
1. The age of power 3
2. The economics of colonialism 5
3. The North American impasse 9
4. To war 10

II. DESIGN FOR FIGHTING
1. The purposes of the campaign 13
2. The force and its matériel 16

III. TRADE-WIND PASSAGE
1. Departure 28
2. Rendezvous 34

IV. INHOSPITABLE MARTINIQUE
1. A Fort Royale reception 39
2. Withdrawal from Fort Royale Bay 51
3. A look into St. Pierre 59

V. GUADELOUPE: BASSE TERRE
1. The island of Guadeloupe 70
2. The bombardment of Basse Terre 75
3. Hopson's choice: To do nothing 90
4. The Marines and the Black Watch at Fort Louis 102
5. Barrington, commander in chief 105

VI. GUADELOUPE: GRAND TERRE
1. The fleet withdraws 113
2. Grand Terre disorganized 120

VII. GUADELOUPE: CAPESTERRE
1. Clavering's advance 127
2. Armistice and capitulation 138
3. Beauharnois achieves an anticlimax 143

VIII. CONSOLIDATION
1. Loose ends 148
2. Consolidation and departure 154
3. "The Recompence of Virtue" 161

IX. THE CAMPAIGN AS A WORK OF ART
1. The British exercise of command 163
2. The defense of the islands 174
3. Significance 181

APPENDIX 186

BIBLIOGRAPHICAL NOTE 199

INDEX 203

The Campaign for the
Sugar Islands, 1759

I.

The Contentious Empires

1. *The age of power*

Before the founding of the United States, the five westernmost kingdoms of Europe were drawn irresistibly to the new world of the Americas. From the late Middle Ages they had been in a state of almost chronic contention over religion and over the merits and territorial claims of their several royal families. The revelations of Columbus and his immediate successors made America's affairs immediately the business of European governments and, in time, complicated the existing struggles by adding a new imperialism as an ingredient of the quarrels.[1]

Although the British people came late in the new field, by the seventeenth century they too were deeply involved in the race for dominion and profit in the new world. As decades passed, a sort of elimination tournament brought two nations ever closer to a final contest: Great Britain and France.[2] At the beginning of the eighteenth century it was clear that Spain, Portugal, and the Netherlands had failed to continue their imperial growth and were hardly able to defend what they had, because of a lack of industrial and naval strength.[3] Thus the rivalry of Great Britain and France became the most conspicuous fact of international relations in the first half of the eighteenth century.[4] The empires

---

1. John R. Seeley, *The Expansion of England* (London, 1891), 98-107.
2. Charles M. Andrews, *The Colonial Period of American History* (New Haven, 1934-38), IV, 5-7.
3. Walter L. Dorn, *Competition for Empire, 1740-1763* (New York, 1940), 251.
4. Charles M. Andrews, "Anglo-French Commercial Rivalry, 1700-1750," *American Historical Review*, 20 (1914-15), 539-556, 761-780.

of the rivals were alike only in external appearance. Actually they were much different. The British empire had been built piecemeal by the expansion of a relatively free society and became a collection of thirty-one relatively well-to-do free provinces, while the French empire was unskillfully but minutely regulated from France.[5]

Because religion was no longer the moving force of politics, and liberalism had not yet become its dynamo, the age of Anglo-French imperial rivalry was an age of power politics, pure and simple. The coexistence of national states competing for territory, for power, and for treasure, brought almost continuous war between powers unable to reduce each other to permanent inferiority. In that deadlock they sought a "balance of power," which is to say they hoped to reform the anarchy of international society by balancing the competitive ambitions of the members. But the many wars brought no steady balance; after all, the notion of preserving a balance of power could easily be used as a cover for aggression.[6]

Personally, the policy makers of Europe saw no benefit to them in permanent peace. The continental nobility provided both the diplomatic corps and the military leaders. They had an ancient tradition of personal advancement and fame achieved in warfare. Their monarchs also found victory in battle useful to add luster to crowns. As Walter L. Dorn well said, the recent tendency of historians to minimize war leads them to forget that "war itself became a basic ingredient of European civilization."[7]

Unlike the continental nobility, the British aristocracy was not a self-conscious military aristocracy separate from the other social elements of national leadership. On the contrary, the landed lords and the merchant princes were closely allied by marriage, by social imitation, and by investment.[8] This was an alliance of agriculture and commerce, with commerce being the dynamic partner. Com-

---

5. Dorn, *Competition for Empire*, 257-267; Lawrence H. Gipson, *The British Empire before the American Revolution* (Caldwell, Idaho, and New York, 1936-), I, 3-4, 8, 8n. Of the British colonies, twenty-one had representative governments.
6. Dorn, *Competition for Empire*, 1-3.
7. *Ibid.*, 5, 12. 8. *Ibid.*, 8.

merce generally favors peace, but Britain was at once commercial and warlike, for commercial men were willing to accept war as part of policy if they were excluded from a field of great promise by some unfriendly foreign government.[9]

In the British Parliament the businessmen, unlike their French commercial rivals, could force the direction of national policy,[10] and they did so in the eighteenth century. French and British imperial competition was therefore a struggle of the French aristocratic and dynastic ambitions, centered on the goals of glory, splendor, and dynastic security, against the British desire to expand the sources of supply, and to find markets to which their productive and growing factories could send their products.

The policy of the British leaders was strengthened by the theory that a nation could only increase its commerce at the expense of the commerce of another nation.[11] If the idea is correct, a nation's prosperity is best measured by the poverty of its rivals. Jean Colbert, the seventeenth-century French statesman, thought the same,[12] but the belief did not appear to govern French policy in the following century. Nevertheless, to some observers, even in France, every nation seemed to get rich by war (except the losers).[13]

Britain and France, poised in precarious balance in the eighteenth century, found themselves pursuing very similar policies for different reasons, the British seeking commercial gain for its own sake, the French hunting profits as a means to strengthen France for reasons of dynastic grandeur, and to fulfill the ambitions of an aristocracy, in short, to get power for power's sake. In both states politics and economic policy were fused[14] and directed toward empire.

2. *The economics of colonialism*

The French and British colonies were closely woven into the fabric of their national economies. Much of the prosperity

9. Seeley, *Expansion of England*, 109-118.
10. Dorn, *Competition for Empire*, 6-7.   11. *Ibid.*, 8-9.
12. Arthur J. Grant, "The Government of Louis XIV," in *Cambridge Modern History* (London, 1902-29), V, 6-7.
13. Dorn, *Competition for Empire*, 10.
14. *Ibid.*, 9.

of both nations was derived from their colonies, and their merchants and politicians knew it.[15] The French had a real fear that British competition would be made worse at any time by military action,[16] while the British colonists and traders were persuaded to tolerate some degree of governmental control by fear that otherwise France would win out. They saw the French as the prime military power of the world, with a population thrice as great as their own, and a dangerous business competitor in many places because of subsidies, fine workmanship, and low labor costs. If the day should ever come when they could weave wool as well as they raised sugar cane, cured codfish, and made hats, England's basic industry would collapse.[17] The interests of France and Britain collided in four remote quarters of the world, North America, the West Indies, Africa, and India. They were militant rivals in several essential commodities, among them Negroes, sugar, and furs. When "special interests" asked the help of their governments, war could easily follow.[18]

A competition most provocative of complaints occurred in the West Indies where the provision and lumber trade of North America and the slave trade of West Africa converged to support rival sugar plantations. The French sugar islands showed greater profits than did the British, largely, it was thought, because of a lively illegal traffic between British North America and the French West Indies, a trade which seemed a very natural arrangement to those concerned in it.[19] The French West Indies were "the richest colonies in the world."[20] Their golden age began at the end of the seventeenth century when French planters switched to sugar cane and began to undersell the British West Indies, just as the British had previously undersold the original sugar planters of the new world, in Brazil. The British West Indian nabobs would have foundered except for the steady expansion of the English domestic market which they monopolized by act of Parliament.[21]

15. *Ibid.*, 252-257.   16. Gipson, *British Empire*, IV, 6-8.
17. *Ibid.*, III, 288-289.
18. Dorn, *Competition for Empire*, 251-252.
19. *Ibid.*, 268-272.   20. *Ibid.*, 115.
21. Gipson, *British Empire*, II, 288-290.

There was no question whether the British would let their Caribbean colonies fail. They must survive. Jamaica alone bought almost as much of English manufactures as Virginia and Maryland combined, and more than any two other colonies of the empire.[22] It was thought that the illegal trade with North America which was carried on by the French islands was a positive danger to a great asset, and complaints were numerous[23] that Americans refused to buy British molasses while consuming a large quantity of French molasses. If the French continued to produce a greater quantity of sugar and to corner the continental European market, as they had done by the aid of their government and the help of Yankee smugglers, the British West Indies might be ruined.[24] It was alleged that the close connection of New England skippers and French planters was deliberately fostered by the French government, in order to hurt the British sugar industry.[25] Plainly the economic interests of British colonists in North America and in the Caribbean were not the same. The French sugar growers had a cheaper supply of labor, greater resources of soil, and a large annual supply of molasses which was barred from France in order to protect the brandy makers but which found a ready market in British North America. From the buyers they received food for their slaves, lumber, and other necessaries.[26] This trade could hardly be broken up by the British government except by severe restrictive action. Such severity seemed, in the 1750's, politically unfeasible.

French competition also brought the slave trade to a crisis. By the 1750's the British slavers seemed to face bankruptcy. If they abandoned their West African stations, the West Indies would have a desperate labor shortage since the life expectancy of a West Indian slave was but seven years. From the British point of view the trouble with the West Indian slave traffic was that the French government subsidized their slave traders, and by various aids and credits made it easier for planters to buy land and slaves. Because of government help and a greater volume of sales the

22. *Ibid.*, I, 63-64. Jamaica's governor was the second best paid overseas official. *Ibid.*, II, 228, 229n.
23. *Ibid.*, II, 299-301. 24. *Ibid.*, II, 257.
25. *Ibid.*, III, 61. 26. *Ibid.*, III, 291-293.

French were able to outbid the British on keenly competitive sections of the African coast and, conversely, by unified policy were able to drive purchase prices down wherever the British did not appear. A reorganization of the British trade, by Parliamentary action in 1750, staved off ruin but did not give superiority over the French. The admission of all traders to a regulated company on payment of a forty shilling fee merely marshaled them in a united front and made them strong enough to compete on more nearly equal terms.[27]

Another grievance of British subjects was French supremacy in the European hat trade. During the War of the Spanish Succession the French controlled the beaver catch of Hudson Bay, and their hat makers were never outdone after that. Because of better workmanship French makers sold hats of beaver felt to all of Europe and British hatters were idle. The Hudson's Bay Company, which exploited northern Canada, did not suffer since it reexported its bales of pelts to France at a higher price than British buyers could pay. Only the hatters suffered. The British fur traders generally did better than their French competitors in America because they could offer higher prices and had more of the goods the Indian trappers wanted[28]—particularly rum, like as not made in Rhode Island from French West Indian molasses.

Fish dealers were also pained by French competition. By the Treaty of Utrecht the French could use the northern shores of Newfoundland to cure their cod by drying. This was an advantage because that coast is less humid than the southern side where the British fishers dried their catch. British cod, poorly cured, lost ground in the world market.[29]

In another area Anglo-French feelings were heated. The British East India Company had factories from St. Helena to Borneo, from which its officials uneasily watched the rising power and prosperity of French far eastern trade. The officers of the East India Company do not seem to have intended to found an empire, but in the end they and their rivals came to strife in efforts to eliminate each other as dangerous competitors.[30]

27. *Ibid.*, II, 294-295, 327, 329-334.
28. *Ibid.*, III, 240-243, 242n., 247-248; V, 63.
29. *Ibid.*, III, 250-251.   30. *Ibid.*, V, 260, 296-297.

3. The North American impasse

The idea that the French were trying to encircle Britain's American colonies was strongly believed by the middle of the eighteenth century. "Encirclement" was not an official policy of the French government but was made in America where local administrators, in an astonishingly swift advance, had linked the St. Lawrence, the Great Lakes, and the Mississippi River system within 110 years of the founding of Jamestown. This linkage was practically complete at a time when Georgia had not yet been founded. While responsible Englishmen were worried about encirclement by their rivals, the French feared that the British would divide Canada and Louisiana and conquer each separately.[31] Knowing that Canada was a drain and not a fountain of wealth,[32] the French motive for defending Canada and underwriting its continuous deficits was political. They hoped the maintenance of Canada as an outpost of France would distract Britain from affairs on the continent of Europe, and when they found it difficult to feed their Canadian garrison, they went so far as to encourage a trade in provisions from New England to Cape Breton Island.[33]

The precise boundaries of French and British America had been long disputed. Each side made demands impossible for the other to accept and during forty years of assertion the disagreements had hardened beyond the possibility of reasonable compromise.[34] While the French were setting up their western chain of posts some English officials thought of doing the same. Said Governor Alexander Spotswood of Virginia, in 1716, "We should attempt to make some settlements on the lakes, and at the same time possess ourselves of those passes of the great mountains, which are necessary to preserve a communication with such settlements."[35]

31. Douglas S. Freeman, *George Washington, A Biography* (New York, 1948-1954), I, 270.
32. Gipson, "The American Revolution as an Aftermath of the Great War for Empire," *Political Science Quarterly*, 65 (1950), 90.
33. Gipson, *British Empire*, V, 33.
34. George M. Wrong, *The Conquest of New France* (New Haven, 1921).
35. Albert P. Brigham, *Geographic Influences in American History* (Boston, 1904), 89.

This would have divided Canada and Louisiana, but, lacking such posts (except for Oswego) the British leaned heavily on an alliance with the Iroquois to shield them from French forays. By mid-century that alliance had weakened. The Iroquois were beginning to compare the disunity of the British colonies with the unity of French policy and were uneasy.[36] In 1754 an attempt at an Albany congress of representatives of the northern colonies to repair this Anglo-Iroquois bond by founding a colonial union failed,[37] although the Iroquois were somewhat mollified by attention to certain of their specific grievances.

This new world maneuvering reflected a feeling in Europe that the balance of power depended for stability upon a balance of colonial power. To the French it seemed that Britain was determined to upset the balance. The upper valley of the Ohio River was a point of collision and British interest in that region seemed indicative of "vast designs on the whole of America."[38]

4. To war

France and Britain were at war in over 50 of 126 years after 1689, a period sometimes called "The Second Hundred Years War." Of course, not all of these wars had identical causes, but their results, before 1815, may be stated generally as the temporary reestablishment of a delicate and easily disturbed balance of power. In this violent relationship the British seem generally to have been guided in their diplomacy by two principles, first, opposition to French domination of the continent of Europe as a danger to the security of the British Isles, and, second, opposition to the consolidation of the French and Spanish empires, which would put in hazard Britain's overseas possessions.[39]

The indecisive War of the League of Augsburg (1689-1699)—known in America as King William's War—was shortly followed by the War of the Spanish Succession (1701-1714)—Queen Anne's

36. Gipson, *British Empire*, V, 110.
37. *Ibid.*, V, 113-142.
38. Max Savelle, "The American Balance of Power and European Diplomacy, 1713-1778," in Richard B. Morris, ed., *The Era of the American Revolution: Studies Inscribed to Evarts Boutell Greene* (New York, 1939), 157-62.
39. Gipson, "The Art of Preserving an Empire," *William and Mary Quarterly*, 3d ser., 2 (1945), 407.

War. These wars were fought to prevent the expansion of continental France, and to prevent the union of the French and Spanish crowns on one head. The problems were temporarily solved by the Treaty of Utrecht which established a three-fold balance, separating the crowns of France and Spain, guaranteeing the unhappily vague American territorial boundaries as of the reign of the English King Charles II, and establishing a legal but very limited British trade with Spanish America. The balance soon began to teeter dangerously as the legal trade was used as a curtain for illegal trade.[40] For the next thirty-five years European foreign offices concentrated on attempts to frustrate real or fancied disturbances of the balance by colonial expansion, an expansion of Europe which could hardly be prevented under the circumstances. Great Britain was seen to be the most dynamic and the most dangerous to the balance, and in time British leaders deliberately upset the balance, bringing on the war with Spain called the War of Jenkins' Ear (1739)[41] which was soon merged with the War of the Austrian Succession (1744-1748)—King George's War. The economic clashes of the rival empires, and the parallel dynastic rivalries which are usefully revealed by the "double names" of this series of wars, effectively make clear the way in which dynastic and economic ambitions were intertwined in the making of policy.[42] When the War of the Austrian Succession came to an end, its Treaty of Aix-la-Chapelle marked only the peace of exhaustion.

Vital issues were left still unsettled. None of the economic pressures of the bitter rivalry had been relaxed, few of the essential political difficulties had been resolved so far as overseas affairs were concerned. After 1748 a common French simile was "bête comme la paix."[43] It is only fair to say that each side wished for peace, but they wished for more than peace with honor; they wanted peace with prestige and profits. When prestige seemed necessarily to require domination of North America there was no

---

40. Savelle, "The American Balance of Power," 141-143.
41. *Ibid.*, 143-157.
42. Dorn, *Competition for Empire*, 122.
43. Freeman, *Washington*, I, 270.

restraining the warriors.⁴⁴ The best that can be said of the situation after 1748 was that war was not quite inevitable. Commissioners met at Paris to negotiate but, again, impossible proposals were made and peace was not made.⁴⁵

The tensions mounted. Jamaica merchants had profited sixty thousand pounds per annum from legal trade with Spanish America, plus an untold amount from illegal trade with Spaniards anxious to escape the excessive mark-ups of Spanish legal monopolists. After 1748 all of that business was lost except the slave trade, and its troubles have already been described. When the Jamaicans complained, their government took them seriously.⁴⁶ War almost started on the west coast of Africa in 1752 when a British naval officer ordered a French squadron away from Anamaboe on the Gold Coast, but the war was postponed when the French chose to obey.⁴⁷ In the West Indies the question of the so-called "neutral islands" caused dissatisfactions. St. Lucia, St. Vincent, Dominica, and Tobago had been declared "neutral," although the commissions of the governors of the British colony of Barbados traditionally included jurisdiction over all of them but Tobago. The actual settlers, although few, were mostly French. British officials found the status of the "neutral" islands intolerable because they were dens of smugglers and, in war, could be privateer bases.⁴⁸ In North America both powers were closing in on the headwaters of the Ohio. The governor of Canada formally claimed the area in 1749, and, at the same time, the British crown chartered a land company with a tentative grant there. In 1752 the Canadians began to fortify the region and Virginia sent a promising young militia officer, George Washington, to protest. In 1754 Washington was sent back with an armed force. There was a border skirmish, a wilderness siege, a French victory, and another world war had started. That it had started in North America is an accident. It might just as easily have started at, say, Anamaboe or St. Lucia.

44. Gipson, *British Empire*, V, 350-351.
45. *Ibid.*, V, 351-352; Gipson, "A French Project of Victory Short of a Declaration of War, 1755," *Canadian Historical Review*, 25 (1945), 361-371.
46. Gipson, *British Empire*, II, 231, 234.   47. *Ibid.*, II, 342.
48. *Ibid.*, II, 260; Dorn, *Competition for Empire*, 272.

II.

Design for Fighting

---

1. *The purposes of the campaign*

Until 1758 the Seven Years' War went against Britain and her allies. The great Frederick had held his own—more or less—against Austrian, French, Russian, Swedish, and Saxon soldiery who lacked only ability to combine their strength in order to annihilate his armies and to gut Prussia. But the British record was not so good. In America the frontier affairs involving Fort Duquesne, Braddock's destruction, the repulses at Niagara, Crown Point, and Louisbourg, the losses of Oswego and Fort William Henry—none of these things was the sort to be commemorated on a regimental flag. In the Mediterranean a British squadron came off second best, Minorca lay in the shadow of the lazily flapping lily flag of France, and Admiral John Byng was shot—rightly or wrongly—for the disgrace. On the continent the Duke of Cumberland's convention of Kloster Seven had surrendered Hanover to the French. Through 1758 the only bright days were those which saw the unusual activities of Robert Clive, "Hero of Arcot," William Pitt's "heaven-born general," who distinguished himself by barely credible military feats at Calcutta and Plassey; also, in America, the ex-physician General John Forbes put on his dogged march to Fort Duquesne and changed its name to Fort Pitt, while, farther north, Louisbourg was captured on the second try.

The British bungling, from 1754 to 1758, is usually and perhaps unfairly attributed to the incompetence of Thomas Pelham Holles, Duke of Newcastle, who was so preoccupied with parliament-bribing and with administrative detail that he had no time for a war even if he had known how to direct one. William Pitt, "this amazing constellation of success" with the eye which "would cut a diamond," the boy patriot of Walpole's day, was Newcastle's opposite number. Honest and self-confident (or vain), precise and able (or extravagant), he led the opposition to Newcastle's conduct of the disaster and ultimately won the support of public opinion for his ideas, or, rather, the opinion of that portion of the public which counted. But Newcastle controlled Parliament while Pitt was leading public opinion. Neither could move without the other. They joined forces in 1757. As Professor Dorn said, "Pitt had become inevitable." Together they produced what was one of the most successful governments in English history.[1]

Pitt had said, "I know that I can save England, and that no one else can." The English believed it. And it was probably true. In the end, Pitt's policies, or the men he chose, brought a brilliant procession of victories: Fort Duquesne, Louisbourg, Goree, Guadeloupe, Quebec, Quiberon, Martinique, Montreal, Havana, Manila. There were other victories in India at Masulipatam, Wanderwash, and Pondicherry, but they probably could have been won by Clive no matter what government ruled at home.

This book is concerned with one of these Pitt-motivated victories: Guadeloupe.

The West Indian actions of 1759 were fought for a new kind of objective in the Seven Years' War. Earlier captains had sought to destroy commerce in those waters, but the conquest of territory was the aim of this expedition. Yet conquest of territory was not the ultimate end. Rather, this was an eccentric attack,[2] a large raid for the purpose of acquiring a definite place and holding it as a permanent diversion and annoyance. Pitt wanted Minorca

---

1. Dorn, *Competition for Empire*, 345, 346. By moving his cross-section date to the end of 1758, Lawrence Henry Gipson can quite properly begin his discussion of the subject with the sentence "As the year 1758 came to its close, the British at home and overseas could look at the balance sheet of successes and reverses with a good deal of satisfaction." Gipson, *British Empire*, VII, 287. But the situation early in 1758 was not at all cheering.

2. On raids, eccentric attacks, and true invasions, see Appendix, Topic 1. An analysis of these problems will also be found in Sir Julian Corbett, *England in the Seven Years' War* (London, 1907), I, 206-209.

back under the Union Jack for reason of long-range imperial policy, the Mediterranean Sea being the "old womb of Empire." Under the circumstances it seemed easier to retrieve Minorca by conquering Martinique (or Guadeloupe) than by a direct attack on the Mediterranean island.[3] As the territorial balance sheet stood at this stage of the war, Britain would have to give back Louisbourg at the table of any possible peace meeting in order to own Minorca once more. But Martinique (or Guadeloupe) would make excellent trading stock and, once it was British, it ought to be possible to trade it for Minorca and keep Louisbourg as a permanently valuable skeleton key to the St. Lawrence gateway.[4] Martinique would be sorely wanted by the French: it was an invaluable French base for developing the line of passage to the St. Lawrence and Mississippi valleys, its capture would give the British the best possible defense of a most valuable seaborne trade for the duration of the war, and the loss of its wealth would be a painful blow to an important French financial plexus. (At least 1400 English merchantmen were taken in the West Indies in this war, most of them by privateers based on Martinique.)[5]

Once started on this line of policy, the British took all of the French Windward Islands and annexed all of the ownerless "neu-

    3. The anonymous compiler of the frequently inaccurate *Historische-geographische Beschreibung der in diesem Krieg von der Englandern eroberten franzosischen Antillischen Inseln* (Stuttgart, 1762)—hereafter cited as *Antillischen Inseln*—has on pages 56-57 an unsupported account of the genesis of the plan to conquer Martinique: Captain Molyneaux Shuldham, taken captive by the French, was carried into Martinique where he was allowed to move freely. Observing the fortifications he devised a plan which he communicated to Moore, naval commander on that station, who packed Shuldham home to Pitt after an exchange of prisoners. The only scrap of evidence to support this is the fact that he was taken in the *Warwick*, 60, near Martinique, by three French men-of-war, in 1756, and was returned in a cartel in 1758.
    J. K. Laughton in his excellent article on Shuldham in the *Dictionary of National Biography* makes no mention of this interesting, if true, origin of the plan to take the French island. Of course Captain Shuldham was a naval officer and would pick up what intelligence he could while a prisoner; it would be mere routine to consult him when laying the plan for the attack on Martinique. On Shuldham, see note on page 34.
    4. Professor Dorn thought Pitt wanted the island for outright annexation. Having read Beckford's and Newcastle's memoranda I am forced to disagree. Dorn, *Competition for Empire*, 362.
    5. Corbett, *England in the Seven Years' War*, I, 375-376; J. K. Eyre, Jr., "The Naval History of Martinique," U. S. Naval Institute, *Proceedings*, 68 (Aug. 1942), 1115-1124.

tral" islands in those waters.⁶ Ordinarily the British West Indian nabobs wanted no more sugar competition in the empire, but the war had entered the stage of collecting chips to cash at the treaty board, and Pitt's West Indian friend, William Beckford, London merchant and M.P., was the one who suggested the desirability of a Martinique-for-Minorca deal.⁷ It might be thought that Pitt would wait until all of Canada was conquered but he knew that to attack in two places at once would disorganize the defense of the French empire. Holding Louisbourg as he did, Pitt thought the conquest of Canada could be postponed indefinitely without loss. Further, he did not think the annexation of Canada was a necessary part of the future peace; what he wished in America was a good military frontier.⁸ This would not necessarily include Canada.

2. *The force and its matériel*

On 17 August 1758 London heard of the fall of Louisbourg. How could this advantage be exploited? In a game of skill and chance, which is a cold-blooded description of war, one needs occasionally to look at the score and reform one's policy. Pitt did so. France was almost beaten off the seas, and a strong French faction wished to concentrate their war effort on land—that is, in Germany. Pitt and Newcastle knew this attitude because they had spies in or very near the French ministry. The land forces of England and her continental allies were in fairly good condition

---

6. The "neutral" islands were left outside the jurisdiction of any nation by the Treaty of Aix-la-Chapelle, 1748. Dominica, to the north of Martinique, and St. Lucia, to the south, were "neutral" islands, although the alleged neutrality was only a public fiction, since the inhabitants usually acknowledged Louis XV.

7. Professor Dorn thought the expedition may have been in the nature of a favor to Beckford, since the French West Indies "were inconvenient rivals of his own estates." *Competition for Empire,* 348. Beckford, who owned much property in Jamaica and who knew the West Indies well, was in Pitt's confidence. He told Pitt of the wealth of the French islands, of their need to import food, and of their political discontents. He may also have provided the topographical and meteorological information needed for planning. A. von Ruville, *William Pitt* (London, 1907), II, 221-224.

8. Richard Pares, *War and Trade in the West Indies* (Oxford, 1936), 185-186. The war had started in the Leeward Islands in 1755 when, the governor of Martinique having taken possession of the so-called "neutral" island of St. Lucia, the British commander on the Leeward Islands station, Thomas Frankland, ordered his ship commanders "to take & detain all such French ships as they shoud [*sic*] meet with." Frankland to Clevland, Nov. 4, 1755, Admiralty 1/306.

and position. From the sea, Richard, Earl Howe and Lieutenant General Thomas Bligh had captured, destroyed, and abandoned Cherbourg, an expensive job, but a great stimulant to the morale of the invasion-fearing public. Late in August Newcastle said he opposed sending men for such purposes as the Cherbourg raid but thought instead three thousand men could well be assigned to America to repair losses there. He thought—his thinking had been a pastime frequently dangerous to England—Louisbourg's fall would cause France to sue for peace, and England's financial tension would require her to accept some sort of peace, perhaps a trade of Louisbourg for Minorca and for a non-French Flanders. Therefore he wanted to destroy Louisbourg while there was time for it. But, he complained, the King and others wanted to keep the Canadian bastion and conquer the whole of Canada. To his surprise he learned in the first week of September that Pitt and John Clevland, Secretary of the Admiralty, were working on a plan to conquer Martinique. He hesitantly admitted this would wound French trade but he was continually worried. Petitions for the retention of Louisbourg were coming in, and the northern industrialists, of whom he stood in awe, wanted the Canadian fort for two reasons: Louisbourg was the focal point of North Atlantic privateer infection, and Canada promised to develop into a market for the midlands' "cheap tin trays." A better judge of military matters than Newcastle also disliked Pitt's plan. Over at the Admiralty George, Lord Anson had his doubts. To win Anson, Pitt gave up all projects except two that Anson approved: that against French Africa, and the foray against Martinique.[9]

This miasma of skepticism undoubtedly floated in through the doors of the London clubs, for that Boswell of the the capital's waggle-tongues, Horace Walpole, wrote, "Martinico is the general notion; a place the strongest in the world with a garrison of ten thousand men. Others now talk of Guadeloupe, almost as strong and of much less consequence. Of both, everybody that knows, despairs."[10]

9. Corbett, *England in the Seven Years' War*, I, 371-374.
10. Horace Walpole, *Letters*, Peter Cunningham, ed. (London, 1857-59), III, 182; cited in Gertrude Selwyn Kimball, ed., *Correspondence of William Pitt, When Secretary of State* (New York, 1906), I, xlvi-xlvii. Hereafter noted as Pitt, *Correspondence*.

The small professional army of the empire during the years of Pitt's tenure as "His Majesty's Principall Secretary at State" was reorganized and strengthened.[11] As soon as Pitt took office he began to reform the establishment. In November and December of 1756 fifteen regiments had been reinforced by adding a second battalion to each. In 1758 Pitt formed ten of these battalions into new regiments.[12]

The manpower of the armed forces of the empire in 1758, including thirty thousand American provincials, fifty-two thousand continental allies, and twenty thousand dock artificers, consisted of more than a quarter of a million men, a third of whom were serving with the Royal Navy. The soldiers were dispersed in India, the West Indies, North America, Gibraltar, and the British Isles. Fifty-five thousand of them were on the home establishment (including artillerymen). Any men Pitt could use for his campaign against the French West Indies would have to come from the West Indian garrison (two thousand men) or from the home establishment. But the British force in the West Indies was hardly a trustworthy unit. Because of the idea that garrisons were immovable, the Thirty-eighth Foot had been in the Leeward Islands, unrelieved for sixty years. It was in miserable condition, only about forty percent effective, ragged, hatless, barefoot, without cartouches and swordless.[13] How much Pitt knew about this ragged regiment is unrecorded, but he never counted on it for more than incidental assistance. The Leeward Islands expeditionary force had the help of a detachment from the Thirty-eighth and a few local volunteers but most of the work was done by Englishmen unused to the tropics.

11. Chapter III of Dorn's *Competition for Empire* gives an excellent account of eighteenth-century military thought and practice.
12. The regiments which were strengthened are shown in the following list, with the new regimental numbers of 1758 shown in parentheses. The information is from Sir John Fortescue, *History of the British Army* (London, 1899-1930), II, 299-300, 299n.-300n. Hereafter cited as Fortescue, *British Army*.

3d (61st)	19th (66th)	32d
4th (62d)	20th (67th)	33d
8th (63d)	23d (68th)	34th
11th (64th)	24th (69th)	36th
12th (65th)	31st (70th)	37th

13. Fortescue, *British Army*, II, 42, 565; *Gentleman's Magazine*, 28 (1758), 254.

DESIGN FOR FIGHTING

In his selection of a commander of the land forces Pitt was overruled by the King. Pitt wanted John Barrington, colonel of the new Sixty-fourth Regiment, to head the army of the tropics.[14] When Pitt carried a list of names to the King, Major General Peregrine Thomas Hopson was selected, probably because the King distrusted younger men.[15] According to Walpole this choice was "not consonant to Mr. Pitt's practice, who, considering that our ancient officers had grown old on a very small portion of experience, which by no means compensated for the decay of fire and vigour, chose to trust his plans to the alertness and hopes of younger men."[16] Hopson accepted the post much as St. Joan accepted the stake and faggots—as a martyrdom for God, for King, and for country. Pitt got Barrington, with local rank overseas as a major general, for second-in-command.[17] As will be made plain, the presence of Barrington in the force can only be explained as part of the standing luck of the British Army.

General Hopson had been commander at Louisbourg when it was restored to the French by the Treaty of Aix-la-Chapelle. He was governor of Nova Scotia in the years 1752-1753 and was promoted major general in 1757.[18] Old but inexperienced, thorough rather than active, he was appointed to command the land forces of the expedition to the West Indies in October, 1758.

For commander of the naval forces Pitt and his king agreed to appoint the senior officer on the Leeward Islands station, Captain John Moore, whose chief impress on history before 1758 had been made as a member of the court-martial which tried Admiral Byng. Along with Augustus Keppel and another captain he had petitioned the throne to show mercy toward Byng.[19] Moore, born in 1718, was the third son of Henry Moore, D.D., rector of Malpas,

---

14. Walpole observed, perhaps truthfully, that Pitt also wished to use Major General John Moyston, groom of the bedchamber, but Moyston declined because he was not fitted for the job. Horace Walpole, *Memoirs of the Reign of King George the Second*, Lord Holland, ed. (London, 1846), III, 170, 170n. Hereafter cited as Walpole, *Memoirs*.

15. Corbett, *England in the Seven Years' War*, I, 376-377.

16. Walpole, *Memoirs*, III, 171.

17. Corbett, *England in the Seven Years' War*, I, 376-377.

18. Pitt, *Correspondence*, I, 24n., in which the editor cited Akins' edition of *Nova Scotia Documents*, 671.

19. Walpole, *Memoirs*, II, 318.

in Cheshire, a younger son of Henry, third earl of Drogheda. After a grammar school education he probably entered active service with the Royal Navy aboard the *Diamond,* under Anson, in 1731. He learned seamanship and war under Anson and Edward Hawke, good masters of those arts. His first command was the *Diamond,* in 1743. His main distinction in the service before the insular campaign of 1759 was under Hawke in the action of 14 October 1747, when his energy as commander of the *Devonshire* caused him to be chosen to take dispatches to London. Moore commanded the *William and Mary* yacht during the peace, and when the Seven Years' War began he was posted to the *Devonshire* again in time to serve on the court which tried Byng. From the *Devonshire* he was moved to the *Cambridge,* and then made commodore[20] and commander in chief on the Leeward Islands station.[21]

Hopson's secret orders were issued in seven parts on 16 October 1758. (1) He was to go to Portsmouth to take over command of the Third, Sixty-first, Sixty-fourth, and Sixty-fifth regiments, and from there, in transports convoyed by Captain Robert Hughes, sail to Plymouth where the transports of the Fourth and Sixty-third regiments would join the squadron. The whole fleet would then sail to Barbados to meet Commodore Moore, who would assume command of the naval forces. (2) The combined force would then attack Martinique. (3) If the attack were successful, Martinique was to be garrisoned and Hopson was to inform the government what supplies he needed. (4) He should enlist any acclimated men he could get from the islands, since they would be useful for irregular warfare and for plantation destruction. He should also secure men from the Thirty-eighth Regiment if the regiment could spare the detachment. He must not stay at Barbados to await these men but should have them join the invading force at Martinique. (5) If the expedition succeeded, and the men could be spared, one thousand were to be drafted from the regiments[22] and sent under convoy to Major General Jeffrey Am-

20. On the title "commodore," see Appendix, Topic 2.
21. Moore died loaded with honors—Admiral, Baronet, Knight of the Bath—in February 1779.
22. On eighteenth-century military drafts, see Appendix, Topic 3.

herst, the commander in chief in North America who was to command the invasion of Canada. If the expedition should fail and the force could not strike elsewhere—a question left to the discretion of the co-commanders—two thousand men should be sent to Amherst and the rest brought home under convoy. (6) Hopson should cooperate with Moore, even to the extent of giving him men to work the ships—Moore would have reciprocal orders. Hopson's orders should be communicated to Moore, who in turn was to communicate his orders to Hopson. (7) ". . . from time to time, and as you shall have opportunity, send constant accounts of your proceedings" to one of the principal secretaries of state, who would send any other information the government would wish Hopson to have.[23] Two or three days later Hopson and his officers were given authority to impress carriage, hospital supplies, and other stores into the service.[24]

The orders to Moore were similar.[25] Joint instructions were sent to the governors of Barbados and the Leeward Islands, calling upon them to assist Hopson with native troops if possible, and to grant aid, provisions, refreshment, and animals to the expeditionary forces. Notice was given to the governor of the Leeward Islands that Hopson would detach men from the Thirty-eighth Regiment, if consistent with the safety of the islands.[26]

Hopson was provided with a small but adequate staff. The Reverend John Tathan served as Hopson's chaplain. Hopson had at least two aides-de-camp: a captain who left the Indies for London on 30 January 1759 with the first good news the government received of this expedition, and a Benjamin Tribe, rank not given. Captain Robert Skene and a Captain Cunningham served the force as deputy adjutant general and deputy quartermaster gen-

23. Colonial Office 5/215, 61-80. Information from Colonial Office papers, throughout, is derived from transcripts in the Library of Congress.
24. Colonel H. C. Wylly, *History of the Manchester Regiment* (London, 1933), I, 8-9. This is a history of the Sixty-third.
25. Colonial Office 5/215, 95-114.
26. Pitt, *Correspondence*, I, 366-370. Part of the expeditionary force was composed of men and ships lately returned from an unsuccessful coastal descent at Lunaire Bay. Ruville, *William Pitt*, II, 224, 224n., citing Berlin archives now inaccessible, if still extant.

eral respectively. They ranked during the expedition as lieutenant colonels. Heading a small group of surgeons was "the physician."[27] The officer commanding the artillery detachment from Woolwich arsenal[28] was Major Samuel Cleaveland; the chief engineer officer was Lieutenant Colonel William Cunninghame; one of his subalterns, or "practitioners" as they were called, was Robert Beatson, the author of one of the best sources for a study of this expedition.

There were, of course, line officers to command units in the field. The six complete regiments were commanded as follows: the Third, by Lieutenant Colonel Cyrus Trapaud, the Fourth, by Lieutenant Colonel Byam Crump, the Sixty-first, by Lieutenant Colonel John Barlow, the Sixty-third, by Lieutenant Colonel Peter Debrissay, the Sixty-fourth, by Major Thomas Ball (vice Colonel Barrington), and the Sixty-fifth, by Colonel Robert Armiger. The detachment from the Thirty-eighth which eventually joined in the expedition after it arrived in the West Indies was headed by its local commander, Major Robert Melville.[29] The second battalion of the Forty-second Regiment, now called the Black Watch, reinforced the expedition after it arrived in the West Indies, and was placed under one of Hopson's officers, a captain who was brevetted major for the campaign.[30]

These eight units[31] functioned as five on the field, the six complete regiments being organized in three brigades, and the Scots and the Thirty-eighth apparently fought independently. The brigades were under brigadier generals.[32] The Third and Sixty-third regiments formed the First Brigade under command of Trapaud. The Fourth and Sixty-fourth regiments were formed into the Second Brigade, commanded until 13 March 1759 by Lieutenant Colonel George Haldane, late of the Third Guards Regiment and

27. Only the physicians were accorded the title of "Doctor." The surgeons were Mister This and Mister That.
28. On the organization of the artillery, see Appendix, Topic 4.
29. On Melville, see note on pp. 65-66.
30. For a list of the regiments which took part in this campaign on the British side, with numbers, names, owners, officer commanding in the West Indies, and brigade of which a part, see Appendix, Topic 5.
31. For a statement of comparable military strength in modern terms, see Appendix, Topic 6.
32. On the ranks in the infantry regiments, see Appendix, Topic 7.

governor-elect of Jamaica, who departed for his post during the campaign. After the departure of Haldane the Second Brigade was commanded by Lieutenant Colonel J. Clavering of the Second Guards Regiment, and, still later, by Byam Crump for a time. The Sixty-first and Sixty-fifth regiments made up the Third Brigade, which took orders from Brigadier General Armiger. The Forty-second's battalion fought independently. Whether the detachment of the Thirty-eighth was brigaded with other troops is not clear. Several hundred Marines from the fleet occasionally saw action ashore with the army, at which times they were commanded by a Colonel (or Lieutenant Colonel) Rycaut.[33]

Hopson had difficulty in organizing this officer corps. Major General George Boscawen was asked to serve as a brigadier but declined.[34] Perhaps he thought such service would be a step down in rank. William, Viscount Barrington, Pitt's cabinet colleague, who held the war portfolio, honorably protested against the elevation of his brother, saying in part, "how earnestly I have wish'd to prevent the perilous honour which has happen'd to fall to my brother's lot."[35] But Colonel Armiger offered the chief difficulty.

33. In the squadron commanded by Commodore Hughes, who convoyed the soldiers to the West Indies, there were eight hundred Marines who, it was claimed, were intended to be formed into a battalion to land with the troops and fight in the line under command of a lieutenant colonel and a major, "expressly appointed by the King for this Service." At Barbados Moore was said to have refused to allow this arrangement "and did, in effect, take away all Command from the Lieutenant-Colonel and Major of Marines." Richard Gardiner, *Account of the Expedition to the West Indies, against Martinico* (Birmingham, 1762), 2. Hereafter cited as, Gardiner, *The West Indies*.

Gardiner, as will be seen hereafter, was not above distorting the story for purposes of his own. Actually, Moore's orders mentioned that Colonel Rycaut and Major Campbell would command the Marines ashore "if it shall be found necessary to land them."—Admiralty, 2/1331. And Rycaut did command Marines ashore in combat, at Fort Louis, Grand Terre, in February. John Moore, "Journal," Admiral's journals, Admiralty 50/22.

Moore's "Journal" covers events laconically and adds little of value to a study of the operation except a precise chronology. It tells what orders were issued, and when, but rarely why; rarely does it speak of results, and never of strategical considerations. It is almost exclusively confined to nautical detail.

34. Hopson to Ligonier, 22 October 1758, Colonial Office 110/1. One lieutenant, two sergeants, and forty men of Boscawen's regiment were drafted into Hopson's force (into the Sixty-third) at Plymouth before embarkation. Wylly, *History of the Manchester Regiment*, I, 8.

35. Viscount Barrington to Newcastle, 9 May 1759, Newcastle papers, Add. MSS. 32891, folio 63, British Museum. Information from the Newcastle papers is from transcripts in the Library of Congress.

From Gosport, on 22 October 1758, he wrote the following self-pitiful letter to the harrassed Hopson, who had much more important business to attend to:

Sir,

Brigadier Barrington tells me that he is to be a major-general. I have served many years longer than him, and seen more service, and if I am not to have equal promotion with him (except I misbehave) I shall be so severely mortified as not to be able to answer for my brooking spirits, and sooner than that should be my situation, and the service suffer, I beg leave to retire to any corner of the world, and there wait my dejected fate.[36]

Perhaps startled by this open show of professional jealousy Hopson hurriedly wrote a letter to John, Viscount Ligonier[37] (then first soldier of the empire) asking him to intervene, and sent copies of these letters to Pitt.[38] To Ligonier he said he had lost one brigadier by Boscawen's refusal to serve. The resignation of Armiger would make the whole project almost impossible. He was to have had one major general and three brigadiers. "I submit to your lordship the now distress'd situation of my command with one major-general and one brigadier, only, and without a colonel." After much expression of anxiety he concluded, "I have already represented the inconvenience of losing one brigadier, and am very likely to lose two."[39] Ligonier was officially commander in chief of the British army but he was seventy-eight years of age and, if Hopson had but stopped to think, it must have been perfectly obvious to him that Pitt was the man who produced the military show. Pitt rebuked Hopson for referring the affair to the venerable hero and settled the tea-pot tornado, either by speaking to his sulky Achilles or by correspondence not preserved, in such a satisfactory manner that Armiger served through the whole campaign without another written complaint—nor did he particularly distinguish himself.

36. Colonial Office 110/1.
37. ". . . when Cumberland fell into disgrace after the convention of Closterseven Ligonier succeeded him as commander-in-chief (without the rank of captain-general held by Cumberland) from 24 Oct. 1757 . . ." He left the office 1 July 1759. Ligonier was born in 1680. Henry Manners Chichester, "John Ligonier," *Dictionary of National Biography*.
38. Hopson to Pitt, 22 October 1758, Colonial Office 110/1.
39. Hopson to Ligonier, 22 October 1758, Colonial Office 110/1.

DESIGN FOR FIGHTING 25

In November orders were sent to the officer commanding seven newly raised companies of the Forty-second Foot to sail under convoy for the West Indies to join Hopson's army. These men were seven of ten new companies making up the second battalion of the Royal Highlanders, or Black Watch.[40] They had but five months' training before they sailed,[41] yet fought as well as any of the troops under Hopson and Barrington and came out with relatively fewer casualties. The explanation of this hardiness is probably that only extremely rugged individuals survived a Highland childhood in the eighteenth century. A few more details of the organization remained to be completed, e.g., bringing the debentures up to date, so that the soldiers would be only about three months behind in their pay when they sailed,[42] and ordering space reserved in the transports for ten women per company.[43] The army was thereupon ready to place itself in the hands of the navy for delivery overseas.

In 1758 the Royal Navy had 310 ships in commission. Of these, 110 were line of battle ships,[44] which can be roughly described as ships mounting fifty guns or more. For the expedition the Admiralty organized a small fleet to be commanded by Captain Robert Hughes until it reached Barbados, where Commodore Moore would assume command. The battleships were: the *Norfolk*, 74 guns, Captain Robert Hughes, 600 men; the *Panther*, 60, Captain Molyneaux Shuldham, 420; the *Lyon*, 60, Captain Sir William Trelawney, 400; the *St. George*, 90, Captain Clark Gayton, 750; the *Burford*, 64, Captain James Gambier, 520; the *Winchester*, 50, Captain Edward Le Cras, 350; the *Berwick*, 64, Captain William Harman, 480; and the *Rippon*, 60, Captain Edward Jekyll, 430. The smaller ships were: the *Renown* frigate, 30, Captain George Mackenzie;[45] and four bomb ketches: the *Kingfisher*, 2 mortars, Commander Sabine Deacon;[46] the *Falcon*, 2 mortars, Commander

---

40. Colonial Office 5/215; C. R. B. Knight, *Historical Records of the Buffs* (London, 1935), II, 194 ff. Hereafter cited as Knight, *The Buffs*.
41. Archibald Forbes, *The "Black Watch"* (New York, 1897), 59.
42. Wylly, *History of the Manchester Regiment*, I, 7.
43. *Ibid.*, I, 8.   44. *Gentleman's Magazine*, 28 (1758), 254.
45. On frigates, see Appendix, Topic 8.
46. For a description of the structure and uses of bomb ketches, see Appendix, Topic 9.

Mark Robinson; the *Granada,* Commander Samuel Uvedale; and, the *Infernal,* Commander James Mackenzie. A hospital ship also accompanied the transports. The *Panther* and the *Rippon* were new ships. The *St. George* was the ship aboard which Admiral Byng had been tried and it was the largest vessel of the fleet which went against the French West Indies.[47]

On 28 August 1758 the Admiralty issued orders for nine thousand tons of transport shipping to be taken up by the navy, and again, on 20 September, called for six thousand more, all to be fitted and victualed for foreign service at "two tons per man."[48] When gathered together the transports numbered sixty. Two more warships were later sent out from England: the *Ludlow Castle* frigate, Captain Edward Clarke, convoyed the Highland troops[49] and the *Griffin* frigate sailed with dispatches from England in March, 1759.[50]

There was a small squadron on the Leeward Islands station under Moore's command, chiefly engaged in protecting commerce and in watching the few French ships in those waters. They were: the *Cambridge,* 80 guns, Captain Thomas Burnett, 667 men; the *Bristol,* 50, Captain Lachlin Leslie, 350; the *Woolwich* (frigate), 40; the *Amazon* (frigate), 32; the *Rye* (frigate), 24, Captain Peter Parker; and the *Barbados* (sloop). Other vessels were on detached duty from this squadron. Their names will be noted as they rejoined it during the course of the campaign. With infrequent exceptions Moore used the *Cambridge* as his flagship. Ships of this squadron had occasional brushes with the French in the months before the attacks on Martinique and Guadeloupe. Moore's most annoying problem was the munition and provision trade carried on between the Dutch islands and the French defenders of Martinique. A second problem was the prevention of the illicit trade of English colonials with the enemy at Martinique, Guadeloupe, and elsewhere. Moore's behavior toward this trade was later to make civilians cry for his head.[51]

47. On the number of men in this fleet, see Appendix, Topic 10.
48. Wylly, *History of the Manchester Regiment,* I, 8.
49. Colonial Office 5/215.
50. John Entick, *General History of the Late War* (London, 1763), IV, 144.
51. Thomas to Pitt, 20 November 1758, in Pitt, *Correspondence,* I, 396-397.

DESIGN FOR FIGHTING

The reservation of two tons of shipping per man gives a good picture of the amount of stores to be taken when Captain Hughes threw out the signal to weigh anchor. There were masts from New England forests, and from Riga and Norway. There were over 1300 extra spars, exclusive of yards and bowsprits. Over a thousand barrels of pitch, tar, and turpentine went into the holds. Among numerous other items were thirty-eight casks of nails, about 8,800 yards of canvas, eighteen "Jacks, Union," and everything else a fleet could use, from ten sailmaker's palms, through twenty paint brushes, to fourteen auger shanks and two azimuth compasses. The whole list covered thirty-three pages in Pitt's letter book.[52] And more was to go, for after Hughes sailed, four months' provisions for seven thousand men were sent after him in freighters convoyed by the *Hampshire*, a fifty-gun ship. These stores were sent in six ships, by three victualers, and tell so well the story of what an eighteenth-century army was fed[53] that the entire table is reproduced below.

Commod'y	Ship					
	Prince William	Dolphin	Juno	Unicorn	Neptune	William
Bread lbs............	71,064	63,336	154,056	110,712	62,048	94,080
Beef pieces..........	10,152	9,012	23,246	15,232	7,506	10,056
Pork pieces..........	10,172	9,178	23,202	14,972	7,326	9,706
Peas, bu. gals........	320 2	288 7	727	475	233 1	307 7
Grotts Bu. & gals.....	241 5	213 1	541 1	356 6	170 1	234 7
Oatmeal Bu. & gals...	237 6	214 7	538 5	354 7	175 2	229 6
Oil gals.............	1462	.....	3009:1½	2521:5½	.....	.....
Vinegar gals.........	645	573	1418	950	419	639

The approximate totals of each commodity are: 500,000 pounds of bread, 75,000 pieces of beef and the same number of pieces of pork, 2,400 bushels of peas, 1,800 bushels of "grotts," 1,800 bushels of oatmeal, 7,000 gallons of "oil," 4,700 gallons of vinegar.[54]

52. Colonial Office 5/215.
53. The weekly ration of each soldier may be deduced from this table. See Appendix, Topic 11.
54. Clevland to Rivers, 8 March 1759, Colonial Office 5/215.

III.

Trade-Wind Passage

General Hopson and Commodore Hughes must have suffered almost constant nervous fatigue during the five weeks which passed between receipt of their orders and their final departure. The elements stormed and so did Pitt. They were between the Secretary and the rough, gray sea. This was not a comfortable place.

1. *Departure*

Commodore Hughes received his orders at the same time that orders were issued to Hopson and Moore. He was to gather a squadron at Spithead and embark troops at Portsmouth and Plymouth. Then he was to sail to Barbados and put himself under Moore's command, meanwhile keeping in communication with the Admiralty, and obeying any orders from the King, from the sea lords, and from Mr. Pitt.[1] While en route he was to send a ship ahead to Moore at Carlisle Bay, Barbados, bearing a message to inform him exactly when the convoy from England would arrive.[2] For the rest of this unhappy period before putting to sea Hughes and Hopson were in almost daily correspondence with Mr. Pitt.

On 18 October Hughes reported from Spithead. "Hard easterly winds" had slowed the loading of stores and provisions aboard the men of war. He promised, nevertheless, to send the transports to Plymouth on the morrow if the weather permitted.[3] Almost

---
1. Colonial Office, 5/215.
2. Pitt, *Correspondence*, I, 369.
3. Hughes to Pitt, 18 October 1758, Colonial Office 110/1.

by return mail Pitt replied with additional instructions to take up any bomb vessels at Portsmouth which were ready to sail when the four battalions were once aboard, and to leave orders for the others to follow under a convoy to be appointed by the Admiralty.[4]

On 22 October the Secretary decided to stir up Hopson, and wrote that the King was "extremely impatient to hear that the troops under your command are sailed." Hopson was instructed to keep Pitt informed of progress toward the departure, and was asked whether there had been any particular event which had delayed matters, "every hour being now precious upon many accounts."[5] Hopson replied on 25 October that he had come on board the day before but about a quarter of the transport masters had ignored the signal to come aboard the commodore. The officers had been asked to report their deficiencies but with the transport masters behaving so badly the reports were not being received. At the moment of writing, he added, the signal had been made to weigh anchor.[6] Hughes's letter of the same day confirmed this information. He said the troops and artillery were embarked at Spithead, and he was sailing that day to join the rest of the ships at Plymouth.[7] But on the following day he reported the squadron as weather bound in St. Helen Roads. Two bomb vessels, he added, had joined him on the previous day, the *Kingsfisher* and the *Falcon*. They had two mortars each, and a previously assigned bomb, the *Pelican,* had but one mortar, so—acting on Hopson's advice—he was leaving the *Pelican* at Spithead.[8]

The little fleet then put to sea but took such a dusting from the weather that Hughes steered back into St. Helen Roads. Some of the vessels had been in serious trouble and Hopson and Hughes reported the damage. On 31 October four or six transports were still missing, according to Hopson's incomplete information. Further, one transport, the *Henry and John,* was sand-borne on Pool Bar, and the ship, he thought, was probably lost although her people were saved. The ordnance transport in which Major

4. Pitt, *Correspondence*, I, 370.
5. Pitt to Hopson, 22 October 1758, Colonial Office 5/215.
6. Hopson to Pitt, 25 October 1758, Colonial Office 110/1.
7. Hughes to Pitt, 25 October 1758, *ibid*.
8. Hughes to Pitt, 26 October 1758, *ibid*.

Samuel Cleaveland of the artillery detachment had sailed had been so damaged that another ship had to be taken up to replace it. The artillery's powder and stores, he also reported, had been sadly wetted down. Hughes knew more of the transports than Hopson did: all were in port except the one which had been stranded at Pool, with part of the Sixty-first Regiment aboard.[9]

More details followed. Major Cleaveland's ordnance transport, the *Anson,* had been examined by three carpenters who reported her to be unseaworthy, her seams open, a thirty-foot plank rotten, and her magazine very wet. The Major agreed with the carpenters' estimate of the *Anson* and reported that other ordnance transports were also in bad condition. The *Providence* needed a new main topmast and should be unloaded and caulked—the work of three or four days. The *Isabella and Mary* should be reloaded and checked since the job had been done hastily with stores lately arrived from the coast of France (probably matériel salvaged from Earl Howe's and General Bligh's withdrawal from Cherbourg). William Cunninghame, the chief engineer officer of the land forces, had his doubts concerning the ordnance transport *Diamond.* She had sailed well in other expeditions but now she leaked and labored and he feared she would roll her masts out the next time she was in a seaway. The final report from the beached *Henry and John,* by one James Randell, the agent to the transports, declared her people were indeed safe, but she was full of water—and that was the end of her.[10]

Again the urgent Pitt replied by return mail. Hughes was ordered to repair the damaged transports, take up any empty transports he could discover at Portsmouth, and get going. (Ah, happy day! when an English-speaking nation at war could float its expeditionary forces by the simple expedient of impressing local merchant shipping.) Hughes was informed that two more line of battle ships had been added to his command, the *Winchester,* which had not been mentioned in earlier orders, and the *Lancaster,* 66 guns, Captain Robert Man. But he was not to wait for them if they were not in condition to go to sea. Rather, he

---

9. Hopson to Pitt and Hughes to Pitt, 31 October 1758, *ibid.*
10. Hopson to Pitt, 1 November 1758, *ibid.*

TRADE-WIND PASSAGE

should leave sealed orders, only to be opened at sea, for them to join him later at such a rendezvous as he thought proper.[11] The soldiers from the stranded transport (one company and half of another) had already been ordered to march to Lymington where, with Hopson's approval, Hughes was to give orders for embarking them.[12] A letter for Hopson came by the same express, according to which Pitt expressed the hope that the transports could be repaired or replaced quickly. This letter closed with pointed and urgent observations on the desirability of sending the expeditionary force to the French West Indies at the earliest possible moment.[13] Pitt's letter arrived at Hopson's transport on the day it was written (2 November) and Hopson promptly answered that the rain and wind were so bad the boats had been unable to pass between the ships in the harbor. He added that the men of the Sixty-first Regiment who had been saved from the *Henry and John* numbered four officers and 160 men.[14] Hughes wrote to the Secretary on the next day that he was doing everything he was told to do and was removing stores from the sodden ordnance transports to newly acquired vessels. He added that he had sent an empty transport to Lymington to take aboard the troops who had been marched to that port.[15]

Hopson sent another weather report the next day. It was still foul outside and there had been only three or four hours of fair weather since they anchored at Portsmouth.[16] Hughes continued the daily exchange on 4 November, submitting that he had been lately ordered by the Admiralty to Spithead to refit and reprovision. He humbly begged to submit that he had been doing nothing else for some time past.[17] Pitt's answer showed a magnificent disregard for the weather, or an ignorance of its importance to seafarers: the King was still impatient for the good news of their departure, and would they please go?[18] Hopson, however, complained that

11. The *Winchester* was ready for sea; the *Lancaster* joined at Guadeloupe in February.
12. Pitt, *Correspondence*, I, 386-387, 386n.
13. Pitt to Hopson, 2 November 1758, Colonial Office 5/215.
14. Hopson to Pitt, 2 November 1758, Colonial Office 110/1.
15. Pitt, *Correspondence*, I, 386-387, 386n.; Colonial Office 110/1.
16. Hopson to Pitt, 3 November 1758, Colonial Office 110/1.
17. Hughes to Pitt, 4 November 1758, *ibid*.
18. Pitt to Hopson and Hughes, 7 November 1758, Colonial Office 5/215.

what he needed was provisions for the army, rather than the authority to acquire provisions, and that he had lost six months' supplies for two hundred men in the *Henry and John.* Furthermore, because of the bad weather he had two hundred sick men who needed rest on shore at New Port or some other hospital. With the pessimism that was habitual with him he predicted that there would be more sick at Plymouth and he wondered whether he could have more soldiers. He hastily concluded this gloomy *communiqué* with the nervous promise that he did not propose to delay the departure on that account.[19] After almost another week of pier head turmoil Hopson learned that seven companies of Highlanders would join his command immediately: when he had finished with them, he was to send them to the most convenient port in North America for joining General Amherst's army.[20]

After all this knocking about in the Channel, the British expedition's condition should have been common gossip among the French fishwives from Cherbourg to Abbeville. It was at this time that François Cardinal Bernis prematurely informed the King of France (via Jeanne, Marquise de Pompadour, as usual) that the British had departed (9 November). He missed it by ten days. He was correct, however, in saying, "It is certain that it goes to attack Martinique or Guadeloupe."[21]

Pitt finally lost patience with the weather and on the day of Bernis' memorandum issued a blunt order to his general and his commodore to move out. They did their hasty best. Hopson, a truly humble and obedient servant, promised that they would sail as soon as the transports got their stores aboard and the weather permitted the squadron to stand out to sea.[22] Hughes, in the same temper, respectfully informed his master that all but one of the disabled ships would be refitted by that very evening and the work on the remaining one would be completed the next day. He assured Pitt that he would fish his anchors as soon as

19. Pitt, *Correspondence,* I, 395-396.
20. *Ibid.*
21. Bernis to Pompadour, 9 November 1758, François-Joachim Cardinal de Bernis, *Mémoires et lettres* (Paris, 1903), II, 333. My translation.
22. Hopson to Pitt, 9 November 1758, Colonial Office 110/1.

the blow allowed, and begged to observe that he could not stow provisions while the wind kicked up the roadstead.[23]

While Hughes and Hopson were learning how a housewife feels when "everything goes wrong," General Haldane, guards officer, governor-elect of Jamaica, and one of Hopson's brigadiers, was approached by one Charles Alexander, who wrote to him, first in French and then in English, that he was a ruined artist and a bankrupt business man who wanted Haldane's aid in returning to the West Indies where he proposed to rebuild his fortunes. Might he not go along to the islands with the expedition? Haldane knew that a relative of Alexander's had been on the losing side in the last Jacobite rebellion, the "forty-five"—1745, when Charles Stuart, "Bonny Prince Charlie," the Young Pretender to the throne, had landed in Scotland in an unsuccessful attempt at revolution. Alexander therefore did not get his wish. Whether he was a spy, as Haldane was convinced, cannot be known. Pitt had the local postmaster watch Alexander's mail, but his name did not occur again in the records.[24] If he was a spy his plan probably was to jump ship in the islands and carry full information of the British force to the local French commanders. If not a spy his request showed that the destination of the force was a poorly kept secret.

Hopson wrote his last letter of the period of preparation on 12 November. He said that a few days previously William Mathew Burt, the King's fiscal agent on the expedition who went along to keep account of the royal booty, had told him the expedition ought to have pontoons, because of a river near "St. Peters" where the French would probably blow up the only bridge.[25] It is unlikely that this advice alarmed Pitt, for in the same letter was proof that Hopson was a pessimist. His prediction of the number of sick to be left behind had been excessively gloomy. Only ninety-four had to remain ashore.

On the same day Hughes dispatched the good news which Pitt claimed was so eagerly awaited by the King: they were under

23. Hughes to Pitt, 9 November 1758, *ibid*.
24. Haldane to Pitt, 9 November 1758; Todd to Wood, 10 November 1758; Pitt to Haldane, 10 November 1758, *ibid*.
25. Hopson to Pitt, 12 November 1758, *ibid*.

way. The *Berwick*, Captain Harman, was sent ahead to call out the ships lying in Plymouth Sound. She appeared off Plymouth at three o'clock in the afternoon of the next day (13 November) with a Dutch ensign flying at the main topgallant masthead, and Captain Shuldham[26] from the *Panther*, at anchor off Plymouth, threw out the signal for the ships there to weigh. The squadron joined two days later in latitude 49° 40′ and made a brave show of seventy-three sail steering out of the Channel into the war.[27]

As a brief anticlimax came two days of foul weather, blowing fresh. The unhappy Hughes resigned himself to more of Pitt's steaming letters and, at four o'clock in the morning, eight bells in the mid watch, on 19 November, made a signal to put back. But thirteen hours later, in the first dog watch, the wind hauled favorably and the commodore "tacked again and stood on his Way."[28] There may well have been extra rum in the *Norfolk* that day.

2. Rendezvous

During the passage to Barbados the nine thousand men and women in the seventy-three vessels suffered from ship-fever, scurvy, dysentery, and smallpox.[29] In the case of a modern expedition such adversity would be enough to bring on a cabinet crisis, but this sort of thing was expected in the eighteenth century, and Captain Richard Gardiner could calmly say that "after a passage of seven weeks and three days, without any very material occurences intervening" they appeared off Bridgetown, Barbados, on 3 January 1759, and came to an anchor in Carlisle Bay, the ap-

---

26. Molyneaux Shuldham (1717?-1798) entered the navy as the captain's servant aboard the *Cornwall* in 1732. He was commissioned lieutenant in 1739, and posted to captain in 1746. As captain of the *Warwick*, 60, in 1756 he fell in with a French seventy-four-gun ship and two frigates near Martinique and, although war had not yet been declared, was taken. He was exchanged in 1758. He immediately went to sea again in the *Panther*, in which he served in the campaign of 1759. He died at Lisbon, Admiral Lord Shuldham, Baron Shuldham in the peerage of Ireland. J. K. Laughton, "Molyneaux Shuldham," *Dictionary of National Biography*.

27. Hughes to Pitt, 12 November 1758, Colonial Office 110/1; Gardiner, *The West Indies*, 1-2.

28. Gardiner, *The West Indies*, 2.

29. Knight, *The Buffs*, II, 193-195.

pointed rendezvous, in twelve to thirty fathoms of clear West Indian water.[30]

M. Lacour-Gayet inaccurately said that the fleet revictualed at Jamaica on the way to Barbados.[31] He neglected to add the obvious truth that it might take a very long time for these square rigged ships to beat to Barbados directly against the force of the trade wind. A ship of the line sailing from Jamaica to Barbados would do well to go by way of Bermuda. The truth is, they were out of sight of land from the middle of November until they arrived at Carlisle Bay. In the state of navigation at that time, the obvious course for a vessel to steer from England to Barbados was southwest from Plymouth to the line of 13° north latitude, thence due west, running free before the trade wind, to Barbados.

Captain Gardiner may have been essaying what Mr. Mencken called "beautiful letters" but his pulsing prose sounded a real tone of sea weariness when he wrote: "As the Ships approached, the Island rose gradually out of the Sea with a delightful Verdure, presenting a most inviting Prospect of the Country all around, which looked like a Garden; the Plantations were amazingly beautiful, interspersed at little Distances from each other, and adorned with Fruits of various Colours."[32] Because of the usual general alarm which was sounded in the West Indies upon sight of a strange fleet, thousands of Barbadians were drawn along shore when the main body of the fleet dropped its hooks in the bay.[33]

As soon as the fleet came to an anchor Commodore Moore "threw out a Signal for all Lieutenants, and took upon him the Command of the now united Squadrons."[34] His broad pennant was hoisted on board the *Cambridge*. On paper Moore's own force was eight of the line and eight smaller vessels, according to a decision of the Admiralty in May, 1757.[35] Actually with him in the bay at the moment of juncture were two of the line, three

---

30. Gardiner, *The West Indies*, 2.
31. Georges Lacour-Gayet, *Marine militaire sous le régne de Louis XV* (Paris, 1910), 392. Hereafter cited as, Lacour-Gayet, *Marine militaire*.
32. Gardiner, *The West Indies*, 3.   33. *Ibid*, 3-4.
34. *Ibid.*, 4. Moore and six of his officers became flag officers, 1762-1777.
35. Pares, *War and Trade*, 268.

frigates and a sloop,[36] other vessels being on detached duty. Because of the detachment of cruisers and the necessity for sending dispatches home in naval vessels, the Leeward Islands squadron was rarely up to its paper strength. Nor had all of Hughes' seventy-three sail arrived in a body, for eleven ships had straggled. Unfortunately, these were extremely important ships, including the hospital ship with all the medical stores and the physician and the surgeons aboard. The artillery ships, considerable baggage, three bomb tenders, and several transport-loads of soldiers were also among the missing. Aboard one of the transports were all of the engineers except the chief engineer, Cunninghame, and two practitioners, one of whom was probably Robert Beatson.[37]

Concerning the missing ships, Hopson and Moore conferred and then Hopson took the opinion of his general officers, who agreed that it was now impossible to surprise the French. Therefore it would be quite proper to await the stragglers.[38] This opinion was sounder than they could know, for, unknown to these officers (although they may have had similar information from Barbados officials), Governor George Thomas of Antigua had written to London on 20 November that an express had arrived at Martinique. The French there immediately set to work entrenching their bays and landing places and mounting all of their spare cannon.[39]

While waiting for the latecomers Moore watered the ships. The men practiced disembarking in the novel flat-bottomed landing boats which came along from England[40] and Governor Charles Pinfold and General Hopson staged a formal review of the troops. Hopson fitted out a hospital ship and engaged local surgeons for

36. Gardiner, *The West Indies*, 4.
37. Pitt, *Correspondence*, II, 20-22. Ships of this expedition were arriving at Barbados from 1 to 11 January. The first in was the *London* transport on New Year's day. The main body anchored on 4 January. Moore, "Journal," Admiralty 50/22.
38. Pitt, *Correspondence*, II, 20-22.
39. *Ibid.*, I, 396-397.
40. "Twelve flat-bottomed boats, of a new construction, were launched at *Portsmouth* to be employed in landing the troops on the enemy's coast. They carry 63 men each, are rowed with 12 oars, and draw not above two feet [of] water." *Gentleman's Magazine*, 28 (1758), 242. More were building in July of the same year. *Ibid.*, 449.

the service. Councils of war were held, and the Council of Barbados was assembled. Proclamations were published. Hopson beat for recruits—men who might not be able to march to the slow cadence of the army, in perfect alignment in the face of blazing volley fire, but who nevertheless were used to the climate and could snap a musket from behind a hedge and touch a torch to thatch. Despite this activity, the only recruits who sailed with the force were three hundred Negro slaves, who went along as pioneers and draft animals.[41] The Barbadians were unwilling to send their trained men away and were hurt by Hopson's refusal to accept an untrained volunteer regiment under a "political colonel." Because Hopson did not think them worth the cost of transportation to the wars they were therefore disbanded. When Barrington later sent to Barbados for help, only two militiamen came forward, out of the militia that numbered about four thousand men and officers in 1762. Similarly, Antigua later feared a depletion of her defensive strength, and the inhabitants smiled to see that the volunteers from that place who joined Hopson were for the most part strangers, which is to say they were probably visiting privateersmen who were on the beach for want of rich French prizes—the fat merchant ships of the enemy being harbor bound by the presence of a strong British fleet in those warm waters. But usually the British islanders were glad to rent out their slaves to the army,[42] since the slave population was not often counted as a defensive asset. The Barbadian slaves who went with Hopson were chiefly used to do the heavy lifting for the artillery.[43]

By 12 January the artillery ships had arrived and the *Ludlow Castle* came running down wind with three of the five transports

41. Pitt, *Correspondence*, II, 20-22. Security precautions were nil. On 13 January the Antigua *Gazette* published news of the departure from that island of the Thirty-eighth Regiment, under Major Melville. It added a list of all ships and frigates under Moore's command, with the number of guns each, size of crew, and name of commanding officer. Furthermore, all the regiments from Britain were listed by number and by commander. The names of all principal officers were also printed. The French at Martinique had a copy of the paper before the end of the month. Archives nationales, Marine et colonies, C^8 A 62.
42. Pares, *War and Trade*, 221-222.
43. Wylly, *The Manchester Regiment*, I, 9-10.

which carried the Scots battalion.[44] Hopson, who had no money except for "subsistence" and "a very small sum for contingencies," had engaged a local gentleman (on Governor Pinfold's recommendation) to dispense funds he raised by drawing on the paymaster-general for £2500. The agent spent freely.[45] Carpenters, working Negroes, and surgeons had meanwhile been hired; stores for the hospital ship had been loaded. Although the strength of the army had been "considerably impaired by Sickness"[46] and 1500 men in all were too ill for duty,[47] this condition could hardly be bettered in a place where a usual defense against naval attack was to prolong the campaign by any means until the attackers from the temperate zone had all sickened and died in their ships. So orders were issued to be ready to sail for Martinique in the morning (13 January).[48]

44. Pitt, *Correspondence*, II, 20-22.

45. Hopson to Martin, 30 January 1759, Treasury 1, bundle 390, f. 96-97. Information from the Treasury papers is from transcripts in the Library of Congress.

A peculiar West Indian supply problem was illustrated when the paymaster-general temporarily balked at honoring a draft in favor of "The Person who owns the water at Barbados." Moore to Clevland, 11 May 1759, Admiralty 1/307. Moore's complaint came in his letter announcing victory; in a celebrant mood, London allowed the draft.

46. Gardiner, *The West Indies*, 4, 4n.

47. Wylly, *The Manchester Regiment*, I, 9-10.

48. Abstract of Hopson to Pitt, 11 January 1759, in Pitt, *Correspondence*, II, 3.

IV.

Inhospitable Martinique

1. *A Fort Royale reception*

At eleven o'clock in the morning of 13 January sails were set and the fleet moved out of the bay, steering for the passage between Martinique[1] and St. Lucia.[2] During the next morning they made land[3] and Captain Leslie was sent ahead in the *Bristol* to sound the anchorage at Fort Royale, chief naval base of Martinique.[4] At noon the highest hill of Martinique "bore N. N. W. half N. ten leagues."[5] In the first faint gray light of the new day

1. Volcanic Martinique is rugged and is chiefly made of lava. The only large plain suitable for a close-order eighteenth-century battle lay behind the fortifications and the citadel of Fort Royale. Except for the excellent and strongly fortified harbor at Fort Royale and a few quiet bays, the coast is uninviting, since it has the various attributes of dangerous shores: coral reefs, shoals, rocky ledges, or cliffs three hundred feet high. The land is scarred by deep ravines. The highest elevation of the 385 square miles is 4428 feet.

Below one thousand feet a tropical rain forest covers the deep ravines and lower slopes of the mountains, in places being almost impenetrable. On the western coast, where the British tried to land, thorn and cactus forests flourish. Part of the shore line of Fort Royale Bay is now covered by a mixture of mangroves and salt grass, and probably was the same in 1759. Such a growth is the habitat of the man-eating mosquito. The rest of the shore of Fort Royale Bay, except for a few beaches, is rocky. Movement on the surface of the island is and was difficult. R. R. Platt, J. K. Wright, J. C. Weaver, J. E. Fairchild, *The European Possessions in the Caribbean Area* (N. Y., 1941), 50-58.

2. Gardiner, *The West Indies,* 4.
3. *Ibid.,* 6.
4. "An account of the expedition against the islands of Martinico and Guadeloupe," anonymous manscript enclosed in Pringle to Loudoun, 2 February 1759, Loudoun Papers, Huntington Library. Hereafter cited as "The expedition," Loudoun Papers.
5. Gardiner, *The West Indies,* 6. The author of this most detailed printed narrative of the campaign was called, or called himself, "Dick Merryfellow," a misnomer if there ever was one. Born in 1723, he was schooled at Eton and was at Cambridge for a while but took no degree. Traveling abroad, he was

of 15 January[6] the sleepy master of a small sloop under sail near the Diamond Rock had what was probably the shock of his life when he looked up and saw the looming misty shapes of almost a hundred ships of a hostile British fleet with all sails set, the nearest ships just four miles away. He raced home to give the first alarm.[7] At seven o'clock in the morning, when the whole fleet was between Martinique and St. Lucia, Moore signalled to the *Rippon, Winchester, Woolwich, Lyon*,[8] and *Roebuck* (three

---

taken by a French privateer and released in 1748. On his return he entered the established church and was said to have been a successful preacher but retired from the clergy in 1751. He wrote a "dull and acrimonious" satire on a young woman who rejected his proposal of marriage, and thereupon he entered the army as a lieutenant in the Twelfth Regiment. He was made a captain of Marines in 1757, in which capacity he served at Martinique and Guadeloupe. His whole life revealed that he had an exceedingly contentious nature. He died in 1781. Alsager Vian, "Richard Gardiner," *Dictionary of National Biography*. As for the name "Merryfellow," the only joke in his military writings was a two-ton pun, in which the catch word was printed in capital letters. His personality is firmly impressed in his writing on this campaign. A critical reading of his animadversions on his superiors, and his badly concealed attempts to inflate the value of his own services, reveal an ambitious, envious man who has come to the realization in his middle years, like most of us, that he is not to be a Great Man, and resents the discovery.

6. From noon of 14 January to seven o'clock in the morning of 15 January (nineteen hours), according to Gardiner's figures, p. 6, the fleet covered seven leagues. If by a league he meant the usual three minutes or twentieth part of a degree, they sailed twenty-one sea miles in the nineteen hours, off the wind, a rate little better than one knot. From mid-channel in Fort Royale Bay to St. Pierre Roads is less than fifteen sea miles. This, under easy sail (Gardiner, 14), took about twelve hours, that is, on a reach they sailed at a speed of about one and a quarter knots.

7. "The expedition," Loudoun Papers. The British intention was known to Governor François, Marquis de Beauharnois, but until the approaching fleet could be positively identified he and his people tried to convince themselves it was a merchant convoy. Ruville, *Pitt*, II, 225, and, Henri Malo, "L'echec des Anglais a la Martinique en 1759," *Feuilles d'histoire*, 8 (1912), 4, hereafter cited: Malo. The MS. on which Malo based his essay I found to be an anonymous narrative in Archives nationales, Marine et colonies, C[8] A 62; I have used Malo, his rendering being fair, and his notes entertaining. I am indebted to Prof. M. A. Fitzsimons of the University of Notre Dame for referring me to Malo's work. A rather free translation of this same anonymous narrative appeared in the St. Christopher's *Gazette*, 25 April 1759, from which it was reprinted in the *South-Carolina Gazette*, 26 May 1759. This wide distribution argues that it was intended by its author to produce an effect in the public mind, probably to enhance the reputation for valor of the people of Martinique and, conversely, to damage Beauharnois.

8. Sir William Trelawney "(d. 1772) sixth baronet . . . was grandson of Brigadier-general Henry Trelawney . . . who served at Tangier and in Flanders, and died M.P. for Plymouth in 1702. Sir William sat for West Looe, Cornwall . . . entered the navy, commanded the Lyon at the attack on Guadeloupe in

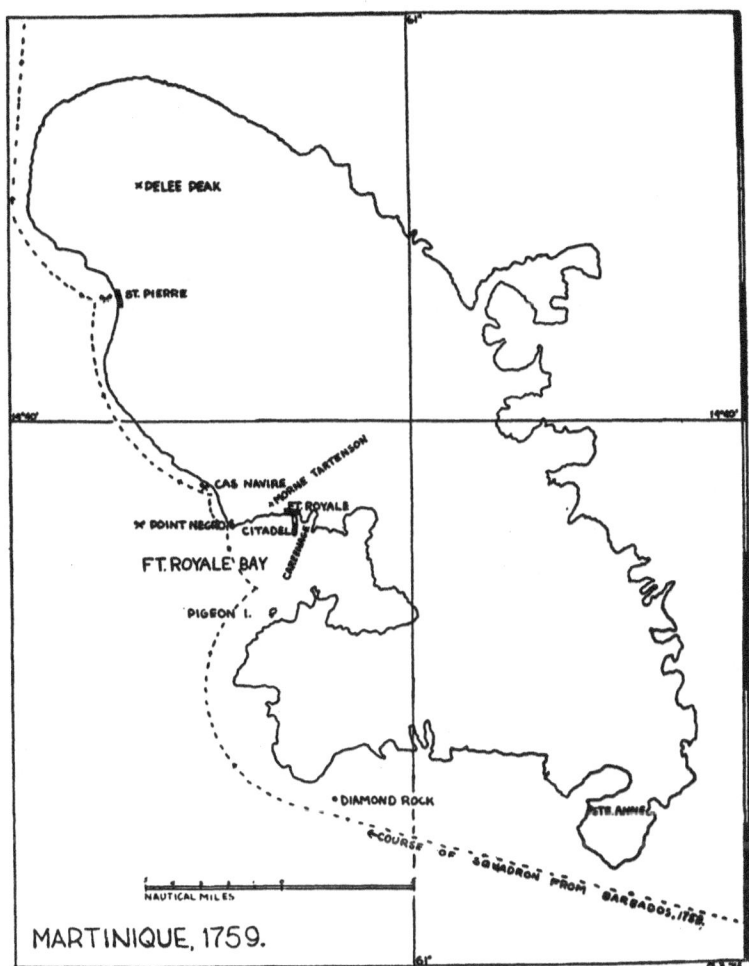

MARTINIQUE, 1759.

ships and two frigates) to draw within hail. When they did so, orders were bawled to them to keep near the flag and clear for action.[9] At the hour when Moore made the signal, the *Bristol* was already tacking in close with the north shore of the bay which was the fleet's objective, and her boats, with pilots aboard, were

---

1759, was governor of Jamaica from 1768 to 1772, and died at Spanish Town on 12 Dec. 1772, receiving a public funeral." C. Alexander Harris, "Sir William Trelawney," *Dictionary of National Biography*.

9. Gardiner, *The West Indies*, 6.

out sounding. She was being eyed with considerable alarm by the masters of a French seventy-four and two frigates which lay at anchor off Fort Royale.[10] At eleven o'clock the whole fleet passed close in with the Diamond Rock, and near a fort in the small bay of Ste. Anne's, and another battery farther along the shore, both of which remained silent.[11] At noon the south point of the bay bore northwest, three miles. Moore consulted his pilots.

The immediate question was whether to attack Fort Royale or St. Pierre, farther up the coast. The pilots said it was very hard to get into St. Pierre Roads because of calms and contrary winds which prevailed there. In entering, the ships would take a beating from the batteries. Then, if disabled, regardless of the outcome, they could never sail against Fort Royale. Further, at St. Pierre there was no anchorage for the transports except within range of every battery. If they hove to instead of anchoring, being of light draft they might be blown to windward and be unable to return. In fact, the whole fleet would drift to leeward if disabled, and never get back to Fort Royale. The French could reinforce Fort Royale if the British took St. Pierre, but could not reinforce St. Pierre if the British took Fort Royale. St. Pierre, however, would fall if Fort Royale were taken. If the British troops landed at St. Pierre they could not hope to march to Fort Royale.

Assuming the attack was projected against Fort Royale, the first job to be done there was to silence the battery at Negro Point, because the ships could go no closer to the citadel than that point.

Moore had each pilot sign this summary of their opinions;[12] it might save him from being shot on his own quarterdeck if the expedition ended in disaster and the inevitable inquiry into his conduct should be made.

At one o'clock in the afternoon the squadron and transports were to leeward of Pigeon Island and the fleet was employed during the rest of the day and night in turning into Fort Royale Bay,

---

10. "The expedition," Loudoun Papers.
11. Gardiner, *The West Indies*, 6.
12. Moore to Pitt, 30 January 1759, Colonial Office 110/1.

a tedious and nerve-tiring job of tacking square-rigged ships in narrow waters against the trade wind.[13] At two o'clock the forts spoke up, firing signal guns and breaking out the flag of His Most Christian Majesty. The *Florissant*, 74, and the two frigates made sail. One of the frigates, the *Bellona*, made a run for it and escaped from the bay.[14] The *Florissant* and the other frigate turned up under the citadel and cleared for action.[15] At four o'clock the battery on Pigeon Island opened fire at the *Rippon*, and thereafter fired occasionally at any ship venturing close enough to make it worth the try.[16] The chief engineer and the quartermaster officer went in a small boat to reconnoiter the shore line for Hopson.[17] At five o'clock Moore threw out a signal for all masters of transports, and signals for the *Lyon, Bristol*, and *Rippon*. He brought to until he was answered, and then made sail again.[18] When Captains Trelawney, Leslie, and Jekyll came aboard him, Leslie was ordered to lead the fleet on and to take the *Rippon* and *Lyon* under his command in the morning for an attack against the fort on Negro Point.[19] Similar orders were given to the *Roebuck, Woolwich, Panther*, and *Winchester* to attack a battery above the beach at Cas Navires Bay at the same time as the Negro Point attack.[20]

Many of the ships arrived too late to anchor and stood off and on all night, while an occasional cannon shot boomed through the darkness.[21] At six o'clock the *Florissant* and the remaining

13. "The expedition," Loudoun Papers.
14. This thirty-two-gun ship was taken after a four hours' engagement by the *Vestal*, 32, Captain Hood, on 21 February and carried into Spithead. She was bearing dispatches for Paris, and thus, on 3 March 1759, the Admiralty had its first news of the arrival of the fleet at Martinique. *Gentleman's Magazine*, 29 (1759), 143.
15. Gardiner, *The West Indies*, 6.
16. *Ibid.*, 6-7. Governor Beauharnois claimed that a shot in the dark from the citadel dismasted one of the British vessels. Beauharnois, Relation, Archives nationales, Marine et colonies, C^8 A 62. No British source mentioned the incident.
17. "Journal of an officer," anonymous paper enclosed in Hopson to Pitt, 30 January 1759, in, Pitt, *Correspondence*, II, 27-29.
18. Gardiner, *The West Indies*, 7.
19. "The expedition," Loudoun Papers.
20. Haldane's "proceedings," Newcastle Papers, Add. MSS. 32887, f. 394, British Museum.
21. *Ibid.*; also, "Journal of an officer," Pitt, *Correspondence*, II, 27.

French frigate had turned into the careenage behind the citadel. They were blockaded.[22]

The fort at Negro Point mounted six or seven thirty-two pounders (witnesses disagree on the number) in embrasures, with a high stone parapet at least twelve feet thick. It had a very narrow gate and the walls were pierced for small arms. Captain Gardiner said it was about three miles from the citadel but the best charts show it to be not more than a mile and a half distant.[23] This would be a difficult but not impossible cannon shot for the gunners in Fort Royale if they chose to annoy any hostile force in Fort Negro.

At half an hour past seven o'clock in the morning of 16 January the commodore and the fleet hoisted colors and the commodore signalled for the attack on Negro Point to begin. The *Bristol* was to windward of the point, while the *Rippon* and *Lyon* were two and seven miles, respectively, to leeward. Captain Leslie in the *Bristol* threw out a signal to his diminutive squadron and ran down to the fort, opening fire a little after eight o'clock, about fifty yards off shore. For forty-five minutes he poured on a hot fire of guns and small arms, while the fort (garrisoned, we now know, by a single company) responded feebly. About nine o'clock the defenders lost courage and fled. A lieutenant of the *Bristol* thereupon took her detachment of Marines ashore in the boats. The Marines, with fixed bayonets and their red coats flashing in the morning sun, clambered up the rocks in single file and entered the fort at one of the embrasures. At the same time the *Rippon* anchored astern of the *Bristol*[24] (the *Lyon* never did beat back in time to be of any use) and the Marines ashore were reinforced by Captain Gardiner with the Marines from that ship.[25]

22. Gardiner, *The West Indies*, 6.
23. "The expedition," Loudoun Papers; Gardiner, *The West Indies*, 7; U. S. Hydrographic Office, No. 1022, *Fort de France Bay (Fort Royal Bay)* (Washington, D. C., 1887, 26th ed., 1931), from a French survey of 1824; Edward Cust, *Annals of the Wars of the Eighteenth Century* (London, 1862-69), II, 284.
24. Beating two miles to windward in an hour and a half may be considered as smart sailing for an eighteenth-century square-rigged ship of the line.
25. In his account of the episode Captain Gardiner gave the impression, without being explicit, that both Marine detachments entered at the same time. But the captain on other occasions seemed to be interested in advancing himself and I have relied on another witness who did not practice studied evasion of the point

While the victorious Marines were successfully searching the fort for souvenirs of the departed garrison, and finding hats, swords, and silver spurs, their officers, including Gardiner, surveyed the prize with an eye to defending it if it was to be held. At half after ten o'clock the Union Jack cracked in the trade wind and sentinels were posted on the parapet. The other Marines were disposed so as to meet any attack from the French. The guns were spiked (these were Marines, not artillerymen) and the content of the powder magazine was taken down to the rocky shore and thrown into the sea, pursuant to Moore's orders of the night before. About eleven o'clock a naval lieutenant returned aboard the *Bristol* and reported to Leslie that the Marine officers considered the place tenable. Leslie ordered them to hold it until he signalled otherwise. Meanwhile the men were knocking the trunnions[26] off the cannon, and breaking up the gun carriages. Shortly before noon Moore signalled for all general officers and at noon ordered all ships to anchor.[27]

A little before one o'clock Captain Leslie signalled to the Marine officers to abandon the fort, which they did immediately. Between two and three o'clock Moore ordered the *Bristol* and *Rippon* to get under way and move down to leeward to avoid a shower of bombs from the citadel.[28]

Earlier, at nine in the morning, the ships which had been detailed to knock out the battery in Cas Navires Bay had been sent in. They silenced the four guns there, blew up a magazine, and stood by to cover a landing of the troops, while the *Bristol* and *Rippon* kept up a cannonade on the shore, once their job at Negro Point had been completed. French troops had been directed from the citadel to oppose any attempt to land at Cas Navires Bay but,

---

but spoke with exactness. Gardiner, *The West Indies,* 7; "The expedition," Loudoun Papers; Malo, 5; Beauharnois, Relation, Arch. nat., Marine et col., C⁸ A 62.

For an example of Gardiner's self-inflation see his "View of the town and bay of Port Royal," reproduced in *American Neptune,* 6 (1946), facing p. 298, on which he managed to get his name inscribed next to Fort Negro, although no source explicitly stated that he helped to capture it.

26. Trunnions are cylindrical projections from the barrel of a cannon, which rest on the gun carriage to support the cannon, and also act as axes for the elevation and depression of the gun.

27. "The expedition," Loudoun Papers.   28. *Ibid.*

on seeing the Marines on the parapet at Fort Negro, the French pulled out to avoid encirclement. This left the beach at Cas Navires undefended and the brigades later landed unopposed[29]—the last bit of good luck the British had at Martinique.

Generals Barrington and Clavering had been out reconnoitering independently. To them and to Haldane the only suitable place to land the troops seemed to be one covered by an entrenchment. On their report it was decided, however, not to try to throw troops ashore in the face of an entrenchment, but rather to exploit the psychological gain at Negro Point and to land the men at the latter place. Moore later told Pitt this was Hopson's idea. It was a rocky place and its only merit as a landing place was that it was undefended. At two o'clock in the afternoon the commodore threw out the signal to hoist out the flat bottomed boats and the soldiers tumbled over the sides of the transports into them. This was an unpleasant operation. It took so long to get the whole army afloat that some of the men must have sat in the boats for three hours under the tropical sun.[30]

At half-past three the troops were ordered to land. At the same time Moore "slipped" and dropped astern, because of the heavy rain of shells which was sent over with the compliments of the commandant of the citadel, one of the shells, as Haldane put it, "almost falling into the commodore." All ships in the squadron were instructed to weigh anchor and drop to leeward to escape the bombardment. The boats alongside the transports perforce went with them to leeward, where the fleet brought up two miles from Negro Point. To carry out the original design would have meant rowing for two miles along a shore which swarmed with hostile snipers. They might have been able to stand out far enough from shore to be beyond musket range, but it was already four o'clock in the afternoon and the army faced a confused and slow

29. Gardiner, *The West Indies*, 8-9; Cust, *Annals of the Wars of the Eighteenth Century*, II, 284. There had been two companies at Cas Navires. Malo, 5.
30. Haldane's "proceedings," Newcastle Papers, Add. MSS. 32887, British Museum; "The expedition," Loudoun Papers. The Haldane account is hereafter cited as, Haldane's "proceedings," Newcastle Papers. Landing drills as carried out at Barbados had taken five hours each, including reembarkation. Moore, "Journal," Admiralty 50/22.

landing after sunset, under sniping fire of French militia, fighting for their homes by the light of the moon. In this emergency they decided to get a footing where they could, so they rowed for Cas Navires Bay, which, as has been explained, was luckily undefended.[31]

It was about five o'clock when Haldane's men of the Second Brigade waded ashore. The First Brigade, Trapaud's, was close behind them. Hoarse and sunburned sergeants barked them into formation while glittering officers affected to be unaware what fine targets their scabbards and gorgets[32] made for whatever irregulars might be hidden in the nearby thorn scrub and cactus brush. At half an hour after five o'clock the commands were shouted the length of the column and the red ranks stepped off. They marched to Fort Negro without waiting for the Third Brigade, commanded by the jealous Armiger, which did not come ashore until half past six in the evening. Having discharged its militant cargo the fleet made sail and spent the night turning up into the bay, nearer the town.[33]

While the unhappy seamen were beginning this night-long canvas drill, the men ashore were not having a pleasure jaunt. Haldane was surprised to learn that what had seemed to be grass from shipboard was heavy brush. It was dangerous and difficult. To reach the neighborhood of Fort Negro they had to pant up a steep hill and pass a deep and rocky ravine where only two men could march in front. This took so long it was dark before they reached a place where they could "sustain" themselves. The unknown author of a journal sent to Pitt by Hopson said this place was the only clearing he saw in the country, and was between two ravines which were covered with trees. On arrival they formed an "oblong square," as he described it, with two regiments in front, two in the rear, and one on each flank. The Highlanders were put in parties on the angles, and a screen of grenadiers[34]

---

31. "The expedition," Loudoun Papers; Haldane's "proceedings," Newcastle Papers.
32. On gorgets, see Appendix, Topic 12.
33. "The expedition," Loudoun Papers; Gardiner, *The West Indies*, 8-10; Haldane's "proceedings," Newcastle Papers; Pitt, *Correspondence*, II, 27.
34. On grenadiers, see Appendix, Topic 13.

was thrown across the front. The diarist passed the night "quietly under a fine tree in the centre sugar canes and an old wall in our front." The men slept on their arms. They were, according to Haldane, "very much heated" and showers occasionally obscured the moon but, he added, "We made the best disposition we could considering the darkness of the night."[35]

While most critics will agree with Sir Julian Corbett's comment that the campaign had been handled "skilfully and correctly" thus far,[36] disappointment was to follow.

At the dawn of 17 January the British outposts saw the enemy advancing through the woods and down the ravines in great numbers. As they advanced in irregular skirmish formation they fired on the covering men from all directions, themselves for the most part hidden in the brush and cane brakes. Hopson ordered out all grenadiers, with two small pieces of cannon, to support the advance posts and to attack a house in the front where the militia were entrenching. This was work the grenadiers understood, and the diggers were soon driven off, but the grenadiers, with "rangers" on the flanks, advanced into a cross fire from invisible enemies. A battalion was sent to support them, and they cleared the woods, but were ordered to retire to the captured house because they could not see the enemy who fired on them. While this skirmishing was going on, the army ashore was augmented by some Highlanders who had not been able to land on the previous evening, because of the lateness of the landing of the first three brigades.[37]

Other British troops advanced beyond Fort Negro, firing into the woods in an attempt to clear a line toward the citadel. Detachments were employed in an attempt to rout the snipers out of the thorny brush surrounding the British "oblong square." Officers reconnoitered the ground between the camp and the citadel and found it blocked by steep hills which were covered by the almost impenetrable rain forest, or by head-high cane brakes, and

---

35. Malo, 7; "Journal of an officer," in Hopson to Pitt, 30 January 1759, Pitt, *Correspondence*, II, 27; Haldane's "proceedings," Newcastle Papers. The diary of the unknown officer is hereafter cited as "Journal," Pitt, *Correspondence*.

36. Corbett, *England in the Seven Years' War*, I, 377-379.

37. "Journal," Pitt, *Correspondence*, II, 27-28; "The expedition," Loudoun Papers.

cut and slashed by dry ravines and gullies with perpendicular walls. These were passable by men at some places, but nowhere passable for the guns or for any sort of wagons. This information was acquired while ducking slugs from snipers' pieces. Meanwhile a few companies of the Third Brigade were landed from the transports and the land force was complete.[38]

The painful bushwhacking continued and casualties increased in number. Colonel Crump was sent to lead the grenadiers against a hill which commanded the camp, but, according to Haldane, "in advancing was fir'd at from ev'ry part, without being able to distinguish from whence the shot came."[39] The French muskets were said to carry farther than Britain's standard fourteen-pound "Brown Bess" musket, and Crump counted casualties when he thought he was out of range. Despite this rough handling he took the hill a little before ten o'clock in the morning. A battery of two light guns, established shortly on the hill top, scoured the woods and probably raised the spirits of the men, but did little else. Taking this hill did not improve the situation for another hill commanded the first. Observing the steady fattening of the casualty rolls Hopson decided there was no purpose in trying "to fight these Indians in a regular way" (Haldane's phrase)[40] so the grenadiers were called off and the durable Scots—more familiar with rough country—were sent out with piece and claymore "to skirmish with them." This brought a relative peace to the camp, and three redoubts were thrown up for use in case of a night attack.[41]

About eleven o'clock in the morning a large party of French was discovered trying to advance across the line from the camp to the transports' anchorage in Cas Navires Bay. Lieutenant Colonel Debrissay was sent out with the Sixty-third Regiment to break it up. For a time the skirmish threatened to become general, the lines were extended, and the whole army en-

38. Gardiner, *The West Indies*, 10-11; "The expedition," Loudoun Papers; Haldane's "proceedings," Newcastle Papers.
39. Haldane's "proceedings," Newcastle Papers.
40. *Ibid.;* Malo, 9.
41. Gardiner, *The West Indies*, 10-11; "Journal," Pitt, *Correspondence*, II, 27-28.

gaged. The sun struck hard and the men "became extremely faint with the heat."[42] This can be understood easily: most of them were carrying on a tropical battle a mile from their water supply. Everything was happening at once. The Scots were harrying the mulatto musketeers through the brush, the Sixty-third Regiment was skirmishing with a French irregular body, the battery on Crump's captive hill was barking periodically, the rest of the soldiery was defending the camp with musket or entrenching tool, two bomb ketches were lofting shells at the citadel, and the dark-skinned pioneers were landing the baggage. At this point Hopson called his general officers into council.[43]

At noon Captain Gardiner, watching the army's work from the *Rippon,* saw soldiers advancing up Morne Tartenson, the hill which overlooked the town of Fort Royale. To him it seemed that he was watching a victory. It is our bad luck that he did not borrow Captain Jekyll's glass and identify the regiment to which the men belonged by the color of the facings on their coats, or by their kilts, if any. They were probably the Highlanders chasing snipers, since there is no record of any other troops being sent out in that direction. Morne Tartenson is roughly a mile from the base of the point of land on which the citadel stood. But the British never reached the top. According to French witnesses it had been neglected by the governor, although it is no doubt one of the strategically important points in the island. On its summit, at the moment when Gardiner saw men ascending it, were some French inferior officers who had resolved to defend it with a body of militia strengthened by the garrison from Fort Negro and by the covering detachment from Cas Navires, neither group of which had acquired any appreciable glory thus far. The British said the defenders were entirely unprovided with cannon,[44] although Beauharnois later claimed to have sent two guns.

Fewer militia had come than Beauharnois had expected, and some of those few had their own ideas of a site for a fight. Rather

---

42. Haldane's "proceedings," Newcastle Papers.
43. *Ibid.;* "Journal," Pitt, *Correspondence,* II, 27-28; "The expedition," Loudoun Papers.
44. Gardiner, *The West Indies,* 10-11; Cust, *Annals of the Wars of the Eighteenth Century,* II, 284-285; Malo, 6-9.

than be cooped up in the citadel they disregarded the governor's wishes (*they* said) and climbed Morne Tartenson, which overlooked the citadel. They had no real training in military matters but they were used to shooting game. As the anonymous narrator quoted by Henri Malo put it, an Englishman once said hunting was like war but here they made war like hunting. And just as Edward Braddock had failed, and John Burgoyne was to fail, Hopson could not cope with a swarm of undisciplined, irregular New World bushwhackers.[45]

For the next three hours the British offensive lagged while councils of war convened and calculated.

2. *Withdrawal from Fort Royale Bay*

The visiting soldiery had spent a hot and harassed morning. One officer remarked that he "never saw such country, the Highlands of Scotland, for woods, mountains, canes and continued ravines is nothing to it." The citadel was five miles from the landing point, across difficult country. Men were collapsing from heat, fatigue, and lack of water. The militia would not stand up and fight, but they did better—they kept up a stinging fire which, Haldane said, "incommoded us extremely."[46] Hopson believed it would be prudent to estimate that the citadel might hold out for ten days after they reached it. Looking over the terrain, he called a council of war.[47]

He and his generals had the professional advice of Cunninghame, the engineer, who had conducted a reconnaissance from the land side. Cunninghame said the troops could advance to within cannon shot, but at that distance (three miles, more or less) would come to a steep ravine. He was asked whether he could bridge it.

---

45. Malo, 6-9; Beauharnois, writing on 27 January when he would have every reason to wish to appear important to the great repulse, said he sent the first companies and two guns to Morne Tartenson, adding that old soldiers advised him the hill was indefensible, despite which advice he kept in constant touch with the situation there. Beauharnois, Relation, Archives nationales, Marine et colonies, C⁸ A 62.

46. Journal," Pitt, *Correspondence*, II, 27-28; Haldane's "proceedings," Newcastle Papers.

47. *Ibid.*; "The expedition," Loudoun Papers; Hopson to Pitt, 30 January 1759, Pitt, *Correspondence*, II, 20-22.

That would be impractical, he thought. What chance would there be to carry around it? Such a portage, in his opinion, would be five miles long, with thirty cannon to be carried, plus mortars, stores, and baggage, by the Barbadian Negroes who numbered only about three hundred. The fleet could not spare more than four hundred hands to assist in this labor. Worse, it would have to be done all at once because the force was too small to risk detaching units to pass that distance alone through woods and fields which were admirable for irregular resistance by men who knew the ground.[48] Worst, there was no water on the proposed road to Fort Royale. Haldane concluded from these uncomfortable remarks that it would take ten days' work by a thousand men daily to make the road passable, and another thousand would have to carry water to the workers. Meanwhile, the French were bringing cannon to another hill commanding the camp.[49]

Hopson may have been swayed by Haldane, or perhaps Haldane was expressing the opinion of Hopson. At any rate the latter sent an aide off with a letter to Moore, who was on board the *Cambridge,* asking him if it would be possible to land the guns nearer than Cas Navires Bay, and in a position to act upon the citadel. Sending Captains Harman, Shuldham, and Gambier,[50] the commodore replied, without doubt on the basis of information received from his pilots on the day before, that he could land the guns no nearer than Fort Negro, but he would be glad to send enough sailors to haul the cannon to whatever place Hopson wanted to use them.[51] Since Fort Negro was no closer to the enemy's chief bastion than the councilling officers were, and the offer did not

48. Hopson was already in a position similar to that in which Burgoyne was to find himself twenty years later, in North America. To have detached a portaging force would have made the analogy even closer; compare Burgoyne's detaching the German auxiliaries and sending them to Bennington.

49. Haldane's "proceedings," Newcastle Papers.

50. James Gambier (1723-1789), of Huguenot descent, was the uncle of the better known, but perhaps less able, James, Admiral Lord Gambier (1756-1833). He was a lieutenant in the Mediterranean in 1743. His first command was the *Speedwell* sloop in 1746. In 1758, after serving as captain of many ships, he was put in the *Burford,* in which he saw service at Louisbourg, Martinique, and Guadeloupe.

51. Inasmuch as cannon had to be transferred from ship to shore on cranky catamarans (light rafts) the best opinion of the eighteenth century was quite against the operation being performed where the landing party could be fired on.

solve the time and water problems, it was not satisfactory to the land staff. It was decided to send Major General Barrington, second in command, in person, with an alternative proposal: could they not make a joint attack on the citadel, and could not Moore guarantee to secure the lines of communication between the fleet and the land force if the army marched without having the cannon landed closer? By this proposal they probably intended that Moore would guard the communication with Marines and sailors. It was now about eleven o'clock. Barrington's return was delayed four hours by the convocation of a council of war among the officers of the fleet.[52]

All captains of ships of the line and of frigates were called aboard the *Cambridge*. Sir William Trelawney was the only one absent—having been blown to leeward again in his shallow, high riding *Lyon*. While the captains' gigs were flashing smartly up to Moore's starboard gangway, the commodore sent officers out to see if there was any practicable landing place on the citadel's side of the bay where the cannon could be landed out of range of the citadel's heavy guns. Also the pilots were ordered up for questioning.[53]

The council took up the whole question of what further aid could be given to Hopson. Thirteen specific questions were put to the pilots, which, with their answers, are paraphrased here.

Q—Can the men of war go up to the fort while the enemy still occupies it?

A—Not until the western battery is silenced.

Q—Why not?

A—Because they would be under fire for hours while tacking up to the fort.[54]

Q—When can the ships be gotten up to the fort?

A—When the westernmost battery is silenced.

Q—How can the battery be silenced?

---

52. Haldane's "proceedings," Newcastle Papers; Hopson *et al.* to Moore, 16 January 1759, enclosed in Moore to Pitt, 30 January 1759, Colonial Office 110/1; "Journal," Pitt, *Correspondence*, II, 27-28; Hopson to Pitt, 30 January 1759, *ibid.*
53. Moore to Hopson *et al.*, 17 January 1759, enclosed in Moore to Pitt, 30 January 1759, Colonial Office 110/1; Haldane's "proceedings," Newcastle Papers.
54. The western battery was the one closest to the ships.

A—By nothing but a land force.

Q—How many ships could lie along the west side of the citadel?

A—Two, afloat.

Q—How high would the battery be in relation to the ships?

A—Above the main top of the *Cambridge*.

Q—Could the ships annoy the enemy fort while themselves enduring fire?

A—Only at the greatest elevation.

Q—If they lay to receive the fire could the troops and matériel be landed on the meadow between the town and the fort?

A—The landing place would be exposed to the fire of the two-deck ship and the frigate in the careenage which could fire across the meadow—only three hundred yards across—and also they would be exposed to the fire of all the small arms in the place.

Q—How many of the citadel's guns would be usable against the ships?

A—About sixty or seventy.

Q—Is there any place above Fort Negro where the landing would not be covered by the whole fort?

A—No.

Q—How far are the transports from the proposed landing place on the meadow by the fort?

A—About four miles.

Q—Is there any better place to land the troops than where they are landed?

A—No.

At the end of this inquisition the pilots volunteered a statement: "We also say if one ship was dismantled or disabled going up, it would stop the progress of the other."[55]

While the briny councillors digested these observations, Moore put the problem this way: Hopson had proposed a joint attack if the cannon could be brought closer to the enemy. If that was

55. The testimony in full was found in Moore to Pitt, 30 January 1759, Colonial Office 110/1. It is not in the published Pitt correspondence. The pilots appear to have been British West Indian merchant skippers who went privateering in war time, and who would have familiarized themselves with these waters in peace time.—*South-Carolina Gazette,* 24 February 1759.

impossible Hopson wanted the seamen to bring him off in the boats "as soon as the moon is up." The commodore added to the pilots' intelligence the information that it "would take two days to beat up to windward to the fort, even unmolested,"[56] while the soldiers might not be able to maintain themselves that long. Officers had been sent to offer the labor of seamen to haul the siege train from Fort Negro, but this had not been accepted. The alternatives were to land the guns on catamarans under close fire of the citadel, or to police some five miles of communications from the fleet to the army. While Barrington waited and the ships tugged at anchor, the council agreed unanimously that they could not comply with the generals' request. Barrington carried the statement ashore to Hopson. Hopson ordered an evacuation,[57] on the ground that they could not sustain themselves where they were for more than two days. It was about three o'clock when it became generally known among the officer corps that Barrington had returned with news which caused Hopson to order a re-embarkation. The operation was to take place between six and seven o'clock.[58]

At four o'clock the boats were ordered made ready. For a ruse, siege implements were landed and the troops began throwing up breastworks as though they intended to stay a while. At five o'clock Moore ordered the *Rippon* to weigh her anchor and warp[59] up to Fort Negro in order to cover the reembarkation. At seven the boats were sent away to pick up the troops on the beach, while other soldiers were employed in burning the brush and cane brakes surrounding them. As darkness fell the pioneers began retiring the baggage under which they had sweated in the noonday sun before the decision to withdraw had been made. Troops were also retiring from up the country, leaving covering posts to amuse any curious French patrols. By eight o'clock boats were passing from

---

56. At the most the distance could not have been more than four or five sea miles. This is a good statement of the inefficiency of square-rigged war ships when sailing into the wind.

57. Moore to Pitt, 30 January 1759, Colonial Office 110/1; Haldane's "proceedings," Newcastle Papers; Gardiner, *The West Indies*, 11-12.

58. *Ibid.;* Haldane's "proceedings," Newcastle Papers.

59. On warping a ship, see Appendix, Topic 14.

the shore to the shadowy transports in the light of the tropic moon. By nine the covering detachments, with the light guns, were drifting down the beach and into the boats. No disturbance marked this transfer of men from earth to deck. By half past ten all were aboard, not having left behind them a single sick or wounded man. Hopson had shown himself a very capable man for any work which did not require a bold imagination and a decisive temper. The men were in generally good condition although a few victims of heat prostration had to be carried to the boats.[60]

Without meeting an enemy force which would hold still long enough to be destroyed, the army had lost what Hopson with his usual pessimism said at first was almost a hundred men. The casualty list shows that the captain of the grenadier company in the Fourth Regiment had been killed in the attack on the hill which Crump had taken; twenty-one of the rank and file had also been killed; Captain Colin Campbell[61] of the Fourth Regiment, and a lieutenant of the skirmishing Scots had been wounded, along with forty-seven men.[62] To persons used to the shocking casualty figures admitted by twentieth-century mass armies, these figures seem trivial.[63] The unhappiest face that could be put upon it was that there was no conscription in this war, and Hopson had lost about one man in eighty in a small force, each man of which was relatively more thoroughly trained than in any twentieth-century army before the decade of the 'thirties. But what is more to the point, he had lost them for nothing to a

---

60. Gardiner, *The West Indies*, 11-12; Robert Beatson, *Naval and Military Memoirs, 1727-1783* (London, 1804), II, 232, hereafter cited as, Beatson, *Memoirs;* Hopson to Pitt, 30 January 1759, in Pitt, *Correspondence*, II, 20-22; "The expedition," Loudoun Papers; Entick, *The Late War*, IV, 145; Pitt, *Correspondence*, II, 27-28; Haldane's "proceedings," Newcastle Papers.

61. The world was and is so full of a number of Colin Campbells it is hard to be sure of identifying a particular Colin Campbell, but a man of this name, a major in the Hundredth Regiment at Martinique, in 1762 was cashiered after a court-martial inquired into the murder of a brother officer, Captain John McKaarg. *Dictionary of National Biography.*

62. Hopson to Pitt, 30 January 1759, Colonial Office 110/1; Gardiner, *The West Indies*, 12. The French lost only three whites and "some Negroes" killed. Malo, 11.

63. Applying my hypothetical manpower ratio of 10:1 (see Appendix, Topic 6) similar losses to a twentieth-century expedition of fifty thousand men would be ten officers and 210 men killed, twenty officers and 470 men wounded, a total of 710 combat casualties.

straggling hide-and-seek irregular crowd of miscellaneous low-trained militia. As to morale at time of evacuation, Sir Julian Corbett said it was a disheartening beginning to the campaign, and a certain depression, true, is reflected in the leaders' correspondence. But eighteenth-century soldiers fought by drilled-in habits and not from emotional or ideological impulses. Barring distrust of their leadership occasioned by bad care or a long train or defeats and always excepting the demoralization of an unusually high casualty rate such as Braddock's men suffered, little psychological harm could come to these men. After sleep, food, and drink, they would fight all the better for the additional seasoning.[64]

It was unfortunate for the invading force that they had no organized intelligence service. Apparently no native offered himself for sale, nor were any prisoners taken by the British, although "un soldat irlandais" deserted to the French, who also took four prisoners. Had the British been able to interrogate any of their enemies Hopson might have stood on the shore for a while longer and the whole campaign have come to a quick and successful end. The one possible weakness of the Martinique defense on which the British did not dare or think to gamble was the will to fight of the French commanders. Unknown to the British the condition of the military spirit of the leaders of Martinique seems to have been low. According to a report which reached England in March, "Three sloops are said to have arrived at Eustatia [St. Eustatius] in *January* last from *Martinico*, having in effects on board to the value of 300,000 *l.* currency, the property of French merchants."[65] This report may have been only a rumor without foundation, but the West Indian nabobs often had extremely accurate information from their estate agents, for example, John Campbell, fourth Earl of Loudoun, who was very well informed of the events of the first month of fighting in this campaign. It would be natural,

---

64. Even a high mortality rate would not necessarily demoralize them if incurred in a type of fighting they understood. Remember Breed's hill.

65. *Gentleman's Magazine*, 29 (1759), 145; Malo, 10; Beauharnois, R'elation, Archives nationales, Marine et colonies, C⁸ A 62. A note in the *South-Carolina Gazette*, 21 March 1759, is also instructive: "The Bellona, taken by the Vestal frigate [Captain Hood], is esteemed a very valuable prize, having a great deal of treasure aboard belonging to the governor of Martinique."

in time of war, to pass it on to the public. Even so, the shipping out of "effects" might represent only an ordinary business precaution, but it does not stand alone.

Information from the French archives shows that at the moment when skirmishers reached the base of Morne Tartenson, about noon on 17 January, Beauharnois at the citadel was so alarmed and desperate that he was ready to demolish his fort if the British gained the hill, and it was with such somber thoughts that he was preoccupied when news of the withdrawal of the British advanced parties reached him. The garrison of Fort Royale was said to have consisted of 480 men detached from the ships in the harbor, thirty-six "bombardiers," and eighty Swiss. The island was also short of provisions. The fort was not nearly so defensible as the pilots had told the fleet officers. The engineer sent out in 1760 to put the defenses of Martinique in good condition, found the entrenchments around Fort Royale far too long for the number of defenders available.[66] Lieutenant General Cust, from sources he did not name, said that when the British troops were leaving, that is, about eight o'clock in the evening, the governor and his people "were at the very moment actually assembled in the public hall in the city, to send deputies to the English General with proposals of capitulation and surrender"; but this does not seem to have represented the attitude of the populace generally, judging by their spirited defense of Morne Tartenson. On 1 January the commanders of the several military districts of Martinique had presented to their commander a jointly signed memorial describing, in cheerless tones, the misery of the island, even before the arrival of the British. They spoke of the stagnation of trade, of the grave shortage of food which

66. Pares, *War and Trade*, 247, 248, citing Rochemore to Berryer, 13 March 1761, Archives nationales, Marine et colonies, C^8 A 63. In fairness to the unknown designer of these defenses it should be added that military engineers in those times usually had nothing but contempt for the work of their predecessors. Two warmly partisan accounts attributed the repulse of the British to enthusiastic defense by the colonists and their slaves, despite timidity in the hearts of the responsible officers. Adrien Dessales, *Histoire Générale des Antilles* (Paris, 1847-1848), V, 145n.-146n., 149-156, and, Malo's anonymous narrator, both of whom show strong anti-officer and pro-militia feeling. Malo's narrator seems on the whole the more credible. But *cf.* Archives nationales, Marine et colonies, C^8 A 62, for the "official" story.

approached famine, of the abuse of special privileges of trade with the Dutch which were used to enrich a few merchants but not for the common good, of the dangerous practice of butchering draft animals for food, and of the real need to put the citadel in condition for defense.[67] Taken together, these scraps of evidence seem to point to low spirits, at least in the French superior officers. A final piece of evidence: hesitant defense does not breed respect for officers, and satirical rhymes and songs concerning the fears of the commandant, Beauharnois, circulated in the French islands for some time after the British left.[68]

3. A look into St. Pierre

During the night the *Cambridge* and the *Norfolk* blew out to sea, and rather than wait for his flagship to beat back to the fleet, Commodore Moore came in by boat and hoisted his broad pennant on the giant *St. George* at six o'clock in the morning (18 January). Shortly afterward the general officers met on the flagship to consult with the commodore as to the practicability of landing to eastward of the fort. He again called up his pilots who maintained, as they had consistently done, that the ships could not beat up to the fort except at too great a risk to the safety of the whole squadron. On receiving this opinion the generals conferred apart and sent to Moore a proposal to attack the town of St. Pierre, to the northward, on the west coast of the island. Although Moore could hardly have forgotten the advice of the pilots that the conquest of St. Pierre would have little or no effect on the defense of the remainder of the island, he had

67. Cust, *Annals of the Wars of the Eighteenth Century*, II, 285; *South-Carolina Gazette*, 21 May 1759. Malo's anonymous narrator tried to make it plain that the judgment of the French commanding general was not trusted by the militia.

68. The eminent naval historian, J. K. Laughton, in his article on Moore in the *Dictionary of National Biography*, gave as one of the reasons for the evacuation of Martinique the statement that the approaches to Fort Royale were heavily mined. This statement was undoubtedly based on a contemporary writer who used the signature "J. J., a lieutenant in the navy," for a pamphlet entitled *Candid Reflections on the Expedition to Martinico, With an Account of the Taking of Guadeloupe* (London, 1759). A reader's digest of the pamphlet is available in the *Gentleman's Magazine*, 29 (1759), 286-287. I reject this alleged source entirely for reasons stated at length in my "A Note on the *DNB* and the Evacuation of Martinique," *American Neptune*, 3 (1943), 168-169.

nothing else to offer at the moment and agreed to steer for that place.[69]

At nine o'clock Moore hoisted his flag once more on the *Cambridge*, and made the signal to bring in the flat-bottomed boats. The signal for the ships to set their sails had been thrown out previously. According to Gardiner, at noon the fleet was employed in turning into the bay, and spent the afternoon at it to occupy the nervous attention of the enemy. No doubt, as was usually the situation, the fleet was pretty well scattered during the night; this would be as effective a way to reassemble the ships as any other. At six o'clock in the evening, the commodore bore away from the bay and ran down along the west side of the island, in the words of Captain Gardiner, "all Night under an easy Sail."[70]

St. Pierre was the commercial capital of Martinique. There was a continued rivalry between it and Fort Royale, the latter being the political head of the island. The governors, on occasion, ordered the merchantmen to lie in Fort Royale Bay for safety but the traders argued that it was most inconvenient for them, and, although St. Pierre roadstead was insecure and ships could be cut out of it, they could not be blockaded there as they could be at Fort Royale. They were correct when they said that St. Pierre roadstead was always open. In 1748 with only a French corvette in the harbor, and a strong English force standing off shore, privateers were able to go out of the roads and—given a little help from shore batteries and small craft—bring prizes back under the bows of the British "blockade" ships.[71]

As seen early in the morning of 19 January the town of St. Pierre had a very attractive appearance. It was built along the bay in the form of a half circle. Behind it the land climbed

---

69. Gardiner, *The West Indies*, 14; Moore to Pitt, and, Hopson to Pitt, 30 January 1759, in Pitt, *Correspondence*, II, 29-31, and, 22-23, respectively; Haldane's "proceedings," Newcastle Papers.

70. "The expedition," Loudoun Papers; Gardiner, *The West Indies*, 14; "Journal," Pitt, *Correspondence*, II, 27-28.

71. Pares, *War and Trade*, 247, citing Bompar to Machault, 20 October 1755, Givry to Machault, 28 October 1755, Archives Nat., Colonies, C^8 A 61, letter from St. Pierre, 12 May 1756, Archives de la Gironde, C 4318, No. 58; Pares, *War and Trade*, 295.

up to a ridge running northward to its culmination in Mont Pelée (which totally destroyed the town in a few minutes of volcanic activity on 8 May 1902). The town's chief strength was the citadel at the north end; there were several new batteries on the heights to the left, and some batteries on the right, with an entrenchment. Gardiner said the fortifications were well built "and well defended."[72] His seniors thought otherwise, and, as Sir Julian Corbett said, St. Pierre would have been fairly easy to take. The shore was steep-to and the roads offered plenty of water for the tallest of ships. The five-fathom line is at no point more than a quarter of a sea mile off shore, and in most places is much closer.[73]

At six o'clock in the morning the town bore E. N. E. five miles. Although the English had been at Fort Royale long enough for word of their unfriendly disposition to have reached St. Pierre, the fleet discovered about forty sail of sugar-laden merchant shipping lying in the roadstead. At seven Moore ordered the *Panther* in to sound the roadstead; Shuldham steered in, sounding from side to side, while several balls from the citadel splashed nearby. At eight o'clock two of the bomb ketches were set to annoying the citadel and stood in, as Gardiner said, "till they had got the true Distance of the Town and the Citadel."[74] At this time the whole fleet was close in with the town and almost becalmed. Nothing much happened during the rest of the morning, while Shuldham ran slowly along, taking a profile of the bottom, his *Panther* partly protected from the shore guns by the fire of the two bomb vessels.[75]

---

72. Gardiner, *The West Indies*, 14-15 Two hundred volunteers from Fort Royale arrived in time to get into the fight. Beauharnois, Relation, Archives nationales, Marine et colonies, C^8 A 62.

73. "Journal," Pitt, *Correspondence*, II, 28-29; Corbett, *England in the Seven Years' War*, I, 377-379.

74. Gardiner, *The West Indies*, 15-16.

75. "The expedition," Loudoun Papers; Beatson, *Memoirs*, II, 233-236. From the perfect synchronization of Beatson's and Gardiner's schedules, it seems probable that Beatson refreshed his memory by reading Gardiner's book, which antedated his by at least twenty years.

Robert Beatson (1742-1818) was born in Scotland. He was probably an ensign (or practitioner, for engineer officers were given equivalent military rank in that year) in 1757 at Rochefort and in 1759 at Guadeloupe.

At noon, when a very light breeze came from the west—very unusual for those parts—Moore sent his flag captain, Thomas Burnett of the *Cambridge,* aboard the *Rippon* with orders to silence a battery about one and a half miles north of the town. As Jekyll of the *Rippon* gave orders to his canvas lieutenant, Moore made the signal for the transports to come under his stern, and Hopson went aboard the *Cambridge.* At one o'clock in the afternoon the breeze had pushed the *Rippon* within range of the fort, while some 390 men stood aboard in battle stations and took the badly aimed fire from the shore. It looked as though a general attack was fermenting, with the *Panther* sounding, the bomb ketches coughing shells, the *Rippon* approaching, stripped (at a speed slightly more than a fast drift), and the transports like chicks clustering under the stern of the flagship. But the co-commanders were below in the flagship[76] and one of them, at least, was a very cautious man. There was a more inspired and natural commander in this expedition but he, Barrington, was still only second in command, and not usually consulted.

Not knowing of the talks progressing behind him, Jekyll went into action, hoisted out his boats, beat to quarters. Flashy Marines were stationed with small arms on the poop, on the forecastle, in the tops. At two o'clock (Gardiner's words) "the *Rippon* brought up against it and let go her Anchor within half a Cable's Length of the Shore in thirty-five Fathom Water," that is, about three hundred feet off a lee shore, in about two hundred feet of water. With the simultaneous explosion of almost thirty guns she let go a broadside, and Gardiner's Marines, he said, "with the Small Arms" helped to silence "the Battery in a few Minutes." Gardiner went on to say he noted great activity ashore and asked permission of Jekyll to lead the Marines ashore to spike the guns of the silenced battery. Jekyll is said to have replied that in the absence of orders from Moore he could not risk having the Marines cut off on shore, unable to return to the ship. Gardiner added, "the Consequence of this Omission . . . had like to have proved Fatal to the Ship."[77]

76. Beatson, *Memoirs,* II, 233-236; Gardiner, *The West Indies,* 15-17.
77. *Ibid.*

Off to the south, unnoticed by the men aboard the *Rippon*, the bomb ketches and the *Panther* were steering toward the open sea. Engineer Beatson later said that, if Moore had thrown his bombs among the merchantmen instead of at the fortifications, the trading vessels would either have been run ashore or else have put to sea where they would have been captured.[78] This is the statement of an engineer officer, not of a naval tactician. If they had broken in every direction, Moore would have had to disperse his fleet to take more than a few of them. And the gunners ashore would have been undisturbed in laying their great pieces in the direction of the *Panther*.

Soon after the *Rippon* delivered her first broadside the enemy opened two batteries on her, one to the north and one to the south. Another battery about one and a half miles north also joined the dance, followed by one of the two bomb batteries ashore. The ship was hulled in several places, was much wounded in her rigging, and had several men hurt. She was engaged on both sides at once as the westerly breeze caused her to tail in toward the shore from her bow anchor. This painful, noisy, smoky contest continued for the next two hours, in Gardiner's economical phrase, "pretty warm." At half past four Jekyll cast accounts aboard his bloody, splintered ship, and saw that Moore and the transports were about six miles off shore, the bomb vessels called off and no other ship engaged or coming to his assistance. He concluded from the position of the ships that the attack was not to be pushed. Meanwhile the King's ship *Rippon* was in grave danger. After an hour more of posing as a target he passed the word for his lieutenants to come to the quarter deck. In Gardiner's hearing he told them of his orders and asked what was to be done for the preservation of His Majesty's ship. The answer came quickly. Since the wind was still blowing inshore, the boats were manned, the axe fell on the cable, and the sweaty, grimy seamen arched their backs over the oars in an attempt to tow the ship out to sea. The batteries ashore still continued at their easy job of pounding an almost motionless tall ship from positions of comparative safety.[79]

78. Beatson, *Memoirs*, II, 233-236.   79. Gardiner, *The West Indies*, 17-20.

The moment when the anchor rope was cut was a moment when disaster was delicately balanced against the weight of the tarry-handed oarsmen. If they could not get enough pull into the oars to overcome her inertia immediately, she would drift ashore and touch fast, the shore being less than her own length astern. If she touched she might be lost, and Captain Edward Jekyll, if he managed to live through it, would perhaps spend the rest of his days in 'long shore pot houses, cursing his half pay.

The colonials ashore, seeing preparations being made to haul the ship out of range, reopened the silenced battery and raked the ship fore and aft, sinking the long boat astern, all the while sniping at the men aboard with small arms. At this time the citadel also opened fire on the ship. The oars dug in, the ship began to head for the sea, and her stern chasers were brought to bear on the battery which had once before been silenced. The Marines fired continuously on the men ashore (who had better cover). For half an hour the crisis period was extended until a short period of flat calm was broken by a ruffling breeze and the trade wind began to blow from east to west, as is its nature. The ship was safe. It was six o'clock. Firing ceased on both sides at half past six, and at seven the *Rippon* joined the fleet. The only help she had received was a reenforcement of one boatload of men, sent by Captain Thomas Lynn of the *Roebuck* frigate.[80]

This engagement lasted four hours and thirty minutes. More than seven hundred great shot had been fired. Of her complement of 430 men, forty were sick in the holds during the fight, and during the towing-off period, fifty men were in the boats. The King's long boat was lost, and for the next few days there was much rope replacement and splicing to be done.[81]

The explanation of the lack of aid to the *Rippon* is simple: Moore and Hopson had decided against an attack on St. Pierre. (Why the ship was not ordered off shore cannot be explained so simply.) That this was a decision by Hopson and Moore apart from any council of war was made plain by Haldane's statement that he (a general officer) "was not consulted about the reasons

80. *Ibid.*, 17-18.
81. Gardiner, *The West Indies*, 18. Two French gunners were killed. Malo, 11.

INHOSPITABLE MARTINIQUE

for not attacking [St. Pierre] as that matter was entirely a transaction between the General and the Commodore."[82]

Hopson had had a while to think the whole thing over, and he and Moore had a long talk while Jekyll was wasting balls, brawn, and blood against the shore defenses. The gloomy phantasms printed in Hopson's brain offered no image of victory in Martinique, for, if St. Pierre were taken, he did not see how he could maintain a garrison there. Such a force could be supplied and fed only from the sea, from ships in an uneasy roadstead. The town itself was commanded by innumerable hills which marched up to the central ridge of the island. Moore, for his part, saw no strategic advantage in taking the town, and said (echoing the pilots) that the fall of this place would not affect the defenses of Martinique in any way. In reading the cautious correspondence of these two gentlemen one must remind oneself that, after all, the island was not impregnable, that it was conquered by a British amphibious force only three years later. But Moore, who had been on the station for several years, knew what he was doing. He was aware that in taking St. Pierre his force might be disabled for any future action. Accordingly, he put in writing a proposal that they steer for Guadeloupe to see what might be accomplished in those parts. Hopson left no record of his emotional response to this suggestion but, from what is known of him from his acts in this campaign, he was probably very much relieved at having Moore assume so much responsibility. He agreed to the Guadeloupe project.[83]

At eight o'clock at night the reassembled fleet steered for Basse Terre Roads, Guadeloupe. During the afternoon the force had been strengthened. Major Robert Melville[84] and a detachment

82. Haldane's "proceedings," Newcastle Papers.
83. Moore to Pitt, Hopson to Pitt, 30 January 1759, both in Pitt, *Correspondence*, II, 22-23, and, 29-31, respectively.
84. Robert Melville, F.R.S. (1723-1809), attended grammar school and the universities of Glasgow and Edinburgh. In 1744 he entered the army as an ensign in the Twenty-fifth Regiment, and served in Flanders. He was promoted captain in 1751. He was promoted major, in the Thirty-eighth, on 8 June 1756, and commanded its detachment at Guadeloupe. He was wounded there, and became blind in later life because of the wound. In a very rounded life he was governor of several West Indian islands, topographer, botanist, antiquarian, and ballistician. In 1759, on this expedition, he invented a piece of carriage ordnance

of two hundred men from the Thirty-eighth Regiment at Antigua, in two transports, had come in a little before three o'clock, under convoy of the *Amazon* frigate and the *Spy*[85] sloop.[86]

A criticism and appreciation of Moore's general conduct of his share of the insular campaign, considered as a unit, are reserved to a later place, but certain specific accusations against him may be considered here, in connection with the Martinique phase. Of the evacuation of the land approaches to Fort Royale some harsh words were said. Horace Walpole remarked, "Moore was blamed by some for want of activity; but his subservience to the Ministry on the affair of Admiral Byng had secured such favour to him, that, in the Extraordinary Gazette published on this disappointment, Moore was treated with great lenity, and the blame made to bear hard on Hopson. . . ."[87]

This statement is a peculiar combination of half-truths and misinformation in the best Walpolian tradition. First, the word "disappointment" was hardly a fair word to use, since they sent no news home at all until 30 January 1759, when they announced very good news—the destruction and occupation of the chief town of Guadeloupe. Second, the reports published in London were from dispatches sent home by the general and commodore, and tell the truth about Hopson's part: he selected the landing place at Martinique, he asked for the evacuation, he agreed to steer for St. Pierre, he said he could not maintain a garrison there if it were taken, and, when Moore proposed to go to Guadeloupe, Hopson agreed to it. There may have been coffee-house chatter and gaming-room gabble which blamed Hopson, and perhaps wishful thinkers could see it reflected in the published accounts of the campaign, but nothing of importance was said or done by any one in authority to indicate that Hopson was in disfavor. Walpole

---

which had a great influence on naval tactics. It was put in production in 1779, and became the world-renowned carronade. He died the oldest general in the army. *Dictionary of National Biography.*

85. In command of the *Spy* was William Bayne (d. 1782), who was first listed as a lieutenant in 1749. He served with Boscawen in North American waters in 1755. In 1756 he received his first command, the *Spy* sloop, in which he served at Guadeloupe.

86. "The expedition," Loudoun Papers; Wylly, *The Manchester Regiment,* I, 12.

87. Walpole, *Memoirs,* III, 170.

can be dismissed as a serious critic of the campaign. It is my own opinion that not only was Hopson not maligned by his contemporaries, but that he got off far better than he deserved. The only excuse I can find for his indecision is that he was probably a dying man.

Another adverse critic of Moore was the contentious Captain Gardiner. After ostentatious show of respect for the obvious fact that the co-commanders would have better information than he would, Gardiner insinuated that the attack on Fort Royale was not vigorous. This was a serious charge; Byng was shot for what amounted to the same thing. A paraphrase of Gardiner's remarks follows: they were near the town, the dangerous moment of landing was past, there were "no unforeseen dangers to alarm, no ambuscades or masqued batteries to pour concealed destruction on the troops," no regular troops in array, only "lurking Negroes here and there" opposed to British veterans. He heard later there were only four hundred regulars on the island and thought it probably true, since he quoted what the governor of Martinique said to the governor of Guadeloupe, on 16 April 1759, that he had no help to offer except arms already sent. Also Gardiner thought the intrepid behavior of the troops at Guadeloupe showed there was no want of courage among the men.[88] This last statement is competent, but otherwise is immaterial and irrelevant; at no time did anyone say that the redcoats or bluegreen kilts were not brave men.

Was the story of Braddock's disaster told to this incredulous Marine? Haldane's reference to "Indians" might mean that the Braddock lesson had been learned in the army outside North America. Gardiner was not far from right when he said there were only four hundred regulars in the island. But neither he nor the commanders had any reliable information on the subject until 16 April, five days before the end of the campaign. Meanwhile a waterless body of troops had been landed from a fleet which could not help them on the last five miles of their way,

---

88. Gardiner, *The West Indies*, 14-16. Counting seamen detached from the three French warships in the harbor, there were about six hundred regular fighting men available for land defense.

in a country without a road, swarming with snipers who knew the ground. It should be enough to know that in 1762 when the British captured the island they took the harbor defenses from the land side, coming up from the south, and did not imitate the Moore-Hopson campaign in any way. The latter two gentlemen were possibly deficient in judgment, but there is no evidence that they slacked at the job. Gardiner was unfair.

Gardiner also printed animadversions on the subject of the *Rippon*. Why the *Rippon* was not called off from St. Pierre is a mystery. Gardiner said Moore ordered the ship to attack St. Pierre at a moment when he was planning to persuade Hopson to go to Guadeloupe, sent it to secure a landing place before he had resolved to make a descent on the coast, and even when he was "determined to dissuade a Landing at all."[89] Two objections to the charges present themselves here: (a) Gardiner could not know at what time Moore determined to suggest an excursion to Guadeloupe, and (b) if what Gardiner said was true, Moore's act in almost throwing away his newest and fastest ship was the act of a madman. Moore showed no other sign of madness. Drunkenness—that favorite charge by those seeking to destroy military or political reputations—was not alleged.

I think the difficulty can be resolved in part. The use of a strong ship to punch at a suspected weak spot seems legitimate. The lee shore formed a semi-circle which would contain the *Rippon* as coffee in an eighteenth-century gentleman's saucer, once she got in it, considering the great leeway the ships of that time made. Did Moore postpone her recall, hoping for a change in the direction of the wind? The direction was certainly unusual, and a change could be expected at any moment. It is a fact that the wind did change while the *Rippon* was towing off. But my favorite resolution of the difficulty is the simplest: perhaps, while Moore and Hopson were below discussing the proposal to steer for Guadeloupe, Moore forgot about the *Rippon*. This would do

---

89. *Ibid.*, 18-20, 19. The only reference to the episode by Moore is this note: "The Rippon being in Shore near to a Fort of four Guns Cannonaded it." Moore, "Journal," Admiralty 50/22.

him no credit, but at least makes him appear more human than does Gardiner's allegation of wilfully wasting his naval resources.

Gardiner and Beatson made a point of the fact that Moore left forty merchantmen undisturbed in the roadstead. Sir Julian Corbett thought this soured the gentlemen because not to attack them meant prize money lost.[90] If Corbett was correct, and it seems reasonable, his theory explains a lot of the criticism directed against Moore, whose orders were not to destroy commerce, but to conquer territory.

In concluding this part of the narrative, it remains to be said that the administration of Beauharnois, military commandant at Martinique in 1759, was one of the worst periods of military inefficiency in the history of the French West Indies. It was hard luck for the British that Hopson and Moore received no French deserters, and, in their absence, were unable to read the commandant's mind.

90. Corbett, *England in the Seven Years' War*, I, 379.

V.

Guadeloupe: Basse Terre

---

1. *The island of Guadeloupe*

A clean-lined yacht reaching across the trade wind along the tropical islands called the Lesser Antilles will pick up a new island every day. At 16° 15′ North Latitude the island will be Guadeloupe, once a very precious stone in the Bourbon crown, producing sugar for the coffee of France, molasses which became rum (for warding off cold New England weather, or for Congo bacchanalia), and a race of swarthy privateersmen who in time of war lived high on the loot from fat British and American West Indiamen.

Guadeloupe is really two islands, separated by a brackish sea arm. Geologically they are not related, for Basse Terre is steep-to and still smokes of volcanoes, while Grand Terre, lying to the eastward, is made of limestone. The two islands are surrounded by satellites, Désirade and the Petite Terre on the east, and Marie Galante and the Saintes on the south. The coasts are irregular. Some parts are rocky and eternally wet with spray, others shoal off in sandy beaches, but everywhere there are little inlets and river mouths where small privateers were based. These shelters were not useful for anything large; today relatively small vessels are steered into Le Moule on the northeast side of Grand Terre by pilots who use as sea marks the anchors of wrecked ships.

Two great bays, the *Grand cul-de-sac au nord* and the *Petit cul-de-sac au sud,* are joined by a narrow channel which separates the islands. Both bays are shoal and choked with alternate coral reefs and sand bars. At the head of the little *cul-de-sac* lies the port

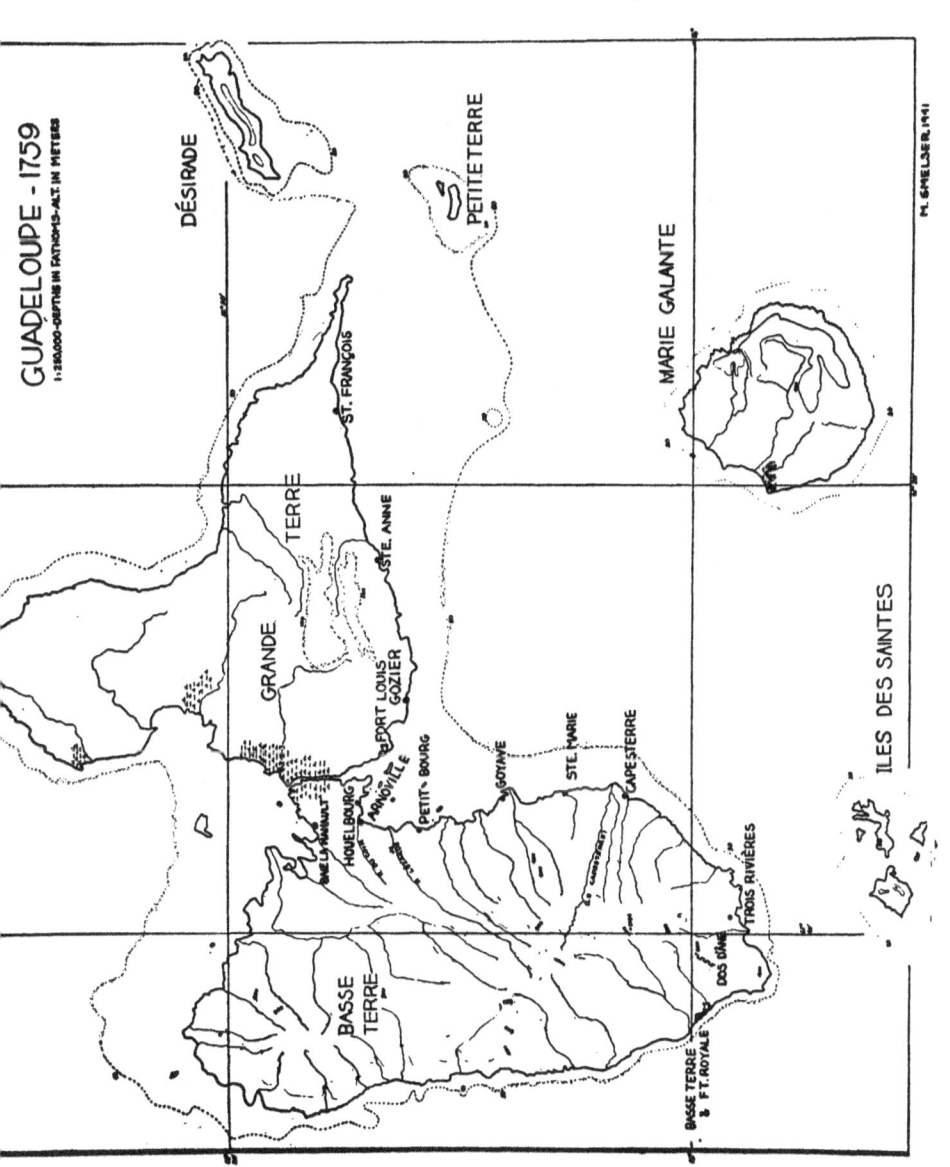

of Pointe à Pitre (which eighteenth-century Englishmen, having little patience with a nation which refused to speak English, called "Point Peter").[1] In 1759 the bay was weakly defended by a bastion named Fort Louis, not far from "Point Peter."

The heat of the islands is endurable to those who do not resist enervation—it has proved fatal to thousands who lived violently, chiefly soldiers. In the low parts the temperature rises and falls in a range between seventy and ninety degrees (Fahrenheit). The inch is too trivial a measure to use in stating the rainfall. Rain falls annually to a depth of thirteen feet, most of it in the latter six months of the year. The trade wind blows fresh from the east or southeast, most of the time. No naval commander in the days of sailing vessels wanted to be caught in those waters during the period from July to October for fear of the dread "hurricanoes." No military commander ever found life pleasant there because, even today, malaria and dysentery are frequent in the lands below an altitude of 1500 feet.

Down Basse Terre runs a spine of volcanic cones, some of which still give off sulphurous steam and hot waters. Of the Lesser Antilles these peaks are second in height only to those of Dominica (the next island to the south). The highest is the Soufrière, which rises to 4867 feet; Ben Nevis and Vesuvius are both lower. But flat Grand Terre's highest point is not more than four hundred feet above the sea. The highlands of Basse Terre are today covered with about 75,000 acres of forest. There are about 25,000 acres of cane fields, mostly on Grand Terre. The only native irrational mammals are the agouti and the bat. The wild raccoon and the mongoose have been imported, probably since 1759. Domesticated cows and zebus, used for beasts of burden, have also been imported. Roots and fruits make up the indigenous vegetable food supply. Fish are everywhere.[2]

In the eighteenth century the population of Guadeloupe was said to have consisted of two thousand Europeans and thirty

---

1. Treasury 1, bundle 390, f. 53-54, has this linguistic curiosity.
2. Société d'éditions geographiques, maritimes, et coloniales. *Antilles françaises*, in G. Grandidier, directeur, *Atlas des colonies françaises* (Paris, 1934), 2-4. Hereafter cited as *Antilles françaises*; Platt, Wright, Weaver, and Fairchild, *European Possessions in the Caribbean Area*, 58-64.

GUADELOUPE: BASSE TERRE

thousand Negroes, which were valued at £1,250,000.[3] Most of these people lived on plantations and in small villages. The town of Basse Terre, on the island of the same name, was the only place of importance. It lay in a natural amphitheater south of the Soufrière, its stone houses partly hidden by tropical trees. The town was divided by a small river. South of the town rose the citadel of Fort Royale, which was the shell of the nut and to be cracked first, if ever. There was (and is) no harbor there, but ships lading and discharging lay in the unsafe roadstead, serviced by lighters.[4]

Guadeloupe was of interest during the Seven Years' War for reasons both economic and military. It was the best of the French sugar islands, and also produced more cotton and coffee than any British island except Jamaica. Unlike some of the Lesser Antilles it was well watered.[5] Sea-weary mariners spoke enthusiastically of its lush plantations. Its chief harbor provided a good, if not entirely satisfactory, shelter against hurricanes, and in fair-weather months the adjacent waters were visited by many trading vessels.[6] Capture of the island would be a disaster to the French colonial carrying trade. The island could produce eighty thousand hogsheads of all sugars, and forty thousand hogsheads of the best sugars sent out of Martinique every year had been packed in Guadeloupe. Martinique also received for transshipment a large quantity of cotton which, because of its high quality, was normally reserved to French manufactures only.[7] And the trade of Guadeloupe was definitely more valuable than the trade of Canada.[8]

In the months following the fall of Louisbourg the economic situation of the French Indies was precarious. With Canada and Cape Breton isolated, there was no place to which the trade could go except to France, and the coasts of France were patrolled by

 3. Entick, *The Late War,* IV, 171n.-175n. The figure for Europeans is probably much too low. *Cf.* Chapter VIII, part 2, *infra.*
 4. *Antilles françaises,* 4.
 5. Antiguans, for example, were sometimes driven to import fresh water by ship.
 6. Entick, *The Late War,* IV, 171-175.
 7. Mackenzie to Pitt (from Turin), 7 July 1759, f. 462-463 (a copy), Newcastle Papers, Add. MSS. 32892, British Museum. Transcripts in Library of Congress.
 8. Pares, *War and Trade,* 217.

British officers who were too close to Anson's desk in the Admiralty to be slack. Except for an occasional French merchant captain who was more daring than discreet, communication with France was kept up by means of Danish or Dutch vessels. But the neutral flag alone was not enough to protect commerce bound Francewards, from either the Royal navy or "les corsaires Anglais," for both the royal fleet and the private ships found British courts quite willing to declare the Danes and the Dutch to be good prizes.[9]

The true wealth of the island was revealed in the reports of governors after it was reduced to British possession. From a one-percent import-export duty, and a capitation tax on slaves, revenue was produced in the sum of 307,284 *livres*.[10] An increase was anticipated when the sugar works which had been destroyed as a part of the warfare were repaired, and when the stream of provisions began once more to flow into the plantations. In October, 1759, it was expected that the normal production of eighty thousand hogsheads of sugar would be restored soon. The wondering Governor Crump reported to his master that this was more sugar than that produced by Barbados and all the British Leeward Islands together, and would bring the revenue up "some hundred thousand pounds a year."[11]

For Pitt's military purposes the conquest of Guadeloupe could hardly be less suitable than the conquest of Martinique. The only good reason for attacking Martinique first was that Martinique's fall would have a better effect on public opinion. A great many persons had heard of Martinique who had not heard of Guadeloupe, since the produce of the latter was shipped to Europe by way of Martinique. Thus Martinique received credit for the fruitfulness of Guadeloupe.

But Guadeloupe was richer, it was not so strongly held, and it was a nest of privateersmen who preyed on the commerce of the British islands and the North American routes. It provided a good harbor on which to base an armed force for the protection of

---

9. Richard Waddington, *La guerre de Sept ans* (Paris, 1899-1914), III, 359.
10. The civil and ecclesiastical lists reduced this figure to 247,509 *livres*. The cost of collection was not stated.
11. Crump to Pitt, 4 October 1759, Colonial Office 110/1.

British shipping. That the protection of British shipping in these waters was a hard problem was shown by the record of the year 1758, when, despite the presence of a squadron on the Leeward Islands station, 113 vessels in the West Indies trade were taken by the French, and of that number 81 were carried into the harbors of Martinique and Guadeloupe. As I have tried earlier to show, the conquest and occupation of territory were Pitt's reason for sending a British expedition to the Leeward Islands and, while other places might offer more jingling prize money and a better chance for destruction of commerce, this island, fat and relatively weak, offered one of the few examples in history of a time when the best apple hung lowest on the bough.[12]

2. *The bombardment of Basse Terre*

At noon on 20 January the fleet was about fifteen miles west by north of the north cape of Martinique. At five o'clock they were about twelve miles south of Dominica, the large, sparsely inhabited island which lies between Martinique and Guadeloupe—nominally "neutral," actually inhabited by a pro-French population. Light winds had died during the night, leaving them to slat uncomfortably in a calm, until the next night. When Dominica was first sighted, Captain Edward Le Cras was sent ahead in the *Winchester* with Lieutenant Colonel William Cunninghame, the engineer, and Lieutenant Colonel Cunningham, the quartermaster, to reconnoiter Basse Terre Roads. Their arrival would be no surprise to the people of Guadeloupe, because Beauharnois had already sent off a small boat to warn the governor.[13]

The ships rolled in the calm most of the day of 21 January, off Dominica. A fresh breeze came up during the night and at eight

12. Corbett, *England in the Seven Years' War*, I, 379-380; *Gentleman's Magazine*, 28 (1758).
13. "Journal," Pitt, *Correspondence*, II, 28-29; Gardiner, *The West Indies*, 20-21; "The expedition," Loudoun Papers; Malo, 11.
  On 21 January Beauharnois sent his two largest privateer vessels to transport about four hundred "filibustiers" to Guadeloupe. Beginning on 27 January Moore had a ship cruising off the southern tip of Basse Terre "to prevent Succours being thrown in from Martinique &ca." Beauharnois, Relation, Archives Nationales, Marine et colonies, C^8 A 62; Moore, "Journal," Admiralty 50/22. The filibustiers got through before this blockade was established. Moore continued his south coast patrol until May, but it was never completely effective.

o'clock in the morning of 22 January, the fleet was fifteen miles west of the northern tip of Dominica, about twenty-seven miles from Guadeloupe. At eleven o'clock Moore signalled for the masters of the warships to come on board the flagship. The trade wind had been at its best, for on this broad reach they made twenty-one or twenty-two miles in about four hours, the best speed recorded for the fleet at any time during the campaign. At noon they were five or six miles southwest of Guadeloupe. The rest of the afternoon was spent in standing back and forth between the Saintes and Guadeloupe, while the commodore and his captains, Hopson and his generals, and the chief engineer, reconnoitered the town and shore at Basse Terre.[14]

At six o'clock in the evening the captains were returning to their ships. Although the chief engineer had said the citadel was too high to be battered by the ships, a general attack was scheduled for the next morning. The ships were to lie off certain assigned batteries, silence them, and await further orders. The night was utilized in turning under the island, while two bomb vessels went in and threw shells against the citadel and the town. Gardiner said they did no damage, and blamed Moore because they were not at their proper distance from the enemy's stronghold, "from being improperly directed in their Station."[15] This shows his animus; the French reported that hits were scored. The chief purpose of the bomb attack was probably to annoy the diggers, for the inhabitants had been sweating over picks and spades since the island was alerted.[16] A few shots were fired from the shore in the evening, but did less damage than a collision of the *Bristol* and *St. George* a little after eight o'clock, which took off the *Bristol's* bowsprit and did other damage, although the *St. George,* standing high above the smaller *Bristol,* was not harmed.[17]

The strength opposed to the British at Basse Terre centered in the large, high, and irregular citadel, which mounted about

14. "The expedition," Loudoun Papers; "Journal," Pitt, *Correspondence*, II, 28-29; Haldane's "proceedings," Newcastle papers; Beatson, *Memoirs*, II, 236-237; Gardiner, *The West Indies*, 22.
15. Gardiner, *The West Indies*, 23-24.
16. On West Indian fortifications, see Appendix, Topic 15.
17. Gardiner, *The West Indies*, 23-24; "The expedition," Loudoun Papers; Beatson, *Memoirs*, II, 236-237.

GUADELOUPE: BASSE TERRE

fifty guns, ranging in size from eighteen to forty-two pounders. It was thought by the chief engineer to be too high for the lower deck guns to batter it, and this was correct. He went on to say that it was impregnable; this was incorrect, for he thus denied the possibility of a moral collapse of the defense. There were also fortifications fronting on the roadstead, all along the town. Under the citadel were two strong batteries, one above the other.[18] These lesser forts cost the defenders very much in blood and treasure. Whether they were worth the expenditure is debatable.

The quality of the arms of the defenders was low if an episode uncovered by Professor Richard Pares was typical: at Guadeloupe not long before the siege the commanding officer bought some muskets for the militia from St. Eustatius, three-fourths of which burst at the first review. "They had not been made to be fired, but only to be bartered in the African slave trade."[19]

The defending force consisted of five companies of Marines numbering twenty men each, and the militia. The French Marines little resembled the hard-hitting *élite* corps of sea soldiers who have made so much British and American history. They were land troops administered by the navy and were used to garrison colonial possessions. Definitely they were not *élite,* for reasons explained later. The militia was augmented by the enlistment of Negroes who were promised their freedom at the expense of the colonial government. Later the defenders were joined by Martinique volunteers and by a company of volunteers from Dominica. Privateersmen from Martinique, their risky trade cut down by the presence of the British naval force, slipped through in small parties from time to time and joined the colonial force. The organized volunteers from the other islands were very few. The attitude of the civilians in general was shown by their preparations when first they heard of the presence of the British. They liquidated their personalty so far as they were able, and moved what else they could to the Dos D'Âne or other strong places in the mountains.[20]

18. Gardiner, *The West Indies,* 22-23; "The expedition," Loudoun Papers.
19. Pares, *War and Trade,* 245, citing Nadau Du Treil to Massiac, 25 December 1758, Archives Nat., Colonies, C7 A 17.
20. Gardiner, *The West Indies,* 29-30, 62-63; Pares, *War and Trade,* 252, citing, Nadau Du Treil to Berryer, 25 December 1758, Archives Nat., Colonies, C7 A 17.

The order of attack for the morning of 23 January was fixed by Moore as follows—with the line of battle given from south to north:[21]

Ship, guns.	Fortification, guns.
Lyon, 60.	First battery, 9.
St. George, 90. }	
Norfolk, 74. }	Citadel (Fort Royale), 47-52.
Cambridge, 80. }	
Panther, 60. }	Third battery, 12.
Burford, 70. }	
Berwick, 66.	Fourth battery, 7.
Rippon, 60.	Le morne rouge, 6.

It will be noticed that the *Winchester* and the *Bristol*, 50 guns each, which were the smallest of the ships of the line, were not to attack. At dawn the wind was from the west as it had been at St. Pierre. The *habitants* attributed this meteorological phenomenon directly to Divine intervention and some of them later told Gardiner the British had come as a scourge for their sins.

A little before seven in the morning the commodore shifted his flag to the *Woolwich* frigate where he joined Hopson, at the general's request, to watch the battle. This freed the *Cambridge* for service in the line. About this time the *Buckingham*, Captain Richard Tyrrel, 65 guns, was known to be approaching the fleet but she did not join in time to serve in this engagement. At half-past seven Moore threw out the signal to engage. Squares'ls broke out all over the squadron, tops'ls which had been loosened now bellied instead of shook, and the line of battle began to move. Then—with the decks cleared—there was a wait of an hour and a half as the ships steered into position in the unusual light air from the west. There must have been many a dry throat, and many a damp palm, as the high-pooped navy moved slowly up from the south, ghosting into action.[22]

At nine o'clock the *Lyon* peeled off the line and ran down on

---
21. Gardiner, *The West Indies*, 23.
22. Beatson, *Memoirs*, II, 237-238; Cust, *Annals of the Wars of the Eighteenth Century*, II, 285; J. K. Laughton, "Sir John Moore," *Dictionary of National Biography;* Gardiner, *The West Indies*, 24-25; "The expedition," Loudoun Papers.

her target as the first battery appeared abeam, firing the first shot of this day's cannonade as she came. Once she had brought to and anchored she had a nasty surprise, as an hitherto unsuspected spot on the hillside turned into a two-gun battery, dead astern of the ship, which proceeded to rake the *Lyon* almost at will. The citadel also brought some guns to bear on Trelawney's ship, and as the other vessels came within range they too were hammered by the citadel's gunners. By half past nine, the *St. George, Norfolk,* and *Cambridge* were within range of the citadel and from that time the men in the island's main bastion were very busy. At ten the *Panther* dropped her hook and opened fire on the third battery. The *Burford,* her partner, seemed over anxious. Her master, James Gambier, caused or allowed her to anchor too soon, and cut loose with a broadside which crashed into the *Panther.* Gambier thereupon slipped his cable and stood out to sea. There were no repercussions of this affair on record, but there must have been some vigorous language aboard the *Panther.* The *Berwick,* next in the line, was putting her flukes into the sand when a small crowd of militiamen were enterprising enough to fire some small craft and send them drifting down upon her. To avoid this danger, her captain broke out his newly fixed kedges and stood out to sea, along with Gambier. These two accidents meant that the *Panther* stood to her enemy alone, that nobody attacked the fourth battery, and the *Rippon* had to bear the fire of that battery and the one to which she had been assigned as well.[23]

At quarter after ten the unlucky *Rippon,* having begun to engage a few minutes earlier, ran down on her opposing battery and let go anchors. The breeze had lightened, but perhaps not as much as Captain Jekyll thought—whatever the cause, whether she made too much leeway or through some other miscalculation, she tailed in toward shore, touched, and stuck fast. She was not more than fifty yards from shore (musket range) and a new and unsuspected battery to the north opened fire upon her, taking her fair on the starboard bow. Thus there were cannon to port,

23. Gardiner, *The West Indies,* 24-25; Beatson, *Memoirs,* II, 237-238.

cannon to starboard, and cannon astern, all pounding the motionless ship.[24]

At eleven o'clock there was a close, hot fire from all the ships which had managed to get to their stations, and the French guns were being well served and laid. The master of the unhappy *Rippon,* his rigging wounded and his ship ashore, fought back. To see if anything would happen he cut the cable. Nothing happened. At noon all ships were still engaged. The forts and batteries were all firing. The *Rippon* was yet aground, and began to be tortured by musket fire as a crowd of militia lined the trenches ashore, having scented big game. Somewhere they found a spare eighteen-pounder and hauled it to a hastily prepared barbette where it could join the fun. Farther south the *Panther* not only pounded the twelve-gun battery to which she had been assigned, but managed to bring some guns to bear on the citadel. Before one o'clock in the afternoon the fire from ashore began to slacken. The *Lyon* had knocked out her batteries and had been called off by the commodore. Apparently other guns had been dismounted elsewhere. Bomb vessels were playing on the shore defenses. All went well, except aboard the grounded *Rippon* where examination of the wounded men showed the colonials were firing nails, bits of iron, broken glass, and other forbidden missiles.[25]

The *Rippon's* contest went on for another hour or two without change, until, by two o'clock, she had silenced the six-gun battery she was originally sent against. By that hour no guns spoke south of the town, but the militia ashore were still raking the *Rippon.* At three o'clock the eighteen pounder began to fire on the ship at very close range, and the exultant gunners ran up the golden lilies of His Most Christian Majesty. But the flag was promptly shot down and was seen no more; it was not flown anywhere else within sight of the British witnesses that day. At that time the first casualties among the officers occurred. Lieutenant Chaundy of the Marines was carried below where the bloodstained surgeon had his leg off in no time, and the lieutenant

---

24. Gardiner, *The West Indies,* 24-25; Beatson, *Memoirs,* II, 237-238; "The expedition," Loudoun Papers.
25. "The expedition," Loudoun Papers; "Journal," Pitt, *Correspondence,* II, 28-29; Gardiner, *The West Indies,* 25-26; Beatson, *Memoirs,* II, 237-238.

GUADELOUPE: BASSE TERRE   *81*

went to join ninety sick and about ten wounded in what must surely have been a foul smelling orlop. Chaundy survived, unlike Midshipman Grey who, about the same time took a musket ball in the thigh and died of it.[26]

At three o'clock, although none of the other ships was in any unusual trouble, of the twenty-eight Marines on the *Rippon's* poop, ten were dead or disabled. Of the eighteen able-bodied survivors, ten were sent to the forecastle where enfiladed seamen had suffered severely. As they left the poop a box of nine hundred cartridges blew up and set the ship afire. Word came from the master gunner that all of the grape had been shot away. A little later it was reported that there was no more wadding to be had, but this was not news, for the captain could see for himself that the gunners were ramming the King's shirts and jackets into the guns for wadding. Thus gun crews carried on, and other men fought the fire on the poop. Jekyll had been engaged for six hours, his ship was aground, afire, and his magazine was showing bottom. It is not to his discredit that he threw out the prearranged distress signal, "an Ensign at his Mast head."[27]

Elsewhere the day had gone well. The *Lyon, Berwick, Norfolk, Cambridge,* and *Burford* had hauled off the shore, leaving the *St. George,*[28] *Panther,* and *Rippon* the only vessels engaged.

26. Gardiner, *The West Indies,* 25-26; Beatson, *Memoirs,* II, 237-238. At the trial of Governor Nadau Du Treil many deponents testified that he had ordered the battery of Morne Rouge to cease firing on the *Rippon* for fear, as one put it, "d'irriter l'ennemy." This seems incredible unless the reason was to stop the firing of illegal missiles which might provoke reprisals. The order included instructions to spike the guns and for the musketeers to cease.—"Guadeloupe/Jugement du Gouverneur de cette isle/Nadau Dutreil," 1759, Archives nationales, Marine et colonies, B⁴ 92.

27. Gardiner, *The West Indies,* 26-27; Moore, "Journal," Admiralty 50/22.

28. With regard to the part played by the *St. George* there is a dubious story. Clark Gayton, her master, with other captains, is said to have stated at the council of war on 22 January that the citadel was too high to be attacked. Moore thought differently and sent him written orders to engage it. Later, seeing the *St. George* suffering, he sent her verbal orders to stand out to sea. Gayton replied that since he had a written order to attack, he could not well cease his attack except on a written order. Before this could be sent the citadel ceased firing and was evacuated.

Nothing that occurs in any of the available contemporary literature can be read that way. The only evidence that is to be found in support of it is that the *St. George* was the last to give up the attack of the three ships sent against the citadel. But the written-order stipulation seems absurd, for all Gayton would

The gunners of the seven cannon in the fourth battery had not had anybody's undivided attention since the *Berwick* stood out early in the bombardment. Now they were to pay for their freedom. In answer to Jekyll's distress signal[29] the *Bristol,* apparently anxious for a quarrel, came running in from the sea and interposed between the *Rippon* and the battery. This brought the Marines on her poop in a position to flank the shore trenches and they made the most of it. Jekyll himself was not through yet; his men knocked out the harassing eighteen-pounder with a parting shot (no doubt rammed home with a tar-collared jacket for a wad). At half past four the *Roebuck* frigate came in and placed herself between the *Rippon* and the northernmost battery. Thus with Le Morne Rouge astern silent, the *Rippon* was completely protected. The *Burford* came in behind the *Roebuck.* At this time all of the forts except the citadel were silent.

At five o'clock the citadel fired its last shot. The *Panther's* and *St. George's* gunners may have taken credit for the unaccustomed silence in the roadstead, but if any gunner gets the credit it must go to an unknown mortarman aboard one of the bomb ketches. Many of the garrison had thrown down their arms and deserted, apparently blind drunk on rum. In the tropic mid-day they had been doing this hot work and cooling themselves with rum instead of water. But they "excused themselves by saying that some bombs had fallen into the cistern, and made the water undrinkable."[30]

---

need to clear himself of any charges brought against him would be witnesses to the verbal order. Mr. J. K. Laughton has wisely dismissed the story. *Dictionary of National Biography,* citing, Charnock, *Biographia navalis,* V, 388. Nothing in Moore's journal supports the tale.

Clark Gayton (1720?-1787?) was captain of a store ship in 1744, and of the *Mermaid,* man of war, in the years 1745-1747. He was on half pay for the next seven years, but went to sea again on the home station 1755-1757. He served in the West Indies, 1757-1759.

29. The signal was not seen by Moore, it was said, and the *Bristol* was acting without orders. Was Moore nearsighted and afraid to admit it? This would explain the St. Pierre episode.

30. Hurault to Beauharnois, 28 February 1759, Archives nationales, Marine et colonies, C^8 A 62. Hurault said that bombs not only had damaged the cistern but also the channels by which other water could be led to the cistern, from which one would gather that there was a reserve supply which could be used if the cistern were cleaned and if the water could be led to the cistern, but not

The commodore threw out the signal for the troops to land and the first two brigades began to clamber down the sides of the slatting transports into the flat-bottomed boats. It was dark when they were ready to pull for shore, and Hopson decided against landing that night. Moore deferred to his wishes. At seven o'clock the boats were ordered to disperse to the ships. The *Panther* and the *St. George* were standing out to sea at that time and came near to running down several boats loaded with soldiers, in the gathering dark.[31]

As the night thickened the bomb vessels were sent in to occupy the attention of the French. The other ships of the fleet relapsed into a routine standing of watches, except the *Rippon* and her sisters at the north end of the town. At half past five the commodore's barge had dropped alongside the *Rippon* and a spruce lieutenant scrambled aboard with orders to tow the ship off shore. He was sent back in a flash of oars against the late sun with the news that she was aground. In a short time Moore had a swarthy local pilot aboard her. It began to look like an all-night job on the grounded ship. The port guns were run to starboard. Nothing happened. Thirty tuns of water were started in the forehold to lighten her forward.[32] Still nothing happened. All the boats were sent out into the night to tow her off the bottom, but she would not budge. The anchors were carried out and all hands bent to the capstan, but the flukes sliced through the sandy bottom and came home. Shortly before midnight Jekyll had exhausted his store of tricks to move a stranded ship and could think of nothing more constructive to do than to post a lookout to warn of weather changes and of the presence of any small boats which might contain islanders with combustibles in their hands and arson in their hearts. But then she gave a sudden start and drifted free. No one aboard could offer any adequate explanation of this hap-

---

otherwise. Only one of the French witnesses at Du Treil's trial mentioned the drunkenness but that seems sufficient confirmation of an episode which any officer would like to veil. "Guadeloupe/Jugement du Gouverneur de cette isle/Nadau Dutreil," 1759, Archives nationales, Marine et colonies, B⁴ 92.

31. Moore to Pitt, 30 January 1759, Pitt, *Correspondence*, II, 29-31; Gardiner, *The West Indies*, 27; Beatson, *Memoirs*, II, 238-240.

32. This water, I assume, was then pumped over the side of the ship.

pening. At midnight Jekyll brought his battered, scorched, and bloody ship to anchor in thirteen fathoms, and had his first easy moment in seventeen hours.[33] The distant explosions of bombs and Basse Terre powder magazines probably did not interfere with his sleep.

Moore later denied that the *Rippon* was more exposed than any other ship. Certainly the casualty figures bear him out. She had two killed and thirteen wounded (mostly Marines) while the *St. George* had six killed and twenty wounded. Considering the relative sizes of their crews, there was about the same proportion of casualties in each ship. But, as Gardiner correctly emphasized, the *Rippon* was the only ship to be attacked by musket fire.[34] On Moore's side it may be added that the *Rippon* had sixty guns against thirteen, and her inability to run away may have been compensated in part by being fast aground. Since she was seaworthy immediately afterward, there was obviously little sea running, and little motion. This ought to have made a firmer platform for her guns and the men who served and laid them. But she was hotly enough engaged. The master gunner reported that she had fired thirteen hundred great shot, and the Marines had used two thousand cartridges.

At ten o'clock that night the town burst into flames from the carcasses[35] which the bomb vessels threw into it. At eleven a magazine blew up and thereafter, as Gardiner put it, "the Magazines of Powder" were "blown about the Enemy's Ears."[36] The whole town was afire shortly, or so it seemed from the sea. The warehouses of the place were packed with sugars, rum, and tar, which burned freely, as did all of the wooden structures of the little town. The *Bristol* and the *Roebuck* fired now and then during the night into the blazing capital and the scene must have given the inhabitants, who had hit out for the hills, a good deal to think about. Moore later felt it necessary to assure Pitt that he did not desire the burning, for, as the King's agent calculated, three of each four buildings in the place were destroyed, with

33. Gardiner, *The West Indies*, 26-28; Beatson, *Memoirs*, II, 238-240.
34. Gardiner, *The West Indies*, 27-29; Entick, *The Late War*, IV, 148n.
35. On the naval missile known as a carcass, see Appendix, Topic 16.
36. Gardiner, *The West Indies*, 27.

a loss of three or four hundred pounds sterling. But the bombing continued all night.[37]

Daylight showed that the ships had suffered much in their rigging from the French[38] shot. As for the town, it continued to burn all the day and most of the next night. Scattered firing broke out from the trenches along shore, opposite the place where the *Roebuck* and the *Bristol* had been berthed. The two ships replied with guns and small arms. The fleet had been blown a short distance to leeward. At half after nine one of the observers commented on a brisk gale blowing off shore. At ten the commodore made the signal for the fleet to anchor in the roadstead (he had spent the night in the *Woolwich*) and at eleven o'clock most of the ships were riding at anchor off the town. In half an hour Moore signalled for the troops to prepare to land and after the usual two hours of boat loading the soldiers of the first two brigades were sent shoreward. Captains Shuldham, Gambier, and Burnett supervised the landing, which was at a place north of the smoldering town where the men were unopposed, any hostile force having been discouraged by the well-laid fire of the *Bristol* and the *Panther* lying there. There was no naval opposition. The French had burned all but a few vessels lying in the roadstead, and those unburned vessels which made a run for it were overhauled and taken by Moore's frigates.[39]

At three o'clock a detachment of two hundred Marines was sent ashore under Colonel Rycaut, and marched some distance up country toward a fort placed so as to command the landing place, but found it abandoned and the guns spiked. A bit later the last two regiments and the battalion of Highlanders were landed. As the troops were being drawn up on a hill north of the smoking town, the bawling of sergeants was punctuated by a single cannon

---

37. "Journal," Pitt, *Correspondence*, II, 28-29; Beatson, *Memoirs*, II, 238-240; "The expedition," Loudoun Papers; Moore to Pitt, 30 January 1759, Pitt, *Correspondence*, II, 29-31; Burt to Newcastle, 30 January 1759, Newcastle Papers, Add. MSS. 32887, f. 410.

38. Other writers have commented on the French theory that the best target on an enemy ship was its rigging.

39. Beatson, *Memoirs*, II, 238-240; "The expedition," Loudoun Papers; Gardiner, *The West Indies*, 29-30; Moore to Pitt, 30 January 1759, Pitt, *Correspondence*, II, 29-31.

shot from the citadel. This was apparently a gesture of honor on the part of the commandant, for at five o'clock the few enemy soldiers left in the garrison made a line for the high land. A party of militiamen who had been entrenching on the high ground back of the town fled also, not having had time for their digging to make their new works defensible. Haldane later said, "A French officer since come in, says that leaving the citadell was owing to a mistake, in the Governors Aid de Camp delivering a wrong message to the commanding officer." How the citadel could have been defended with so many of its garrison already gone is not clear. Perhaps the French officer did not wish to confess the intemperance of the militia; perhaps he did not know of it. Whatever the reason for the afternoon's final abandonment of the strong place, the engineers had no siege problem to solve. At half past five the Sixty-first Regiment was sent into town to approach the citadel. Major Charles Teesdale, backed by four hundred men, called on the citadel to surrender. No answer. The major led his men in. They found the guns spiked, which was evidence of an ordered withdrawal. At six o'clock the British flag fluttered over the fortress.

Seeking to determine the cause of this collapse, French interrogators later pressed two questions on practically all witnesses at Du Treil's court-martial: Who ordered the evacuation? (Apparently the Governor did.) Were Chevalier Le Roy de la Poterie, the commandant of the citadel, and the Governor on good terms? (Absolutely not.) The aide de camp denied that he had garbled the verbal order to Poterie. It was generally agreed that Du Treil and Poterie were "indisposés l'un contre l'autre." Whether this difference affected the quality of the defense was not agreed upon by the witnesses. Other deponents testified that they thought the citadel was under-armed and one said the powder supply had been condemned during the tenure of the previous governor. Still others pointed to heavy casualties and the absence of a surgeon, and one claimed many of the wounded had been left behind in the withdrawal, although it seems certain that many wounded were carried out by the defenders. Abandoning one's wounded is the mark of low grade or desperate soldiery.

GUADELOUPE: BASSE TERRE

Most deponents (quite naturally) asserted that they had wished to continue the fight from their respective batteries but had been called off by their superiors. However, they seemed more martial in the court-martial than they were in their enemy's combat reports, where one always expects to see the opponents rated high.[40]

To return to Teesdale's men in the citadel, a train of powder had been led to a magazine containing three hundred barrels of powder. The chief gunner, a Genoese, remained hidden in the fort when the French abandoned it and, when brought to Teesdale, warned him of the danger. An immediate search discovered a drunken Negro staggering through the cellars with a lighted torch. He had been promised freedom if he would touch off the powder train. A method of escape had been drilled into him but, as in the case of the militia, the rum ration had been his undoing, and although his courage was high, his powers of concentration were low.[41]

During the night the troops were so disposed as to offer a defense against any possible counter attack. Part of them lay on their arms on rising ground overlooking the town. The Third Regiment moved to an advantageous post on a hill about a mile east of the citadel. The rest, excepting Teesdale's companies in the citadel, entered the town and lined its streets. It must have been uncomfortable, for the town was still billowing with smoke. Some of the men were employed at limiting the fire.[42]

Now it appeared that the expedition was in a very strong posi-

---

40. "Journal," Pitt, *Correspondence*, II, 28-29; "The expedition," Loudoun Papers; Haldane's "proceedings," Newcastle Papers; Beatson, *Memoirs*, II, 240-241; Gardiner, *The West Indies*, 29-30.

"Guadeloupe/Jugement du Gouverneur de cette isle/Nadau Dutreil," 1759, Archives nationales, Marine et colonies, B⁴ 92. The only immediately contemporary document, Hurault to Beauharnois, 28 February 1759, stated explicitly that the aide delivered an order, and that upon its receipt Poterie (without consulting his officers) ordered the evacuation of the fort. Judging from Hurault's phrasing it sounds as though the order was verbal: "vint dire par ordre de Monsieur Le Gouverneur a Monsieur de la Poterie. . . ." Archives nationales, Marine et colonies, C⁸ A 62.

41. "The expedition," Loudoun Papers; Beatson, *Memoirs*, II, 240-241; Gardiner, *The West Indies*, 29-30. The unfulfilled intention of blowing up the powder is confirmed in French sources, but without this detail. Hurault to Beauharnois, 28 February 1759, Archives nationales, Marine et colonies, C⁸ A 62.

42. Gardiner, *The West Indies*, 30; Haldane's "proceedings," Newcastle Papers; Hopson to Pitt, 30 January 1759, Pitt, *Correspondence*, II, 23-24.

tion. The guns of the citadel had been spiked with old nails which were quickly drilled out by the armorers. The troops had suffered no loss in the landing. The inhabitants seemed to be terrorized by the tremendous amount of force turned against them. The capital of the island had been bombarded, burned, and occupied. Beyond these results of their own efforts another ship of the line had been added to the fleet when Captain Tyrrel in the *Buckingham* joined. He had been on detached duty and was considered a first-class fighting man. In addition the *Rye* frigate came in from Barbados, bringing the missing hospital ship with the physician and the surgeons aboard. In the next week or so the remainder of the Highland battalion arrived also.[43]

On the debit side these facts may be noted: the inhabitants had entrenched the only pass which led from the town of Basse Terre to the rest of the island; the fleet was still splicing rigging a week later;[44] and worst of all, while two of the dread Horsemen, War and Death, had treated the British not too unkindly, their brother, Pestilence, was saddling to ride through them with awful effect.

The last day of January, 1759, was the end of a period in the literary history of the insular campaign, because on that day dispatches, letters, and diaries were packed to be taken to London. Haldane's "proceedings," the "Journal of an officer" which Hopson sent to Pitt, and the anonymous account which Pringle sent to Lord Loudoun and which I have cited as "The expedition"—all went off in the mail bags. Thereafter the witnesses of war were not nearly so articulate and the stream of British documents was much thinner. Except for Captain Gardiner's account, the sources for events after 30 January are nearly all official documents, British or French.

From the records of the week preceding the sending of dispatches, the aftereffects of the occupation of Basse Terre can be easily summarized.

Because of the fire the loot was not great. William Mathew Burt, the King's fiscal agent with the forces, sent in his report. "The effects which have come to my hands as his Majesty's agent,

---

43. Gardiner, *The West Indies*, 29-30; Moore, "Journal," Admiralty 50/22.
44. *Ibid.;* Moore to Pitt, 30 January 1759, Pitt, *Correspondence*, II, 29-31.

are yet so trifling, & scattering thro the remains of this miserable town that 'tis impossible for me to send any acct. of them." The only things of real worth he had acquired for the royal account were 168 slaves.[45]

Forty-seven casualties had been added to those suffered at Martinique. In taking Basse Terre seventeen had been killed and thirty wounded. No officers had been killed, but Captain Peter Innes of the artillery, Lieutenants George Leslie and James Hart, of the Forty-second and Sixty-third regiments respectively, had been wounded by 30 January. The navy's butcher's bill is not known. Nor is a French record now available, but it has been said that in the shelling of the citadel the fort major and the engineer-general had been killed.[46]

The political situation on the island, in the week after the landing, remained unchanged. On 26 January Hopson and Moore sent letters to Governor Nadau Du Treil, of which more later.[47]

Meanwhile the British had been strengthening their position. On 25 January the chief engineer reported that the citadel could be made tenable against an interior force, even after the army left. On the advice of the general officers and the engineer, Major Cleaveland of the artillery ordered the citadel repaired, and Moore gave twelve guns for it. The only warfare in the period 24-30 January was a bushwhacking, sniping fight such as the invaders had encountered at Martinique, but less intense, casualties being daily about one-tenth the number suffered near Fort Royale.[48] Hopson settled down to perfect his position and to try to think of some way to force the passes which led to the other side of the island. He never succeeded. Like another and better general officer, King David, his eyes anticipated the watches; he was troubled and he spake not.

Captain Tyrrel, due for a leave, was sent home with the dispatches—where he arrived on 6 March, and was taken by First

45. Burt to Newcastle, 30 January 1759, Newcastle Papers, Add. MSS. 32887, f. 410.
46. Hopson to Pitt, 30 January 1759, Colonial Office 110/1; *Gentleman's Magazine*, 29 (1759), 142.
47. Hopson to Pitt, 30 January 1759, Pitt, *Correspondence*, II, 23-24.
48. Hopson to Pitt, 30 January 1759, Pitt, *Correspondence*, II, 23-24; "Journal," *ibid.*, II, 28-29; Moore to Admiralty, 6 March 1759, Admiralty 1/307.

Sea Lord Anson to the King at St. James to tell the story of the campaign thus far.⁴⁹ The army at Guadeloupe relaxed—and then rotted.

3. *Hopson's choice: To do nothing*

The most serious problem faced by this army henceforward was the problem of disease. Hopson was to die within a month, and his last month of command was a month in which a sickening army was headed by a dying man. It was recognized by British colonials that military operations in the West Indies were a race between death on the field and death in stinking pest-ridden tents. Beckford, one of the most influential of West Indians, had written to Pitt in September of 1758, "Whatever is attempted in that climate must be done *uno impetu;* a general must fight his men off directly, and not give them time to die of drink and disease; which has been the case in all our southern expeditions."⁵⁰

On 30 January Hopson reported fifteen hundred men sick, and blamed it on the heat, the hard work of provisioning the outposts, and a shortage of Negroes for heavy labor.⁵¹ This, as he mildly put it, was embarrassing and made planning difficult.⁵² On 14 February the *Rippon* and the *Spy* set sail for St. John's, Antigua, with a convoy of eight transports containing five or six hundred of the sick, "the greatest Part of which Number died soon after their Arrival, and many on their Passage."⁵³ The surgeons, as was usual, had been sent ahead to make preparations for receiving the sick "and to buy Water."⁵⁴ St. John's was the capital of the Leeward Islands. On the same island was English Harbour, the chief naval base of the area. Gardiner added the grisly note, "*English Harbour* has, for many Ages, been the Grave of *British* officers."⁵⁵ Less than a fortnight later it was estimated that near

---

49. *Gentleman's Magazine*, 29 (1759), 143.
50. Pares, *War and Trade*, 286, citing Beckford to Pitt, 11 September 1758, *Chatham Correspondence*, I, 353.
51. This in an age when a favorite military hygienic precaution was to set off a pinch of gunpowder in each tent daily, to purify the air.
52. Hopson to Pitt, 30 January 1759, Pitt, *Correspondence*, II, 24-26.
53. Gardiner, *The West Indies*, 39.
54. *Ibid*. The water came by ship from Montserrat, about twenty-four sea miles south southwest.
55. Gardiner, *The West Indies*, 40.

GUADELOUPE: BASSE TERRE   91

eighteen hundred of the army were sick or dead. Nor were the sailors immune—"Twenty Men a day fall down in Fluxes on board some of the Ships," wrote Moore early in March. Antigua was so crowded with the sick, and the transports being unable to beat up to Barbados, the Commodore added that General Barrington was thinking of sending some of his invalids to North America. When Barrington had taken command of the army at the end of February, the army numbered about half as many effectives as when it took its departure from England. A trivial number had died of gun fire.[56] A later commander blamed the inexperience of the English surgeons, and engaged a French physician to oversee them;[57] this hardly seems sufficient explanation—after all, the British had as great an experience of tropical life as the French. Stephen Vincent Benét once spoke of a place

> where our tall young men in turn
> Drank death like wine.

That place was not Guadeloupe. There the tall young men drank a death which tasted of bilgewater and untreated sewerage.[58]

Confronted to the decomposing army were the acclimated French, French colonials, and their Negroes, busily digging themselves in, in the Dos D'Âne and in advanced posts. They probably could not be starved out of their hill lines, for the island produced a wonderful variety of vegetable foods, manioc, yams, potatoes, and fruits. For flesh they had their flocks.[59] But war materials had to be shipped in to them. Could Moore stop that traffic? Supplies from France did not often get through, and on 30 January the *Brilliant* took two merchantmen of over three hundred tons each "freighted and loaded with provisions on the *French*

56. Moore to Admiralty, 6 March 1759, Admiralty 1/307. Later in the year, in the six months after Barrington departed, thirteen officers and 775 men died of disease.
57. Crump to Pitt, 4 October 1759 and 26 December 1759, Colonial Office 110/1.
58. Gardiner, *The West Indies*, 42. Thirteen months later, a Frenchman said they had known by mid-February that the British were weakening fast and had heard that all captured positions had been mined as though for a withdrawal. (Actually, the citadel had been made ready for demolition as a routine precaution.) "Guadeloupe/Jugement du Gouverneur de cette isle/Nadau Dutreil," 1759, Archives nationales, Marine et colonies, B⁴ 92.
59. *Antilles françaises*, 4.

king's account for *Martinico,* having also on board some cloathing, and 500 stands of arms for the soldiery."[60] Supplies did come in from the Dutch, however.

The chief French concentration, in the Dos D'Âne, was about six miles southeast of Basse Terre. The French islanders used the term for any cleft.[61] The ascent to it was very steep; the road was rocky and gullied. Under the most favorable circumstances it would have been hard to storm, but Gardiner asserted that "some Officers" thought it could have been done if the assault had been attempted on the day the troops came ashore, when the enemy was still panicky.[62]

The strongest defense the colonials had, apart from the climate, was topography. In personnel the defenders were not strong. Negroes were early put to work by order of Guadeloupe's hard-talking but soft-fighting governor. Each company of militia was required to furnish able Negroes for distributing stores and doing other heavy work. The Negroes of the religious houses were to be employed in non-combatant services, as were the slaves owned by the hospitals. The white people complained of the insolence of the slaves, once the blacks discovered themselves to be indispensable. The governor regretted having to arm some of them: "Perceiving most of their masters in great fear and poverty, and their own services in great demand, they have assumed an impertinent and insubordinate air for which we have to punish them." He took the precaution of putting them in companies with whites, instead of forming them into separate units.[63] Nor was the handful of French regulars to be accounted of very much value. The "men" were often only boys. The officers came out to the islands as youths and matured without professional improvement. The cost of living being very high, the regular troops were often hired out as servants in time of peace, and the officers married heiresses or cadged off their economic betters.[64] No intensity of professional

60. *Gentleman's Magazine,* 29 (1759), 92.
61. And a V-bottomed boat was called a *bateau fait à dos d'âne.*
62. Gardiner, *The West Indies,* 31.
63. Pares, *War and Trade,* 253-256, citing, Nadau Du Treil to Berryer, 25 December 1758, Archives nationales, Marine et colonies, C⁷ A 17; and, "Guadeloupe, note of measures to be taken in case of an invasion," *ibid.*
64. Pares, *War and Trade,* 263.

feeling, or pride in the skilful practice of the profession of arms, could be expected from such a corps.

The traditional means of defending the West Indies were three. Shore batteries were everywhere, but were useful only against small raids by few ships, such as privateers. Citadels, like the ones at Fort Royale, Martinique, and Basse Terre, Guadeloupe, were maintained so that trading ships could lie under the great guns. Refuges in the mountains, called "dos d'ânes" or by some other term, were made use of at Nevis, Montserrat, and Guadeloupe.[65] Thus it is plain that by the last week in January the islanders of the western slope had fallen back to their last defensive position. An energetic officer might have done something on the other side of the island. Hopson was not an energetic officer.

The record of the next month is not inspiring but it may be examined profitably in detail for its contrast with the brilliant activity of Barrington in March and April. Only one well-thought-out action was fought; that was conducted by the sea forces and will be considered later.

The day of 25 January was spent in landing tents and the light artillery, and in marking out ground on which to encamp the battalions on the different heights in back of Basse Terre so they would be mutually supporting. Beatson, writing almost thirty years later, said a corps of light infantry was formed under command of Major Melville of the Thirty-eighth. This seems doubtful, as the idea of separate battalions and regiments of light infantry is generally thought to have originated later, probably not much before the 1770's.[66] Be that as it may, Melville was given

---

65. *Ibid.*, 245-246. At his trial it was alleged against Du Treil that he proposed to his people a general withdrawal from all posts to the Dos d'Âne, in February. If purely military considerations were to govern the defense, a strong case could be made for such tactics (if he really made the suggestion, which is doubtful). Deponents said it was rejected unanimously. It would have been safer than the risky, ill-considered war of defensive detachments which the French fought thereafter, but would have allowed the British to destroy a vast amount of wealth, something the civilians were not prepared to accept.—"Guadeloupe/Jugement du Gouverneur de cette isle/Nadau Dutreil," 1759, Archives nationales, Marine et colonies, B⁴ 92.

66. For an introduction to the subject, see, C. F. Atkinson, "Infantry," *Encyclopaedia Britannica*, 11th edn. See also "The Grenadiers," Appendix, Topic 13.

command of a body of men which seized an advanced post about four miles northeast of the town, on a plantation owned by a Madame Ducharmey. This post was held as long as there were any British troops on this side of the island, outside the citadel. Whenever any unusual activity was seen by Melville among the French, he signalled to the Third Regiment below him, which in turn signalled to the headquarters "to march off the Picquets." Three days' provisions were landed this day. The Fourth, Sixty-fourth, and Sixty-fifth regiments were encamped back of the town, where the artillery park and the camp of the Scots detachment were also fixed. The Sixty-third covered the citadel, while the Sixty-first supplied its garrison. General Hopson made his headquarters among the ruins of the governor's house in Basse Terre. Sailors were employed in moving captured cannon to the citadel, and also in bringing cannon from the ships to the same place. The staff reconnoitered, inspected the new posts, and examined the citadel. The great fort was in good condition, and so were its cannon for the most part. As Haldane optimistically said, they "took every necessary step for the reduction of the island" including preparation of the previously mentioned letter to the governor.[67] But wars are not won by inspections and paper work.

At dawn the main body of the colonial defenders had retired to the hills from the high ground back of the town. About two thousand of them, according to Gardiner's estimate (which seems excessive), threw up breastworks near a house about four miles southeast of the town, where Governor Du Treil made his headquarters.[68]

The next day, 26 January, the British held the same positions, their tents already pitched. At ten o'clock in the morning a small British party attacked French stragglers in the country, and some shells were thrown from the citadel into the woods where a small body of the enemy had appeared. The letter which had been drawn up on the previous day was sent by an officer toward the French lines, but the French—probably because of ignorance rather

---

67. Haldane's "proceedings," Newcastle Papers; Beatson, *Memoirs*, II, 241, 245; Gardiner, *The West Indies*, 32.

68. "The expedition," Loudoun Papers; Gardiner, *The West Indies*, 30.

GUADELOUPE: BASSE TERRE

than malice—fired on his flag and he returned. One of the colonials was then sent with another note to the governor. He was received by Du Treil who sent back word by a French officer that he would receive British officers. Brigadier Clavering, who bore the letter which called on the French to surrender or to take the "fatal consequences," was sent to treat with him. The governor asked Clavering to withdraw and return later for an answer. On 28 January Clavering went back with two naval officers, Captains Shuldham and Gambier, who represented Moore's interests, and a Captain Cleiland of the army, and brought out a reply. Du Treil thought the British had been rendered overconfident by their easy progress thus far (he said), but he denied they had a sufficient force to do more than possess the extremities of the island. He trusted that the laws of war would be observed and took it upon himself to point out that, if they were not, he had a "Master who is powerful enough to take Revenge for what we may suffer." Gardiner thought this a strong reply from a commander whose activity had thus far been rather listless; better, he mused, to point the bayonet than the pen.[69] It is a simple fact that the militant spirit of Du Treil's letter was not shared by all his force. On the day Clavering first visited the governor, about a hundred of the enemy, with an officer, surrendered to the British, under no immediate compulsion.

Military activities of 28-30 January were confined to sniping and anti-sniping work. Detachments of redcoats were sent to scrub the countryside. The enemy gathered in mass only at great distances from the British, and then in small parties, which became objects of attention of the gunners in the citadel. The cane fields offered excellent cover for the natives, and on 30 January a French party hidden in cover near the squadron's watering place killed

69. Gardiner, *The West Indies*, 32-35; Beatson, *Memoirs*, II, 242-243; "The expedition," Loudoun Papers. The governor's letter is in Beatson's account. See also, Hopson to Pitt, 30 January 1759, Pitt, *Correspondence*, II, 23-24. During these parleys there was a twenty-four-hour armistice which was used by the British to dig three more entrenchments, make two redoubts, and mount a battery. Defenders of Du Treil said the people murmured because the Governor did not surrender at this time. Father Roger Magloire, an Irish Jesuit parish priest, said the inhabitants murmured because they disapproved of discussions with the British.—"Guadeloupe/Jugement du Gouverneur de cette isle/Nadau Dutreil," 1759, Archives nationales, Marine et colonies, B[4] 92.

three Marines and a seaman. To stop this sort of thing troops burned the cane fields and houses nearby.[70]

By this time Moore had a vessel ready to go to England with dispatches (the *Weazel* sloop) and Hopson wrote his report. He had not yet made up his mind what to do next, although his second, General Barrington, had been urging him for the past three days to allow him, Barrington, to go with sixteen hundred men to the other side of the island.[71]

Hopson did not know yet what provisions would be needed but promised to send an account by the next ship. He had been hoping to receive supplies which had been sent from Portsmouth on 8 November. He dared not wait for them, he continued, but was sending to Antigua, which place could probably not produce so much on such short notice. If the Antiguans had not enough provisions for him, he did not know what he should do. He closed this pessimistic letter by praising the naval officers for their work in the expedition and enclosed maps which would be explained by the bearer, his *aide*.[72]

On 1 February a detachment commanded by Major John Trollope of the Sixty-third repulsed a considerable party of the enemy and took thirty prisoners. Two days later Major Melville set fire to several villages near his outpost at Madame Ducharmey's and burned the cane brakes around them. Colonel Crump also led a cane-burning detachment from the camp. The events of 4 February were the most exciting since the town had been taken: a ship arrived from England, a gun burst in the citadel—killing one and wounding three—and Major Melville fought a small battle with Madame Ducharmey and her private army. Melville sent a force against a fortified house on an entrenched hill opposite his post, commanded by Madame, who had armed her Negroes and now appeared wherever the fire was hottest, encouraging her dusky helots to hold off the swarming redcoats. Melville carried the trenches by storm, losing two officers and ten men killed, three officers and twenty-seven men wounded. He took

---

70. "Journal," Pitt, *Correspondence*, II, 29; Gardiner, *The West Indies*, 35.
71. Barrington to Pitt, 2 March 1759, Pitt, *Correspondence*, II, 45-46.
72. Hopson to Pitt, 30 January 1759, *ibid.*, II, 24-26.

some prisoners, several of them females, but their amazon commander made her escape. The defenders lost only ten killed. The wounded officers were two of the Sixty-fifth, and a lieutenant of the Forty-second. The latter lost his arm but later became a great favorite among the ladies of the island;[73] there is probably a profound psychological lesson in that happy result.

Two days later another skirmish was fought. This time the defenders had mounted a battery on a hill south of the citadel, whereby they commanded the line along which reliefs were marched to the outposts beyond the river Galion. Colonel[74] Debrissay, with the grenadiers of the Sixty-first and Sixty-third regiments, some pioneers, and one hundred other men, was ordered to silence it. Two companies of the Sixty-first were sent with the pioneers directly against the battery. Their commander misunderstood his orders and went against a different battery which was half a mile south of the one Debrissay sought to silence. On marching out he had fired about a dozen Negro huts which would have given cover to anyone harassing his withdrawal, but the smoke was an alarm beacon and rallied the islanders. He soon saw that he was too weak to carry out the mission and had no cover for a retreat. He marched back a short distance and, upon being joined by half the grenadiers, then stormed and took a steep hill which was already conveniently entrenched. This was the strongest available place to maintain himself until Debrissay could extricate him. Just as his panting, sweating soldiers settled down on the hill top, he saw the main body of the enemy marching past him to attack the remaining grenadiers below, and he abandoned his "island" of refuge to attack the uncautious colonials on the flank. In a heated scrimmage lasting ten minutes he disorganized them, and the citadel's gunners poured their fire on the rapidly dissolving and retreating French. The British loss was eight killed and wounded; the French loss was estimated at

---

73. Gardiner, *The West Indies*, 36-37; Beatson, *Memoirs*, II, 244; Forbes, *The "Black Watch*," 63.

74. I am using the titles "Lieutenant Colonel" and "Colonel" interchangeably when speaking of "Lieutenant Colonels," just as soldiers often do in conversation.

70 killed and 130 wounded. The citadel fired cohorns[75] the rest of the day.[76]

Except for these raids which were used as counter-irritants, the army was chiefly concerned with its own consolidation and administration during the last period of Hopson's command. On 11 February Debrissay was made governor of the citadel, and the Sixty-first marched in to relieve the Sixty-third, which in turn settled on the camp grounds of the relieving force. A flag of truce was sent on the same day to Martinique to arrange an exchange of prisoners. On 14 February the joint command issued a manifesto to the inhabitants. In the manner of St. Valentine, Hopson and Moore invited the residents to become British subjects. They also confirmed the free Negroes and mulattoes in their freedom. Moore had wanted to wage sharper psychological warfare, and proposed an additional clause addressed to Protestants and slaves which guaranteed the Protestants civil equality with British subjects and promised freedom and ten acres of conquered land to any slave who might desert his colonial master. He was overruled, probably because two nations could play that game, there being slaves and Catholics in the British West Indies, both under political restrictions. A nation which meddled with religious and racial lines could easily suffer from the precedent it established. In his letter to Pitt, Moore deprecated the proclamation. "I had no Opinion of that alone being sufficient to bring the Inhabitants to terms, nor have they taken any Notice of it."[77]

From that time on there was no serious fighting by the defending forces on that side of the island. There were, however, numerous alarums and excursions designed to bring the British out under the sun and tire them out. When the pickets would begin to march and the rest of the men in camp stood to arms, the enemy would withdraw. Such a show would last about four hours[78] and no doubt had considerable nuisance value for the

75. A cohorn was a small mortar with two handles by which it could be carried for short distances. It was sometimes spelled "coehorn."
76. Beatson, *Memoirs*, II, 244-245; Gardiner, *The West Indies*, 37.
77. Gardiner, *The West Indies*, 38; Moore to Pitt, 6 March 1759, Colonial Office 110/1.
78. Gardiner, *The West Indies*, 38, 42.

French. In that way they may have added hundreds to the total of British soldiers who answered to sick call.

On 16 February six hundred more of the sick were evacuated to Antigua in transports. About this date Hopson wrote to Governor Thomas of the Leeward Islands asking him to raise men up to the number of six hundred, black and white. On 20 February a council of war was held but what decisions were made is not known, since the minutes were apparently not sent to Pitt. Two days later the governor of Barbados was asked to send supplies, but the governor's reply and the supplies did not arrive until after Hopson's death. John Barnes, commissary of artillery, delivered to Robert Patrickson, clerk of the stores in the citadel, as much material as Major Cleaveland thought necessary to defend the great fort. Hopson's last official act was to authorize an auction (24-28 February) of the loot—all tangible wealth except the Negroes—which brought in a little more than £350. in six different coinages.[79]

The naval force had also been occupied with a good many relatively unimportant affairs.[80] The flotilla had been reenforced, as previously stated, by the arrival of Captain Tyrrel of the *Buckingham*, 65 guns. He was a local hero, having successfully attacked a munitions fleet of sixteen sloops, convoyed by three Frenchmen in the previous November.[81] For a week after the bombardment

[79.] Barrington to Pitt, 2 March 1759, Colonial Office 110/1; Burt's account, Treasury 1, Bundle 390, f. 108-116.
[80.] The fleet's major action of 14 February is treated in the next section of this chapter.
[81.] Governor George Thomas of the Leeward Islands reported Tyrrel's fight in a letter to Pitt from Antigua, 20 November 1758. On 3 November Tyrrel engaged a convoy of three ships of war and sixteen sloops, mostly Dutchmen, bound from St. Eustatius to Martinique with munitions and provisions. The French ships of war were two frigates of thirty-six and twenty-four guns respectively, and the *Florissant*, 74 guns,—probably the vessels discovered at Fort Royale, Martinique, by Moore's ships. Tyrrel drove off the frigates and silenced the *Florissant* in three hours, leaving not a man on her deck. Tyrrel, many times wounded, made ready to board her but before his exhausted crew could undertake it, the *Florissant* limped away and escaped. Aboard the *Buckingham*, of 450 men, Tyrrel had seven killed and forty-six wounded. Pitt, *Correspondence*, I, 396-397. Tyrrel's account of the bloody match was printed in the *Gentleman's Magazine*, 29 (1759), 39-40.
When the chastened master of the *Florissant* saw Moore's ships turning into Fort Royale Bay he probably thought the oak-hearted Tyrrel had come back with his gang.

of Basse Terre the crews had been engaged in patching hulls, splicing hemp, and sewing canvas to repair the considerable damage done by the shore batteries on the day of the attack. It was not until 28 January that Moore hoisted his broad pennant on the *Cambridge,* and not until two days later that he had time to write a report to Pitt and send it off by the *Weazel.* The *Weazel* was placed under Tyrrel who was sent home for kudos and a rest. Peter Parker was promoted to command the *Bristol*;[82] Lachlin Leslie became captain of the *Buckingham.* On the last day of January a lieutenant and twenty men from each ship were ordered to help the soldiers move captured guns to the citadel. On 2 February the *Ludlow Castle* frigate and the *Spy* sloop, neither of which had been in the bombardment of the island's capital, returned from knocking out a four-gun French shore battery to the northward. On the next day the ships' boys were sent to choke and sneeze among the ashes of the town, collecting usable cannon balls which had been fired against the French. By this time it was charged among the sailors that the French had used all sorts of langrage shot,[83] stones, and chewed musket balls. Some men in the eighteenth century excused the use of such missiles on the ground that they were intended to rend an enemy's rigging, but the loads were warmly resented by the seamen.[84]

On 4 February, the day Melville fought Madame Ducharmey, the *Lancaster,* 66 guns, Captain Robert Man, arrived at Basse Terre. It will be remembered that the ship had been ordered to leave with Hughes in the previous November but had not been ready for sea. Captain Man brought news that four months' provisions for seven thousand men were being prepared and that Pitt had hoped to have the supply fleet sail by 30 December. From

---

82. Admiral Sir Peter Parker (1721-1811), son of an admiral and father of another, received his first ship command in this campaign. See the author's "Admiral Sir Peter Parker's First Ship of the Line," *American Neptune,* 3 (July 1943), 266. To Americans the interesting fact of Parker's life was that he commanded the British naval force which unsuccessfully attacked Charleston, South Carolina, in 1776, where Parker lost a ship. He is more happily remembered in Britain as a patron of the young Nelson.

83. Langrage shot was composed of miscellaneous scraps of iron for tearing sails and rigging. It would of course make ugly wounds in human flesh.

84. Gardiner, *The West Indies,* 30, 35, 36; Haldane to Newcastle, 30 January 1759, Newcastle Papers, Add. MSS. 32887, f. 392.

7 to 9 February, the *Rippon,* the *Lyon,* and the *Winchester* were trying to land heavy guns from the restless roadstead by means of catamarans. The guns were towed ashore by ten boats each and carried to the citadel by Negro drudges.[85]

All the while ships were being sent against the little batteries which were to be found in almost all of the creek mouths, where they gave a limited protection to enemy privateers and other small vessels. Moore attempted to arrange a blockade of the island with all of his "cruizers,"[86] but he complained that it was almost impossible to expect important results from the blockade because of the fertility of the soil and the great number of cattle on the island. He went a little farther than some international lawyers of the period might have been willing to follow when he blockaded the neutral Dutch island of St. Eustatius which was a source of supplies for the Guadeloupe defenders. Meanwhile the ships were growing sickly, the crews diminishing in numbers, and Moore could not legally impress men of this part of the world into the service. Because he was short handed, because hurricanes were sure to come sooner or later, and because he would have to detach ships to convoy the trade home to England before the season of great storms, Moore was growing impatient of the lethargy of the army command. Perhaps it was irritation and impatience which impelled him to refuse a request from Du Treil which from this distance of time seems humane and reasonable. Du Treil asked for ships to carry the island's women and children to a French port in the West Indies. Moore's refusal was blunt, and the women and children who had already been assembled for the departure had to trudge back up to the Dos d'Âne.[87] I assume—

85. Gardiner, *The West Indies,* 36, 38; Pitt, *Correspondence,* I, 386-387, 386n., and, Pitt to Hopson, 30 November 1758, *ibid.,* I, 411-412; Man to Pitt, 1 December 1758, Colonial Office 110/1.

86. For "cruizers" frigates were usually employed, but when a fast ship was to be had—such as the song-worthy *Rippon*—it was used for such work too.

87. Moore to Pitt, 6 March 1759, Pitt, *Correspondence,* II, 54-56; Amherst to Pitt, 28 February 1759, Colonial Office 5/54. French sources show that men, arms, and intelligence moved freely in and out of Guadeloupe in small French vessels throughout the stay of the British. "Guadeloupe/Jugement du Gouverneur de cette isle/Nadau Dutreil," 1759, Archives nationales, Marine et colonies, B^4 92. Barrington reopened the subject of evacuating the women and children, in April, but his letter to Du Treil on the subject was not answered. Clainvilliers' narrative, Archives nationales, Marine et colonies, C^8 A 62.

without any foundation, to be sure—that the women and children to be transported were only the refugees of the hills. It would not have taken much shipping to move them. But perhaps Moore thought Madame Ducharmey was a typical Guadeloupe female; if all of them were like her no one would dare trust them aboard a King's ship.

All of this dilly-dallying with a dying army and a sickening fleet came to an end on 27 February when tired Hopson—old in the eighteenth-century way, at what we would call middle age—died of the fevers which had more than decimated his idle troops.[88] He was succeeded by Major General John Barrington[89] who was as energetic as his predecessor had been slack. Things began to happen. But before going on with the events of his command let us turn back to the only important action fought in the period 23 January-27 February.

4. *The Marines and the Black Watch at Fort Louis*

Early in February Moore borrowed some of the Scotsmen for use at Grand Terre. Although Barrington had unsuccessfully petitioned Hopson for permission to lead a force against the other side of the island, Moore, being co-equal in command, needed no permission to wage war. With the aid of the Scots, Moore's force on 14 February wrested Fort Louis, the chief strong point of Grand Terre, from the hands of the French commander of those parts, Lieutenant Joseph de Beaulés. On 2 February Brigadier Clavering and the sub-engineer sailed in the *Berwick,* accompanied by the *Bonetta* bomb, to reconnoiter the south coast of the islands from Trois Rivières to Grand Terre. The *Bonetta* returned alone very early on 6 February. Although the Commodore does not say what

---

88. Barrington to Pitt, 2 March 1759, Pitt, *Correspondence*, II, 45-50.

89. This general was one of at least five well-known sons of old John Shute Barrington, first Viscount Barrington (1678-1734). His eldest brother, the second Viscount, was secretary at war under Pitt. Daines Barrington was a lawyer and a respected constitutional historian, who also published speculations on how to reach the North Pole. Samuel Barrington was an admiral who was almost continuously afloat for twenty-two years, took St. Lucia from the French in 1779, and relieved Gibraltar in 1782. Shute Barrington was Bishop of Durham, known chiefly for advocating toleration of Catholics in all but political matters. Note how this family typified the aristocratic tradition. A son for the title, one for the law, one for the church, one for the navy, one for the army.

word she carried, she stood off and on for orders and the result was the dispatch of the task force which took Fort Louis.

At two o'clock in the afternoon of the same day Captain Harman in the *Berwick* came back from the reconnaissance and with three frigates, the *Roebuck, Renown, Woolwich,* and several bombs and tenders under his command, set sail again on the difficult beat to Grand Terre. He had an augmented force of Marines under Colonel Rycaut, and several companies of the Highlanders aboard. Nothing more was heard from this force until the lieutenant of the *Berwick* returned four days later, probably in a sailing boat, with a request to be allowed to attack Fort Louis at closer range than had been ordered. The difficulty was that his force was rather weak for close-on bombardment in such a bay. Moore ordered Harman to go in, and he told off the *Panther*, Captain Shuldham, to reinforce. Shuldham got away on the next day (11 February).[90]

When the detachment arrived off Fort Louis, it was all regular "shores of Tripoli" stuff, complete with a beach-head landing under fire, and plenty of heroism. For six hours the ships of the "task force" bombarded the French shore positions: fort, low-lying batteries, and two redoubts of four guns each which were built up on two nearby hills. Every house in the fort was burned by bombs, the wall was breached, and the men on the shore batteries found it too unpleasant to stand to their guns. Three fire ships had been moored across the channel, but sailors, extemporized into 1759 "commandos" with cutlasses between their teeth, boarded them and towed them to the Isle des Cochons and burned them on the beach there. The Marines and the Scots who had been in the boats for five cramping hours were now urged in to the sands. The landing boats were impeded by pilings driven into the bottom for the purpose, and also by mosquito-infested mangroves and other water plants; nevertheless, led by a major of the Marines, the men splashed over the gunwales at armpit depth (wetting their powder) and, streaming with sea water, emerged on the beach in a rush of foam to scatter the horrified defenders with bayonet alone.[91]

90. Gardiner, *The West Indies*, 37-38; Beatson, *Memoirs*, II, 245-246; Moore, "Journal," Admiralty 50/22; *South-Carolina Gazette*, 14 April 1759.
91. I suggest that this was easier than it may seem, on the premise that these

The loss among the attackers was considerable; a lieutenant aboard the *Berwick* was killed and many of the seamen and landing party were casualties.[92]

The local militia had been more harm than help, as they so often were during this campaign. In the first place, they refused to enter the fort because they disliked the noise of its cannon. Again, when the powder magazine exploded and Beaulés knew the day was lost, his officers had to beat the militia to get them to approach the fort and remove the stores which had not yet been damaged.[93]

During the following week the men of this expedition got news of Keppel's victory at Goree on 29 December. The troops were drawn out, salutes were fired, and much hearty celebration was undertaken.

On 22 February Moore sailed to view the captured bastion, leaving the fleet under Leslie's orders. Moore was back at Basse Terre by 25 February. The Marines and Scots at Fort Louis were later relieved by a detachment under Major Thomas Ball of the Sixty-fourth, but they were still there as late as 7 March and, said the critical Gardiner, "on account of the scarcity of Provisions and Water, and not being supplied with Tents like the rest of the Army, they were growing sickly" and two captains of the Marines had died.[94] No one else complained of such shortages, and over on Basse Terre men with plenty of food and tents were also dying, at about the same rate.

The capture of Fort Louis cut the communications between the two halves of Guadeloupe.[95] When Pitt heard of the victory he wrote Harman's name down to remember.

---

were militiamen who ran, and the less one knows about the bayonet the more one fears it.

92. Gardiner, *The West Indies*, 38-39; Forbes, *The "Black Watch,"* 63; Beatson, *Memoirs*, II, 246-247.

93. Beaulés to Beauharnois, 21 February 1759, Archives nat., Marine et colonies, C⁸ A 62. The fort had been under fire daily since 8 February when the British task force began to accumulate off shore. "Guadeloupe/Jugement du Gouverneur de cette isle/Nadau Dutreil," 1759, Archives nationales, Marine et colonies, B⁴ 92.

94. Gardiner, *The West Indies*, 38-39, 41, 44.

95. Moore to Pitt, 6 March 1759, Pitt, *Correspondence*, II, 54-56.

5. *Barrington, commander in chief*

Hopson died at one o'clock in the morning of 27 February. He had been ill for a month. This is known from a private note to Pitt sent with his "publick letter" of 30 January in which he spoke of "my having been very much out of order for some days past."[96] This one letter only proved he was ill during the last week of January, but there was nothing in his behavior of the next four weeks to indicate much recovery.

On the following day Barrington convened a council of war, attended by Brigadiers Armiger, Haldane, and Trapaud. Clavering was ill and could not attend, but he agreed to the articles when they were read to him on 5 March. The generals viewed the facts and set them down in five articles, which are paraphrased here.

1. Only 2796 men were fit for duty.

2. The physician said the standard of health of this body of men would worsen instead of improve.

3. The position they now held had a three-mile chain of posts, which were so extended as not to have a complete relief. Clavering held a hill commanding the left flank, with six hundred men. On an eminence in front the Third Regiment was posted. To secure the rear 120 men had been assigned. In Fort Royale the garrison numbered five hundred men.[97] The ordinary guards numbered 160. In addition there were the "picquets" and men assigned to ordinary camp duty. In summary there were 1380 men, plus the Third Regiment, plus pickets, plus men assigned to ordinary camp duties. (I estimate the total at about two thousand of the 2796 able-bodied men.)[98] A complete relief was

---

96. Hopson to Pitt, 30 January 1759, Colonial Office 110/1.

97. The regiment in garrison must therefore have been augmented by drafts to complete its paper strength.

98. Considering that almost half the men were on the sick list, and that the outside regiments must have been drafted upon for men to serve in the citadel, the Third Regiment could hardly number more than three hundred men. From the previous statement of their use we know that the pickets were a reserve held in readiness for any alarm. I can only guess at their number, but if the regular guards numbered 160, my own experience would indicate that the picket would be the same number, 160. The men assigned to ordinary camp duties would be cooks, kitchen police, men assigned to quarters, and sergeants to see that they did what they were told to do. The camp-workers would probably average

therefore impossible. Conclusion: because of the number of men required, this position was untenable.

4. All the works of the enemy, including plantations, which the British could reach, they had already destroyed by burning or otherwise, and the enemy's Negroes had been driven away, so they had exhausted all possibilities of distressing the colonials on this side of the island.

5. The chief engineer said the citadel was tenable against any interior force.

From the above facts the council unanimously agreed to remove from their present camp.[99]

But to what place should the army be removed? They agreed that the best means to reduce the island could be learned by answering two questions: whether to attack the enemy in his camp, or to go to Fort Louis, which could be used as a base from which to destroy the defenders of Grand Terre. With regard to the question of attacking the French camp in the Dos d'Âne, they agreed to four propositions.

1. It was strongly posted, entrenched with cannon, had a mountain and a wood on each flank, and the river Galion in front. The banks of the river Galion were steep precipices at that place. There was another steep gully in front, which the French passed with ladders. These ladders were drawn up nightly.

2. Some of the general officers had reconnoitered these gullies within half a musket shot (about 100 feet) and reported they could not pass any number of men in the face of the enemy.

3. The only other place to go was one where the men must march in single file, very close to the citadel, and then must pass a mountain and a wood.

---

three or four men per company. With more than sixty companies outside the walls of the citadel these men would number about two hundred.

          Number given 1380
          Third regt.   300
          Pickets   160
          On camp duty 200
                                    ─────
                                    2040 required on duty at
                                         any given moment.

99. Barrington to Pitt, 2 March 1759, Colonial Office 110/1.

4. One otherwise unidentified man had said there was a "road" to the French flank, passable in single file, but this was guarded by an officer and one hundred men who must be surprised and disposed of silently, without any gun play.

From these pieces of intelligence they deduced that they must go to Fort Louis. All present signed the articles (Clavering on 5 March).[100]

In such a cool and rational way did these gentlemen demonstrate that they belonged to "the age of reason" at its best. Readers who have served on committees and councils may envy the logical integrity of the document represented by this summary. Not for nothing did the Anglo-American cultural tradition insist upon the study of logic and rhetoric as part of the training of gentlemen.

On 1 March Barrington received word from Governor Thomas that three hundred Negroes were on the way. This was welcome information. The men would be extremely useful for work among the woods and mountains. On the next day Barrington made a disturbing discovery while reading through Hopson's papers. It was a letter from Pitt which ordered Hopson to send the Highland companies to North America after the attack on Martinique. In his next letter to Pitt Barrington protested this, saying they were extremely diminished by sickness, death, and injury. Some were in the hospital at Antigua. If he sent the remainder to America, he would be too weak to carry on, since he would have the whole of the enemy force against him. Without the Scots he would not be able to leave a sufficient force on Basse Terre to contain the inhabitants who were then roosting patiently in the Dos d'Âne. Thus it was necessary to keep the Highlanders for a while, especially in view of the fact that he intended to try what might be done on the other side of the island. However, he promised to send them to North America with an additional draft of a thousand men, if so many were left over from the neces-

---

100. Barrington to Pitt, 2 March 1759, Colonial Office 110/1. English prisoners told the Jesuit missionary, Father Roger Magloire, about this time, that spirits were low in the army and they had a rumor that the force would withdraw if not successful at Grand Terre. "Guadeloupe/Jugement du Gouverneur de cette isle/ Nadau Dutreil," 1759, Archives nationales, Marine et colonies, B⁴ 92.

sary garrison forces, after a successful campaign.¹⁰¹ Pitt later approved of this proposal completely.

This letter to Pitt was a competent and complete document, the healthy Barrington panting optimism where the sick Hopson had sighed pessimism. He was leaving Debrissay in the citadel and with him instructions, money, and a letter of credit on the contractors at Antigua, on whom the army would continue to draw until the food promised to Hopson arrived in the West Indies. As to the sick, the number was still increasing;¹⁰² 1649 were being sent in thirty-three transports to Antigua, since nothing else could be done with them.¹⁰³ Inasmuch as there was not enough fresh food in Antigua, he had ordered more from Barbados. With respect to the condition of the citadel he enclosed the signed opinion of the engineer:

> This garrison in its present state with the proportion of artillery allotted for its defence, is not only above insult, but equal to sustain a siege against any interior force of this island.
>
> Will. Cuninghame
> Chief Eng^r:

A casualty list of 55 killed and 140 wounded, covering the period 24 January-3 March, was also enclosed.¹⁰⁴ The Thirty-eighth, the smallest unit of the line, and the Forty-second, possibly the toughest unit, were hardest hit by combat. The losses of the Thirty-eighth were probably men spent in Melville's fight against Madame Ducharmey's slaves. The levy of death on the Forty-second was the penalty of merit. These rugged, hardy youngsters of a shiny, new battalion were sent in wherever there was a particularly difficult job to do, and they did the jobs well with sword and gun.

Barrington was fast learning his new job, and four days after writing the letter which contained the casualty list, he found it necessary to write again to convey more news to Pitt. In the

---

101. Barrington, to Pitt, 2 March 1759, Pitt, *Correspondence*, II, 47-48.
102. Barrington to Pitt, *ibid.*, II, 45-50.
103. This made a total of almost three thousand men separated from the army because of illness.
104. Barrington to Pitt, 2 March 1759, Colonial Office 110/1. The casualty list was tabulated as follows:

interval 181 men had fallen sick, and eight men had died.[105] Thus the sickness rate had risen to forty-five per day, the death rate to two a day. At this rate only sixty more days need pass for the entire army to have been attacked and immobilized by disease.

Several soldiers had deserted to the enemy. Governor Thomas had written that he could get more men only with the greatest difficulty, unless the army were prepared to pay more money—which, he added, would be very expensive.

On 6 March Barrington completed the Sixty-third Regiment to five hundred men by drafts on the other regiments;[106] this was the regiment which garrisoned the citadel. He was leaving them two-thirds rations for four months, and said he must have full rations for six hundred men for five months, including fresh food. And there must be forage for the animals to eat.[107] He also wanted two hundred recruits from England, and was writing to Barbados for about four hundred men. With understandable pride he said all the men had been embarked with their baggage for the new campaign and not a man had been lost in the maneuver.[108]

Unit	Killed	Total	
3d	1 ensign, 1 sergeant, 7 men	9	
4th	8 men	8	
61st	3 men	3	
63d	4 men	4	
64th	1 man	1	
65th	5 men	5	
38th	1 lieutenant, 1 sergeant, 9 men	11	
42d	1 ensign, 10 men	11	
Artill.	1 lieutenant-fireworker, 2 matrosses	3	
		55	

Unit	Wounded	Total	K&W
3d	1 lieutenant, 1 sergeant, 17 men	19	28
4th	5 men	5	13
61st	16 men	16	19
63d	1 lieutenant, 17 men	18	22
64th	1 lieutenant, 1 sergeant, 2 men	4	5
65th	1 lieutenant, 1 ensign, 7 men	9	14
38th	1 major, 1 ensign, 1 sergeant, 34 men	37	48
42d	2 lieutenants, 2 sergeants, 28 men	32	43
		140	195

The major of the Thirty-eighth who was wounded was the aggressive and scholarly Melville, whose blindness in later life was attributed to this wound.

105. Barrington to Pitt, 6 March 1759, Pitt, *Correspondence*, II, 52-54.

106. I do not know whether this was a second draft or merely the first record of the draft which had obviously taken place by the date of Barrington's first council of war, 28 February 1759. See p. 105, note 97.

107. Since there were no draft animals it may be deduced that fresh food meant fresh meat to an eighteenth-century army.

108. Barrington to Pitt, 6 March 1759, Pitt, *Correspondence*, II, 52-54.

His medical staff was in pitiful condition. When the expedition left England its medical service was provided by a physician, a purveyor, an apothecary, two surgeons, and ten surgeon's mates. In early March only the purveyor, one surgeon, and two surgeon's mates were fit for duty in Guadeloupe, all the rest being sick or dead, except the apothecary who was with the invalids in Antigua—these invalids including two prostrated surgeon's mates. The original fifteen medics had been reinforced at Barbados by the addition of a surgeon and eleven surgeon's mates. The surgeon was at Antigua and, of the mates, eight were at Antigua, of whom three were sick.[109] In short, Barrington had a surgeon and six mates in good condition with his army of 2615 able-bodied men![110] At Antigua with the feverish invalids there were a surgeon, an apothecary, and six mates. From this sorry compilation one can reasonably say the diseases the men were suffering from were probably so not much deficiency diseases such as scurvy, but contagious fevers and dysentery, since the percentage of the medical men disabled was higher than that of the rank and file. The fact that a quarter of the Barbadian staff was down with sickness supports this conclusion, for the assumption is warranted that they were acclimated and knew something about a correct diet to support life in their islands.

Governor Thomas' attempts to raise men at Antigua were interesting. He called for six companies to consist, each, of one captain, three lieutenants, four sergeants, four corporals, and one hundred "private men." The officers were to have the same pay as the King's officers. The privates were to receive "three bits a day" which was about equal in purchasing power to the dollar a day paid to American privates until the 1940's. Any Negroes who were killed or lost in any way were to be paid for out of the King's funds according to an appraisal made at time of embar-

---

109. Barrington to Pitt, 2 March 1759, Colonial Office 110/1, enclosing return signed "G. Corryn."

110. The tables of organization of the infantry arm of the Army of the United States in recent years have provided that in a regiment containing 2,985 enlisted men—approximately the number Barrington had—there be ten medical officers and eighty enlisted men of the medical department (excluding veterinary officers and men). This is about twelve times the number Barrington had available in Guadeloupe.

kation. All men were to be transported and victualled at the expense of the Crown. White volunteers and officers were promised bounty lands at the end of the war.[111] The results of this proclamation were negligible; only a few "strangers" came forward, barely enough to embody in a unit.

The embarkation at Basse Terre was made easier by a ruse of Barrington's devising. On 28 February he ordered tents to be struck and the army to hut as though they planned to settle down for a long stay. This job was completed on the next day. During the next three days the artillery, the baggage, and the sick were embarked. On 5 March the town batteries were blown up. Early next morning the outposts were drawn in, and all were on board by dawn of that day except the Sixty-third Regiment and some of the artillery which was remaining in the citadel. The *St. George* and the *Buckingham* were left in the roadstead to cover the garrison. The enemy suspected an ambuscade and it took him six hours to work his way, unopposed, into the town. About noon the suspicious colonials set fire to the army's jerry built huts. Debrissay allowed them a short while in which to get comfortably settled in the town, and then opened fire from the citadel, beating down and burning the houses they occupied and at the same time making a sally and taking some prisoners. The rest of the colonials left in a hurry for the salubrious air of the Dos d'Âne.[112]

The fleet sailed for Fort Louis—shortly to be renamed Fort George—on 7 March, with not more than two thousand healthy soldiers aboard, although they had numbered just a few less than six thousand when in their prime, counting services men, the detachment from the Leeward Islands, and the Scots. The trade wind and the leeward current held up passage, and before all arrived at Fort Louis some twenty-five vessels had been driven to leeward, for days finding it impossible to weather the Saintes. Subtracting the garrison it would be necessary to keep at Fort Louis, Barrington had only about 1500 effectives with which to carry out his grand design of conquering both halves of Guadeloupe from the new base on Grand Terre. The general himself did not arrive until 11 March, but that indefatigable soldier was

111. *Gentleman's Magazine*, 29 (1759), 241.
112. Gardiner, *The West Indies*, 43-44; Beatson, *Memoirs*, II, 247-248.

off the next day in a ship's boat, reconnoitering both coasts of the bay to find a good place at which to make a descent from his new base.[113] He had a large program to get through.

News of the change in leadership was sent to England in the *Spy* sloop, Captain Bayne, which set sail on the day the troops embarked for the captured Fort Louis. Coincidentally this was the day Pitt received Hopson's dispatches of 30 January. Bayne arrived in England in May, coming to Whitehall on the 6th. His account covered events from 14 February to 6 March. This was typical of Barrington. The government was usually from six weeks to two months behind in the news from the West Indian "front."[114]

When intelligence that Hopson's command had devolved upon one of the active Barrington boys reached Viscount Barrington at the war office, he desired "the feathers and emoluments" of commander in chief for his younger brother. Writing to Newcastle to that effect, he asked the Duke to do what he could if Pitt were unable to secure the desired privileges. He cited precedents and added that "nothing on earth could distress and mortify me so much as that he should not have the feathers and emoluments which have been invariably granted to others in like situation; and if ever a general wanted & deserved ten pounds a day, it must be at Guardeloupe [*sic*] where a bad turkey costs five and twenty shillings and all other things in proportion." His brother, he urged, had many mouths to feed and "unavoidable expense is inconceivable."[115] It may be assumed that General Barrington had written to his brother in the same express that brought his dispatches to Pitt. But it should also be remembered that in a nepotistic age Lord Barrington had protested his brother's elevation in the beginning. *P.S.* General Barrington got his feathers.

---

113. Gardiner, *The West Indies*, 44; Corbett, *England in the Seven Years' War*, I, 382-383.

114. Gardiner, *The West Indies*, 44; Pitt memoranda of 6 May 1759, Colonial Office 110/1.

115. Lord Barrington to Newcastle, 9 May 1759, Add. MSS. 32891, f. 1. The last quoted phrase above is an intellectual illusion, appearing to make sense when it really does not. I have translated it: it is inconceivable that there *not* be unavoidable expense.

VI.

Guadeloupe: Grand Terre

1. *The fleet withdraws*

Moore had gone to look at Fort Louis, and had returned to Basse Terre on 25 February, where he ordered a sermon of thanksgiving for the victory to be preached aboard every ship of the squadron.[1] Then he had cooperated completely with Barrington in moving the army to Fort Louis. But he received disconcerting news when only half the force had arrived at Grand Terre. A French fleet of war ships, carrying troops, had arrived in the Leeward Islands.

Lieutenant General and *chef d'escadre* Maximin de Bompar, a former governor of Martinique, had arrived at Martinique with eight ships of the line and three frigates, bringing with him a battalion of Swiss and other troops. The rumor was that they had intended relieving Martinique if they found it besieged and blockaded, and were now lying at anchor between Pigeon Island and Fort Negro, ready to weigh at a moment's warning. Sir Julian Corbett later summarized Moore's problem very well: he was trying to conquer Guadeloupe and to protect British commerce at the same time. The protection of British commerce was to be a secondary consideration until shortly before the hurricane season when he would have to send off large convoys with the "trade" for the home ports. This would reduce his strength when he was already short (he had previously written for reinforcements). St. Eustatius had been blockaded. All of these operations had seemed necessary, but Moore now saw that he must mass his ships where

1. Gardiner, *The West Indies*, 42.

he could most easily strike at Bompar if the visiting Frenchman tried to relieve Guadeloupe.[2]

He put the matter before a council of war. Prince Rupert's Bay, in the northern part of Dominica, which lies between Martinique and Guadeloupe, seemed the most suitable anchorage for the purpose of attacking any French relief. Moore summarized its advantages as follows: it was the only place in which he could assemble his scattered ships in a hurry. The crews could be refreshed there. It would be possible to keep up communication with Barrington from Prince Rupert's Bay by means of small vessels. The anchorage was located within easy reach of Moore's base at Antigua. From Dominica he could still support the operations of the army.

At this point the reader should consult a chart of that part of the world, and observe that every advantage he cited for Prince Rupert's Bay was to be had in the bay at Fort Louis, between Grand Terre and Basse Terre, except that of refreshing the men. Note also that Prince Rupert's Bay was to the south of Barrington's headquarters. Apparently Moore's council did not consider this alternative, an omission which almost wrecked this expeditionary force. The only other alternative to Prince Rupert's Bay they considered was that of blockading Bompar where he lay in Fort Royale Bay.

The proposal to blockade Bompar in Martinique was dismissed for these reasons: If the fleet sailed to Fort Royale, they could fight only at the discretion of Bompar. They would lengthen their line of supplies and all of their cruisers would be in use merely to bring water and stores. From a position of blockade opposite the mouth of Fort Royale Bay they could not communicate with Antigua under seven days. These all seem valid objections to such a proposal, and the councillors agreed that Prince

---

2. Gardiner, *The West Indies*, 44-45; Corbett, *England in the Seven Years' War*, I, 383-385. The withdrawal opened St. Eustatius again, and supplies from there strengthened both Guadeloupe and Martinique. Bompar, "Extrait du journal tenu par M. de Bompar," Archives nationales, Marine et colonies, B^4 91. According to deductions from Moore's journal, St. Eustatius was "open" in January and February, and for one week in March and for the last week in April. See the account in Chapter VII, *infra*.

GUADELOUPE: GRAND TERRE

Rupert's Bay was the place for them.³ Of the dangerous omission to discuss the advantages of the best harbor in Guadeloupe the reader may later judge.

In the fleet the junior officers apparently thought Prince Rupert's Bay the best place of refuge, for Gardiner, who frequently seemed to be echoing mess chatter, said it was "where he [Moore] could be early acquainted with any Motions made by the Enemy, and be ready to follow if Occasion required, as he would then be to Windward of Guadelupe, and at a Distance of only nine Leagues."⁴ True, Moore would be to windward of Guadeloupe, that is to say he would be to windward of Basse Terre and the Saintes, but he would be to leeward of the eastern half of the double island. I have considered the possibility that the sailors were so sickened that it was absolutely necessary that they be refreshed by putting them ashore where desertion would be uninviting. But Moore did not emphasize the necessity of refreshment to that degree.

The commodore notified the general of the arrival of Bompar and of his (the commodore's) determination to go to Dominica. Barrington made no complaint, but called his general officers to council. They decided to hold the fort, literally. This fort was not intrinsically so strong as the one at Basse Terre but at least the enemy could be approached from it. From the citadel at Basse Terre one could only defend. From Fort Louis one could attack. And they were full of the spirit of attack. Their cooperation with Moore was admirable. When Moore requested additional soldiers to serve as Marines aboard the fleet, probably to replace men taken sick,⁵ Barrington, who had just received 350 volunteers from Antigua, bravely made the commodore a present of three hundred regulars, complete with a sergeant to command each platoon. According to my estimates this generosity cut Barrington down to 1200 regulars and 350 Antigua militia who were free to be used in an offensive. Or, the militia could be put in the fort to release some hundreds of regulars; militia always fought

3. The council's deliberations were summarized in Corbett, *England in the Seven Years' War*, I, 383-385.
4. Gardiner, *The West Indies*, 45.
5. On eighteenth-century naval hygiene, see Appendix, Topic 17.

best when their legs were hidden from the enemy's view, anyway. Moore sailed on 14 March for Prince Rupert's Bay, leaving the *Woolwich,* 44, to guard the transports, but taking Debrissay's supporting ships from Basse Terre Roads. Bomb ketches and a few sloops were also left with Barrington,[6] but for the rest of his naval force he was on his own native ingenuity.

At this distance of time we know more about Bompar than Moore did. Bompar's orders were rather broad: to recover any French islands that had been taken by the English, or to compensate for the loss of any islands by seizing British possessions. French naval policy for the West Indies differed from British policy. There was no intention of keeping a regular squadron on the station but the marine ministers sent "task forces" or convoy ships as needed. French home naval bases were slow in fitting out, especially when the British blockade broke up the coasting trade. If a squadron was promised to sail in November so as to depart immediately after the hurricane season, it might get away in January. Bompar had been delayed two months in 1758 and, as will be shown, got to Martinique too late. In addition, any French naval force was limited, by the amount of supplies it could carry, to a campaign of not more than six or seven months. If more supplies were carried, the heavy lading endangered maneuverability. Frigates could not even carry enough for half a year's work.[7]

Bompar was under-armed. For store ships the French sometimes used war ships with the lowest tier of guns unworkable because the hold was so crammed with stores as not to leave sufficient room for the gun crews, and sometimes the ships were so low in the water that it would have been dangerous to open the lowest ports. Bompar's *Vaillant* and *Amétiste* went out in this condition, with their guns in the hold, that is, *en flûte,* but could

---

6. Barrington to Pitt, 9 May 1759, Pitt, *Correspondence,* II, 94-97; Corbett, *England in the Seven Years' War,* I, 385-387.

7. Pares, *War and Trade,* 185, citing private instructions to Bompar, 15 November 1758, Archives nationales, Marine et colonies, B² 359. See also Pares, 268-270. The names of Bompar's ships, their armament, and their commanders were common knowledge in Antigua no later than 26 March. So much for French security precautions, if any. *South-Carolina Gazette,* 28 April 1759.

GUADELOUPE: GRAND TERRE 117

not find men for completing their armament at Martinique. Bompar was also under-provisioned. Naval officers carried *pacotilles* to the islands—small ventures of European goods, received on commission from French merchants—which were sold to the colonists. The proceeds of the *pacotilles* were used to purchase indigo or white sugar on the merchants' accounts. This trading distracted the officers from the naval operations at hand, cut the throats of the regular traders, and caused the ships to be too heavy-laden. Bompar was sensitive on this point. After the campaign he hotly denied the charge (of a person or persons unnamed) that he had been distracted by his *pacotille*—"que je n'avoir été [*sic*] occupé que de ma pacotille"—during his stay at Martinique, or that any other *pacotilles* had interfered with the proper ordering of the squadron's affairs.[8] But the fact that they carried these private goods in a squadron for which supplies had to be shipped in freighters without convoy speaks for itself.

Moore's condition was better than Bompar's. Two important British practices contributed to it. The English ships were generally well supplied from the provision provinces of North America, and the navy maintained dock yards where most of the vessels could refit. Thus a British squadron could usually stay out in the islands as long as the admiralty wished and the weather allowed. This is not to say that the Leeward Islands bases were perfect. English Harbour at Antigua was not an ideal base. Its artificers were slaves or freedmen, and not well trained. It was hard to get in or out of the harbor since the channel was too shallow to take the very largest ships without their having been lightened. If they were lightened at St. John's harbor they rode too high out of the water to beat up wind to English Harbour, so the biggest ships were sent to Jamaica or to Nova Scotia for refitting.[9] But despite these disadvantages, British facilities were infinitely superior to anything the enemy had.

To return to the squadron—Moore arrived at Prince Rupert's Bay on 16 March with all of his ships of the line except the *Rippon*,

8. Bompar, "Mémoire justificatif," and, Bompar to Berryer, 2 May 1759, both in Archives nationales, Marine et colonies, B⁴ 91; also, Pares, *War and Trade* 270-271, citing several other French sources.
9. Pares, *War and Trade*, 273-274.

which was at Antigua, and the *Bristol,* which had been sent to blockade St. Eustatius (of which more later). The bay was spacious and deep, capable of sheltering a large fleet from the trade wind, since the peaks of Dominica lay to the east of the anchorage. Sounding parties found seven fathoms near shore; farther off the bottom dropped rapidly.[10]

Dominica was one of the so-called neutral islands, having been given a kind of extra-national status at the end of the preceding Anglo-French hostilities (the War of the Austrian Succession). These islands were in part peopled by folk who—as late as 1740—went there to get away from government. The neutral islands had been occupied by but few people, but of these few the chief part were French. Of St. Lucia, its commandant complained that it took a week after an alarm was sounded to assemble 150 men. Three reasons account for the sparse population. There was constant danger of conquest, and no home government to appeal to. The infrequent *corvées* on the Negro population were, when they came, oppressive. The future of the islands was very uncertain, a situation which would discourage all but the most venturesome from laying out heavy investments in plantation improvements. On the first arrival of Moore's ships, said Gardiner, the inhabitants were very frightened, but Moore made an agreement of neutrality with them and they began a brisk trade of provisions for English gold, and brought in their herds which they had previously rounded up and driven into the interior.[11]

The agreement of neutrality appeared later to be no more than a working agreement, valid so long as the inhabitants were within range of Moore's guns. As soon as he left, the civilians returned to their "natural allegiance."[12] Militia volunteers from Dominica, in fact, served under the governor of Guadeloupe in this campaign, despite the "neutrality."[13]

10. Gardiner, *The West Indies,* 21, 42, 45n. See also United States Hydrographic Office, Chart 513.
11. Pares, *War and Trade,* 196, 197, 215; Gardiner, *The West Indies,* 21; Moore, "Journal," Admiralty 50/22.
12. Beauharnois to Du Treil, 9 April 1759, Archives nat., Colonies, C^8 A 62. Bompar sent an officer in disguise to Dominica to keep him informed. Bompar, "Extrait du journal," Archives nationales, Marine et colonies, B^4 91.
13. Gardiner, *The West Indies,* 62.

GUADELOUPE: GRAND TERRE

For almost six weeks the British ships lay in the bay with little more to do than to change the scope of the anchor rodes as the tide changed. Naval events of this period can be summarized quickly. Three days after they dropped anchors their move was announced in Antigua with an explanation of why it was made, and an exhortation to the effect that the enemy was probably inspired to new efforts by Moore's withdrawal, that everybody must support the war effort, and so on. On 21 March General Haldane sailed for Jamaica, of which he was governor-elect, in the *Renown* frigate. He intended to put its defenses in order in case Bompar decided to attack there. On 1 April the *Emerald* frigate arrived from home with dispatches, and was promptly sent off to look into the harbor of Grenada to report what she could see. On appearing off the port, she was approached by the master-attendant and several civilians who mistook her for a Frenchman and came aboard where they were made prisoners. The odor of alcohol floats about in this operetta episode for, as Gardiner said, "upon finding their Mistake, they burst out into a violent Fit of Laughter, and soon after fell a singing." On 17 April Moore lost a vessel and received more mail from Whitehall. The vessel lost was the *Falcon* bomb, which had been stationed off the Saintes to prevent passage of supplies to the embattled *habitants* of Guadeloupe. Chasing a privateer she missed stays[14] and stranded. Her men, stores, and small mortar were saved, and her master was honorably acquitted by a court of inquiry on 26 April. The dispatches from England arrived in the *Griffin* frigate, which had made a speedy passage of only twenty-eight days from England.[15]

But in a fortnight this quiet existence was rudely upset. Moore had received a shocking rumor: Bompar had landed on the eastern side of Guadeloupe, well to *windward* of Moore, had taken sixteen pieces of cannon and sixty prisoners, with a loss of twelve dead and forty wounded. More than that (and it was very inaccurate information that he had) the unhappy commodore knew not. On 8 March this commodore had written to Pitt that from an inter-

---

14. On the embarrassing accident known as "missing stays," see Appendix, Topic 18.

15. Gardiner, *The West Indies*, 49, 51, 58; Beatson, *Memoirs*, II, 249; *Gentleman's Magazine*, 29 (1759), 144; Moore, "Journal," Admiralty 50/22.

cepted letter he had learned not to fear an enemy attack.[16] Despite Moore's later explanation of this event, it seems obvious that he had been asleep on his watch. We will leave the startled sailor at this point and take a look at what was happening ashore, but not forgetting that his enemy was out in force, to windward of him.

2. *Grand Terre disorganized*

While the squadron had been drowsing in the spring air off Dominica, Barrington's army had been using a compound of blood, tears, and sweat to write an honorable chapter in the history of the British arms. An estimate of the situation, such as Barrington himself might have presented, will make the narrative of battles and skirmishes easier to understand.

The mission of the land forces was, in general, to take and hold French territory. The particular territory already chosen by the commanders in the field was the island of Guadeloupe, on which two beach heads had been established, one at Basse Terre (not much use) and one at Fort Louis (very good for the purpose). The enemy consisted for the most part of militia. For their actions thus far it could reasonably be deduced that they were not well trained, that their equipment was at best mediocre, their resources—other than food—slender, and their hearts not in the fight. If this was thought to be too sweeping a condemnation of the enemy, the best that could be said was that they fought well only as guerillas. The British troops had been considerably crippled by disease, but those on their feet were the toughest of the lot. Since they were drilled until they could go through the motions of war without thinking, the question of their morale was not so important as it was in the case of the French civilian-soldiers. But they seem to have been in good spirits anyway, despite the terrible toll of disease. Their equipment and munitions were entirely adequate by the standards of the age. The chief defect of the British situation was that the force was intended to be amphibious but was in danger of losing its ability to swim. There was also no immediate prospect of support from other

16. Moore to Pitt, 11 and 14 April 1759, Pitt, *Correspondence*, II, 83, 83-84.

GUADELOUPE: GRAND TERRE   121

troops, and the fleet could not well be expected to come to their aid (according to Moore's arrangement) except in a grave emergency, such as a forced evacuation. The ground they fought on gave the advantage to the enemy. It was his own field, and its terrain, temperatures, and diseases were familiar to him. It furnished good cover for snipers. The only advantage it offered to a force on the offensive was that there were plenty of covered approaches to most enemy positions.

Plans open to Barrington seem to have been these.

1. He could endeavor to bring the enemy, in mass, to battle in the formal eighteenth-century fashion on a flat plain somewhere and use continental European tactics to disorganize him and to capture him.[17]

2. He could move his whole force overland to attack each post in turn.

3. He could fight a war of detachments, attacking several strong points at approximately the same time in order to keep the scattered defenders from uniting.

He adopted the third plan. He did not leave a written record of his estimate of the situation, so no one can be sure that he considered anything but a war of detachments. But if he had considered the first and second plans, he no doubt would have ruled them out. There would be two defects in the first plan. The enemy had shown that he had no intention of fighting in the open, which was a wise attitude as students of battles between long-term professionals and low-trained civilian-soldiers well know. Secondly, the ground offered no place to fight in that fashion, even if the colonials had been willing and able to try it. The second plan—to attack the strong points in turn—would require that Barrington sweep the defenders before him as a housewife sweeps floor litter. If their spirits were not broken, they would accumulate numbers and experience with each defeat and offer stronger resistance with each engagement—while Barrington could expect to be steadily drained of power by such tactics. It would have been imprudent of him to anticipate that their spirit would steadily deteriorate. Indeed, with men fighting in their own front yard

17. On infantry tactics, see Appendix, Topic 19.

the reverse might well be true. The third plan offered a further advantage. It allowed Barrington to exploit the gain he had already made, namely, the splitting of the defense forces by his grasp of Fort Louis. Thus the principle of division and conquest was applicable. And the men in the citadel at Basse Terre could be expected to pin the defenders on the Dos d'Âne in their places, thus further weakening the potential resistance to Barrington's high-trained compact force, by requiring a relatively large force to be kept near Colonel Debrissay's garrison regiment in the citadel. The cleft called the Dos d'Âne led directly into the richest part of Guadeloupe. It was not likely that it would be left open.

So Barrington set to work on his "war of detachments." His first step was to maintain the sea power he had begun with. One rarely thinks of the British army as carrying out naval operations, but Barrington did. Moore had left him a forty-four gun "frigate," some bomb ketches, and some sloops. Using these and the armed transports as cruisers, he hired and armed local craft and ultimately made his little army once again completely amphibious.[18]

Moore sailed on 14 March, taking Haldane with him, as previously mentioned. Had Haldane been a brake on Barrington's enthusiasm back in the Hopson régime? His journal of "proceedings" as sent to Newcastle indicated hearty concurrence with the opinions of the futile Hopson—and this was an age when professional soldiers were as jealous for their professional freedom of thought as college professors are today. Whether he had a pessimistic influence or not, once he left, the army began to earn the King's shillings. And, as the doughboys said, they "earned some tough iron men" in their time.

While building up his "naval army" Barrington directed the works at Fort Louis and awaited the rest of the transports. Although desertions from the French militia began to be more numerous, the British were harassed by snipers, whose lack of skill with the musket was in part made up by their numbers. Three days after Moore's departure the chief engineer made port in one of the slower transports. His opinion of the tenability of the fort was not cheering. As he pointed out, it was commanded by sev-

18. Corbett, *England in the Seven Years' War*, I, 385-387.

eral hills and its water supply was inadequate. Barrington freely credited him with those opinions in dispatches, but added on his own responsibility that he intended to hold the place. By the twenty-third of the month he was ready to strike his first blow.[19]

Sometime between 18 and 23 March he ordered Crump to take six hundred men of the Fourth and Forty-second regiments to attack simultaneously the two small towns of Sainte Anne and Saint François. It was planned to land on the beach between the villages, march inland, divide the force and attack each place from the land side. Lieutenant Colonel Barlow of the Fourth Regiment was second in command of the brigade. They sailed on 25 March. Since the small sailing vessels had to tack in plain sight of the shore, it is hard to see how the defenders could have been surprised, but whether the defenders were surprised or in a funk, the attack was a complete success. Both towns were destroyed and the attacking force lost only one man killed and two wounded. Their activities drew off about three hundred of the enemy force at Gozier (the enemy post nearest to Fort Louis), a weakening which Barrington promptly exploited. Having accomplished their mission, the troops under Crump set sail for Fort Louis again.[20]

On the day that Crump received his orders (sometime between 18 and 23 March), 350 volunteers had arrived from Antigua, St. Christopher, and Montserrat. This enabled Barrington to embark another expedition without awaiting the return of Crump's brigade. On the same day nine transports came in, sixteen days out of Basse

19. Gardiner, *The West Indies*, 47; Barrington to Pitt, 9 May 1759, Pitt, *Correspondence*, II, 94-97, 98; Beatson, *Memoirs*, II, 248. By March the defenders had organized a counter-desertion force with headquarters at Trois Rivières. A witness at Du Treil's court martial said that when he first met Du Treil, in March, the governor was complaining of the inhabitants ("tous les habitants") against whom he was conducting "enquêtes." "Guadeloupe/Jugement du Gouverneur de cette isle/Nadau Dutreil," 1759, Archives nationales, Marine et colonies, B⁴ 92. All evidence points to low morale.

20. Gardiner, *The West Indies*, 48, 50; Barrington to Pitt, 9 May 1759, Pitt, *Correspondence*, II, 94-97, 98. Officers on Grand Terre later testified that they had about fifteen hundred men in January, of whom the best seven hundred had been promptly sent to Basse Terre. After Fort Louis fell, many returned without arms—probably deserters or else men who preferred to fight on their own island. "Guadeloupe/Jugement du Gouverneur de cette isle/Nadau Dutreil," 1759, Archives nationales, Marine et colonies, B⁴ 92.

Terre Roads, for a distance which a modern destroyer could run in less than an hour. It was the arrival of these transports which probably occasioned the issue of orders to Crump. Of the British colonial volunteers it should be remarked that they were generally more efficient than the militia of England, chiefly for psychological reasons. They lived in the constant presence of powerful native and European neighbors, they could expect little help from home under a period of months after a crisis was upon them, and they lived in perpetual fear of Negro uprisings. During the seventeenth century Barbados is said to have been able to produce six regiments of foot and two of horse, totalling six thousand men. Jamaica could call seven regiments totalling four thousand men. The West Indian magazines were replenished by charging port dues in gun powder. Some of their equipment came from England, and, less frequently, sometimes money aid was to be had from the London government. The British West Indian governors were often military men.[21] Of course the motives making for merit in the British colonial militia should also have operated in the French islands but their weaknesses, which have already been discussed, seem to have enervated them completely.

The next action was against the defenses and defenders of Gozier, where, by rapid movement, surprise, vigorous attack, and concentrated blows, Barrington not only reduced the place but relieved the growing pressure on his own none-too-strong headquarters. Gozier lay two miles to the east of Fort Louis, and on 29 March Major Teesdale of the Sixty-first Regiment lay off the town just outside the surf with three hundred men. On the next day[22] the detachment landed in flatboats in the face of the defenders' guns, burned the town, drove the enemy into the woods, and destroyed the cannon and battery.[23] The absence of the three hundred militiamen who had gone to help in the defense of Sainte

---

21. Beatson, *Memoirs*, II, 249-250; Fortescue, *British Army*, II, 39-40.

22. Sir Julian Corbett in his discussion of this phase of the campaign (*England in the Seven Years' War*, I, 385-387) said the attacks on Sainte Anne, Saint François, and Gozier were simultaneous. Barrington's dispatches gave the dates I have used.

23. Beatson, *Memoirs*, II, 250-251; Barrington to Pitt, 9 May 1759. Pitt, *Correspondence*, II, 97-98.

Anne and Saint François may well have been the determining factor in the outcome of this small battle.

There followed (on the same day) a bewildering operation which was executed almost perfectly. Its only flaw, as will be seen, was a minor one. Teesdale was ordered to force his way back to Fort Louis by land. The garrison at Fort Louis was ordered to make two sallies, one to the right and one to the left. The attack to the right would place the enemy's left flank between two fires, that of the sally party and that of Teesdale's battalion. The party on the British left could loot the besieger's camp, since the French there would probably be drawn off by Teesdale's attack from the rear. As Teesdale came overland, his flat boats were rowed along shore parallel to his advance in order to take him off if he found himself in difficulties. As the red coats issued from Fort Louis, the transports feinted to the west as though they were to land troops behind the besiegers. All went well, except that the party which was to go to the French camp did not march out, owing to a mistake in the orders. With fire on his left flank, a large party attacking his left, and the transports reaching ominously across his right flank, the enemy wilted. Teesdale brought his men, with some loss, through a strongly entrenched pass and took three twenty-four-pound guns which next day would have played on the fort. In the language of 1914-1918, the enemy "took foot in hand" and went away from there. The garrison at Fort Louis was thus relieved of the constant danger from gunfire directed from commanding positions, and its water supply was assured. The action—with Crump's—had disorganized all resistance in Grand Terre and, when Crump's force returned, Barrington could safely give his attention to the defenders of the western part of Guadeloupe. The job was half done. The disorganization of Grand Terre had cost (excepting Moore's capture of Fort Louis) one officer and eight men killed, two officers and twelve men wounded.[24] About this time desertions from the French militia began to be more numerous.[25]

24. Beatson, *Memoirs*, II, 250-251; Barrington to Pitt, 9 May 1759, Pitt, *Correspondence*, II, 94-98.
25. Dubourg de Clainvilliers' narrative, Archives nationales, Marine et colonies, C[8] A 62.

Between 23 March and 1 April Barrington received the only bad news heard since that of the arrival of Bompar. A report from the citadel informed him that on 23 March Lieutenant Colonel Peter Debrissay, Major Trollope, a lieutenant, some artillery men and several men of the Sixty-third Regiment had been killed by an explosion. Many more were wounded. The loss was practically as great as that suffered in the four operations on Grand Terre. The death of Debrissay was particularly regretted, he, by all accounts, being a living example of the eighteenth-century military tradition at its best. The loss was part of the price paid for the withdrawal of the fleet. Since Moore had called the *St. George* and the *Buckingham* away, the inhabitants surrounding the citadel had grown steadily bolder. Debrissay, governor of the fort, had ordered cannon to be fired at them whenever they appeared. For this purpose powder was placed in the sentry boxes. On this occasion two barrels were in a sentry box on the flank angle of the southeast bastion. When a body of the enemy appeared on 23 March the gunners opened fire on them. Wadding sparks drifted toward the powder barrels. Debrissay sent two bombardiers to cover the barrels. Again the gunners fired, sparks got into the barrels, and the costly explosion was the result. The enemy immediately attacked, but, according to Beatson, were driven off with considerable loss.[26]

Barrington appointed Major Melville to be governor of the citadel vice Debrissay. The casualties were made good by detaching men from Fort Louis and the chief engineer was sent to repair the breach. Melville learned that the enemy had mounted a thirteen-inch mortar to play on the citadel, and sent three hundred men against it. The sally was successful and the attackers spiked two other pieces of ordnance at a cost to the British of six killed and six wounded.[27] The mortar had come from Martinique—additional proof that Moore's blockade was not so effective as he thought.

26. Beatson, *Memoirs*, II, 251-253; Barrington to Pitt, 9 May 1759, Pitt, *Correspondence*, II, 97-98; Gardiner, *The West Indies*, 47-48.
27. Barrington to Pitt, 9 May 1759, Pitt, *Correspondence*, II, 97-98; Gardiner, *The West Indies*, 49-50; Beatson, *Memoirs*, II, 251-253.

VII.

Guadeloupe: Capesterre

1. *Clavering's advance*

The British force had so far nullified resistance on the leeward side of Basse Terre Island and had so disorganized the forces of Grand Terre Island that the defenders no longer had a will to resist. What remained was to subject the inhabitants of the windward side of Basse Terre. This part was the richest and most populous section of the island of Guadeloupe. Its topography was suitable for the use of British regiments in traditional close order fighting since it possessed a gently rising coastal plain which extended back from one to three miles from the sea before rugged country was encountered. This coastal plain was the site of the richest plantations of Guadeloupe. Its chief settlements, from north to south, were: Baie la Mahault, Houelbourg, Arnoville,[1] Petit Bourg, Goyave, Sainte Marie, Capesterre, and Trois Rivières. Capesterre was a cluster of dwellings at the foot of the valley of the same name, a sugar valley full of fat, sweet fields, as wealthy as any similar agricultural area in the world of the eighteenth century.

On 1 April, Barrington could write (in the journal he kept for Pitt) that all of the transports had at length arrived from Basse Terre Roads. He had been intending to attack the other side of

---

[1] Of Arnoville, Sir John Fortescue said, "Though I have searched multitudes of maps of all periods I have been unable to discover Arnouville [*sic*] in any of them. Its position, however, may be guessed by its relations to Mahault Bay."— *History of the British Army*, II, 354n. He placed it at the head of Mahault Bay which is across the isthmus from the river du Coin. Lieutenant Archibald Campbell's contemporary map (in the Widener Library at Harvard) has located the town as I have placed it on my map (*supra*, p. 71).

the bay on which his troops lay and, now that his force had been completed and his base on Grand Terre was secure, he began earnestly to interview Negro guides and pilots. From their information he judged it practical to plan surprise attacks from the sea against Petit Bourg, Goyave, and Sainte Marie, at the same time. This plan was entirely consistent with his war of detachments so successfully waged on Grand Terre. Against a well-organized enemy Barrington's plans might have been more complex than the situation demanded or allowed, but, against the forces of irregulars he was opposing, the advantage of an opportune bewilderment of the enemy outweighed the risk that all of the parts of a complicated machinery might not function perfectly.

According to the General's plan of operations, Negro watermen were to pilot the troops in the flat-bottomed boats. Brigadiers Crump and Clavering[2] were to have the field commands. Crump was to land at Petit Bourg, then march to Baie la Mahault, the north shore port, and there destroy its batteries and also the stores supplied by "our good friends the Dutch." Clavering was to strike at Sainte Marie and Goyave simultaneously, combine his forces and then march south to ravage the Capesterre. The plan seemed perfect to Barrington,[3] and, indeed, at this distance of time still seems good.

But generals cannot plan the weather. When the boats put off on their surprise mission the night was so foul (Beatson described it as "tempestuous"—probably a soldier's exaggeration) and the "Negroe Conductors were so frightened" that several of the boats ran aground on shoals—of which there are plenty off that shore. Although Clavering did get ashore with about eighty men, his landing place was so crowded with mangroves and so deep

2. Lieutenant General Sir John Clavering, K.B. (1722-1777), was named by Horace Walpole "the real hero of Guadeloupe." This was an unnecessary detraction from the able but obscure Barrington, whose almost unnoticed death in Paris in 1764 may have lost the empire a greater soldier than has been recognized. But that Clavering was an able man is not open to doubt. He served in the Coldstream Guards until 1758 when he was given local rank as a brigadier in the West Indies. As a mark of appreciation for his services there he was made a royal aide-de-camp in 1759 with rank as a colonel of foot. He died in Bengal, commander in chief of the Bengal army in the régime of Warren Hastings, with whom he was not congenial.

3. Barrington to Pitt, 9 May 1759, Pitt, *Correspondence*, II, 98-99.

in mud that he had to return. The mosquito-bitten expedition had also been noticed by the enemy, and Barrington realized that power rather than guile would have to be used thereafter.[4]

At this critical point in the campaign Barrington fell ill; as he himself put it, he "was then laid up in a most severe fit of the gout in my feet, head and stomach." From his bed he sent Clavering and Crump to reconnoiter the coast near Arnoville. Their report encouraged him to order 1300 regulars and 150 Antigua volunteers to land under the guns of the *Woolwich*. Barrington then resigned direction to Clavering for the period of his illness.[5]

Thus began, on 12 April 1759, the final drive of the campaign. At a small bay near Arnoville 1450 weathered and veteran men were disembarked. The very sight of them seems to have been enough to deter the enemy from making any resistance; for the colonials offered no opposition to the ticklish operation of landing that many redcoats but retired to entrenched positions behind the line of the river du Coin. This place was very strong naturally and much strengthened by artifice. The British commanders discovered only two narrow passes to the river, each occupied by a redoubt and palisaded entrenchments, defended with cannon and manned by all of the militia of that part of the country. They could only be approached on a contracted front, which at length narrowed to the width of a cart track and was intersected by ditches. This scheme of defense seems to have been as thoughtful as any the British had met, but sharp Clavering and blunt Crump were equal to it. They used artillery in a way that twentieth-century soldiers would recognize: a "brigade" of four field pieces and two howitzers played on the enemy positions, under cover of which the Fourth Regiment and the battalion of the Forty-second advanced, keeping up a regular platoon fire as they came. This cool and resolute approach in what the colonials had thought to be an almost impossible situation for the redcoats was too much for the nervous militia on the British right, who broke from their cover at sight of the nerveless advance. The Highlanders and

---

4. *Ibid.*; Beatson, *Memoirs*, II, 253.
5. Barrington to Pitt, 9 May 1759, Pitt, *Correspondence*, II, 98-99.

part of the Fourth entered their line and chased the fleeing enemy into a redoubt.[6]

On the British left the French were not so easily frightened and stood to their pieces, keeping the British under a painful musket and gun fire. Those British who had broken through on the other flank continued moving to the rear, yet the resistance on the left could not be overcome until a bridge was built. This job of engineering took half an hour but, despite the loss of time, when the thrust was pushed home seventy prisoners were taken. The total bag of guns was six. The butcher's bill: one officer and thirteen men killed, two officers and fifty-two men wounded—a high casualty rate for this campaign.[7]

As soon as the river du Coin was forced, men advanced with spades and filled in the ditches which the defenders had dug in the road, in order that the field guns could go rolling along toward Petit Bourg. The enemy meanwhile "dug in" on the left side of the road at a point a half mile south of Arnoville, but left a flank in the air. Clavering sent parties out to his right, as if to flank them, and the French withdrew. Although they had been roughly handled this day, the colonials were still under the control of their officers and fought an intelligent and effective rear-guard action, the last element falling back slowly, about two hundred yards ahead of the British. They augmented their fire-power by burning the cane fields which lined the road, and the heat and the flying sparks endangered the British powder supply, while the smoke obscured their vision. By sending out patrols on the flanks, the rear guard forced the British to advance cautiously, and the advancing force had to leave the road from time to time in order to assure that there would be no ambush in the luxurious cane growths which hid the sniping French.[8] Clavering must have wished for a few troops of horse at this time.

At this prudent rate of progress an advance of two miles con-

---

6. Clavering to Barrington, 24 April 1759, *Gentleman's Magazine*, 29 (1759), 273; Cust, *Annals of the Wars of the Eighteenth Century*, II, 288.

7. Clavering to Barrington, 24 April 1759, *Gentleman's Magazine*, 29 (1759), 273.

8. Clavering to Barrington, 24 April 1759, *Gentleman's Magazine*, 29 (1759), 273-274; Archives nationales, Marine et colonies, B^4 92.

sumed the rest of the day, and the victors arrived in the evening at the Lézarde River. The ordinary means of passing this obstacle was by a ford,[9] but the ford was covered by the fire of French musketeers in strong trenches and a brigade of four guns was placed on a hill so as to command the passage. Clavering's estimate of the situation was clear: to force this strong point would be unnecessarily expensive. By a stratagem which has probably been learned by every company officer since troops began to use missiles, he gained the passage without loss. During the night the British pinned the French in place by firing across the river, while at the same time men were being ferried across in two canoes, at a point a mile and a half downstream. In the morning the uninformed colonials found themselves menaced on front and flank, and decided they would be more comfortable within the lines of the fortified town of Petit Bourg. No man was lost by the British in this routine operation.[10] It is hard to reconcile the colonials' gullibility at Lézarde Ford with the skill they showed in their delaying action from Arnoville to that point. To allow oneself to be surprised is one of the cardinal sins of the military code.

The British—who must have been a dusty, sweaty lot of lobsterbacks by this time—rolled on down the road to Petit Bourg, meeting no more resistance until they reached the outskirts of the town itself. It was fortified with trenches which were supported by a redoubt mounting a number of cannon. Life in this redoubt was unhappy and hard to preserve, because offshore lay the *Granada* bomb, leisurely dropping bombs within the position.[11] Petit Bourg was commanded by one large hill and several lesser heights, and when Clavering's men began to occupy these elevations the desperate French withdrew to the south without offering

9. Sir John Fortescue, *History of the British Army*, II, 354, said that the French retreating across the river Lézarde broke down a bridge behind them. There was no citation of his source, and the documents now available are either silent or else speak only of the ford.
10. Clavering to Barrington, 24 April 1759, *Gentleman's Magazine*, 29 (1759), 273-274.
11. There is an anchorage off Petit Bourg among the shoals with about twenty feet of water, less than half a mile from the town.

further opposition. The British, who sadly needed rest and food, lay in Petit Bourg on 14 April to receive provisions.[12]

At dawn on the 15th Brigadier Crump with seven hundred men (about half of the British force) was sent back over the road down which he and Clavering had come, to visit Baie la Mahault[13]—the small shoal bay where most of the supplies imported by the defenders had been landed. Most of this matériel came from the Dutch island of St. Eustatius. It would be well at this point to examine the Anglo-Dutch relationship.

An Anglo-Dutch treaty of 1674 excepted naval stores from the category of contraband, and, what is more important to this study, acknowledged the then rarely-held doctrine that "free ships make free goods." According to this doctrine the Dutch ships could carry almost anything during a war involving Great Britain and some other power. But there was a joker in the deck. There was also an unequivocal treaty of 1678, an alliance "which required either ally to come to the assistance of the other with stipulated forces in case of war."[14] Thus if the Dutch hid their aid to France behind the treaty of 1674, the British could neutralize the acid of aid-short-of-war by calling the treaty of 1678 into operation. And the only time when the treaty of 1674 could operate to embarrass the British would be during a war. Certainly the British officers were justified in regarding the aiding of French troops via a Dutch island as an unfriendly policy on the part of allies.

St. Eustatius was the chief base of Dutch commercial activity in any West Indian Anglo-French war. A mere dot on the map, it is neither large nor fertile. Its area is about seven square miles.

---

12. Clavering to Barrington, 24 April 1759, *Gentleman's Magazine*, 29 (1759), 273-274.

13. *Ibid*. Engineers in a small boat had earlier reconnoitered Baie la Mahault, coming from the sea. On being discovered they threw out a white flag for a parley but were arrested as spies. Du Treil freed them, to the disgust of their corsair captors. "Guadeloupe/Jugement du Gouverneur de cette isle/Nadau Dutreil," 1759, Archives nationales, Marine et colonies, B⁴ 92. The episode was not recorded in any British source.

14. Samuel Flagg Bemis, *A Diplomatic History of the United States* (New York, 1936), 36-37. It will be recalled that wrangling over these treaties and the obligations of their signatories was a major cause for the opening of hostilities between the British and Dutch during the war for American independence.

In the middle of the eighteenth century it supported a peacetime population of about 1320, of whom slightly less than ten percent were whites. Its planters produced annually about six hundred barrels of sugar. J. F. Jameson, certainly an authority, stated its importance well: "When war prevailed between England and France or Spain, and the prohibitions of mutual intercourse between the islands were enforced by vigilant cruisers and eager privateers, the neutral trade of St. Eustatius flourished still more, and drew in a far larger population than that of peaceful days."[15]

Captain Gardiner, who claimed to have seen service in a "vigilant cruiser" off that island in 1759, spoke of it with less restraint. It was "the barest and least fertile [island], notwithstanding the *Dutch* carry on a very powerful Trade in the *West-Indies* from it, and it has been for some Years the Market of *Europe:* Being poor and naked in itself, and in all Appearances like a ragged Rock, it thrives by borrowed Commodities and a clandestine Traffic with the Powers at War; transporting the Produce of one Enemy to another, under the Pretence of neutral Bottoms. The Town is badly built, and the Houses very indifferent; ... It is an Island of *Smugglers,* and the common Receptacle of all the *Thieves* in Europe."[16]

In the previous November, Governor Thomas had written to Pitt from Antigua that three Dutch fleets had left St. Eustatius in the past four months. They carried materials of war and rations to the French islands and returned with produce which was then shipped to the Netherlands. To protect this trade the Dutch had armed several vessels, no doubt on the much more firmly established principle that armed ships make free goods. Thomas thought the French at Martinique and Guadeloupe would have been unable to carry on their plantations without this help. The food the Dutch carried, according to Pares, came from Ireland or North America.[17]

15. J. F. Jameson, "St. Eustatius in the American Revolution," *American Historical Review,* 8 (1902-03), 683-684.
16. Gardiner, *The West Indies,* 88. Moore's journal shows the *Rippon* to have been at Antigua, not engaged in the blockade of St. Eustatius. Admiralty, 50/22.
17. Thomas to Pitt, 20 November 1758, Pitt, *Correspondence,* I, 396-397; Pares. *War and Trade,* 456.

On 27 February Moore seems to have decided to leave the subtle dialectic of international law to the home governments and to get on with his war. He ordered the *Bristol* (one of his fastest and sleekest) to proceed to St. Eustatius and dry up the leak at its source by blockading the island, despite the neutrality of the sovereign Dutch. No statement of the exact period of time British ships passed there is to be found but the duration of the blockade can be deduced. The *Bristol* was ordered out late in February and probably arrived in the first days of March, since St. Eustatius was about four days' sail from Basse Terre (and one day more distant from Prince Rupert Bay). On 13 March an order was sent to the *Bristol* to return to the fleet and to join Moore at Prince Rupert Bay. She arrived at the bay on 20 March, seven days after the order was sent, whereupon the *Ludlow Castle* was sent to cruise off St. Eustatius for twenty days. Working this out on a calendar will show that St. Eustatius was blockaded from 2 or 3 March to the 16th or 17th, and then again from about 25 March to about 23 April, the latter tour having been extended until Moore ordered the *Ludlow Castle* back to the fleet on 18 April—she returning to the bay on 28 April.[18]

No one could rightly maintain that this was merely a "paper blockade" but to what degree it was successful in a military sense is very difficult to decide. Certainly its duration was too brief to be decisive. Gardiner asserted that the French had been receiving provisions ever since the bombardment of the citadel at Basse Terre Roads, and French sources support this assertion—indeed Bompar said that Dutch supplies made it possible for him to get to sea. Gardiner quoted Moore[19] as saying that Captain Harman and other captains had been detailed to patrol the coasts of Guadeloupe after the fall of Fort Louis. Moore is said to have evaluated their

---

18. Moore, "Journal," Admiralty 50/22. The blockade orders sent to the master of the *Ludlow Castle* were strong: "to cruise before the Port of St. Eustatius, Twenty days to Intercept Vessells, going in or coming out, to Seize and detain all Vessells of what Nation soever bound to or from that Island, laden with the produce of the French Islands . . ." or carrying provisions or naval or ordnance stores. *Ibid*.

19. Gardiner several times referred to a published statement on the campaign by Moore. He gave neither title nor date and I have been unable to locate it.

work: "and this service they *effectually performed*;[20] for the Enemy, by their own Confession, had no Provisions . . . nor any Sort of Supply, but what they drew from their Stores in *Basse-Terre.*" Gardiner then quoted Clavering's statement that there were plenty of supplies in Baie la Mahault in April, and made Clavering's contradictory information the occasion of some incisive criticisms of the truthfulness of the commodore.[21] Since Gardiner did not give the source for the quotation from Moore, it cannot be verified, and Gardiner's record where his remarks are subject to verification does not encourage one to accept his unsupported word. *If* Moore said it, he might not have been wholly wrong— perhaps the material Crump found at Baie la Mahault had been landed before the blockade or during one of its intermissions, when ships were changing stations.

To return to the combat. When Crump had departed for Baie la Mahault to destroy the depot, an officer was sent south against Goyave, five or six miles away, with a hundred men. At Goyave there was a battery, and its destruction was their object. This was not difficult. At the approach of the British the guns were discharged at them—and then the gunners ran, although Clavering reported the post might have been held against an army. The British spiked[22] the seven pieces of ordnance there and returned to temporary headquarters at Petit Bourg on the same day (15 April).[23]

By the following day Crump was also back, having found the town and guns of Baie la Mahault abandoned. The town and the provisions there he burned, and on his return sent his men ranging through the fields and plantations, laying waste the whole countryside between Baie la Mahault and Petit Bourg, a distance of six or eight miles.[24]

20. Italics are Gardiner's.
21. Gardiner, *The West Indies,* 42-43. It is barely possible that the stuff came from the Danes in the Virgin Islands. The capture of a French merchantman bound from what is now Haiti to the Danish islands aroused a suspicion that the Danes had replaced the Dutch as wholesalers of French trade after St. Eustatia had been blockaded. *South-Carolina Gazette,* 5 May 1759.
22. On spiking guns, see Appendix, Topic 20.
23. Clavering to Barrington, 24 April 1759, *Gentleman's Magazine,* 29 (1759), 274.
24. *Ibid.*

During the next two days heavy rains fell, and the immobilized Clavering used the time to strengthen the defenses of Petit Bourg. When the rain ceased, the Antigua volunteers retook Goyave and were supported there by a detachment under Lieutenant Colonel Barlow who was ordered (19 April) to repair the road for the passage of the artillery. Leaving 250 men to hold Petit Bourg against wandering colonial irregulars, the main body moved forward to Goyave on the next day (20 April). Clavering had intelligence[25] that the enemy was concentrating at Ste. Marie, two or three miles beyond Goyave, to oppose further British advance. Entrenchments and barricades were thrown up on the road to impede the movements of the invaders, but the British were fortunate in their "guides" who showed them how to get to the rear of these works by trails which the French, in the manner of so many bunglers since, had thought to be impassable, and had indolently left unguarded. Barlow was given a detachment with which to carry out a flank movement against this system of road blocks. He attacked from the rear, the artillery showered shot from the front, and the defenders—who were becoming very skilled in the operation—took to "precipitate flight" and did not stop running until they reached Ste. Marie. They were closely pursued by the gaudy, panting British soldiers who were ordered into their bright battle formation outside Ste. Marie.[26]

While the redcoats stood at rest in their line outside Ste. Marie, Clavering examined the ground and decided to try his usual flanking movement. For once the attack was not executed in concealment, and the defending partisans showed that they were beginning to learn from the enemy and to understand the value of protecting their flanks. They moved troops to the left to meet

---

25. Having no cavalry for scouting, these British generals seemed to have relied almost entirely for their information upon deserters and slaves. The information seems generally to have been accurate. Perhaps a disinclination to trust such sources explains Hopson's indecision. It has been shown how unfortunate the lack of such information was at Martinique.

26. Clavering to Barrington, 24 April 1759, *Gentleman's Magazine*, 29 (1759), 274. Small bodies of armed men had already been landed via "pirogues" from Bompar's squadron before the fall of Ste. Marie (20 April) but not enough of them to affect the conduct of the defense. "Guadeloupe/Jugement du Gouverneur de cette isle/Nadau Dutreil," 1759, Archives nationales, Marine et colonies, B⁴ 92.

the advancing British. Clavering ordered a halt. His guns were still being laboriously brought up from the rear and the pioneers were still perspiring over their work on the roadblocks. But he correctly measured his enemy, and, despite the lack of gun support, ordered a frontal assault on the entrenchments in the face of musket and cannon fire. The brilliant redcoated line marched forward in time to the famous slow cadence with what Clavering described as the "greatest vivacity." Just as at Arnoville, the sight of the steady, regular approach of a disciplined mass frightened the enemy out of his wits—and out of his prepared positions. The French abandoned all of their artillery "and went off in so much confusion, that they never afterwards appeared before us." French interrogators later regarded this action as the decisive one. The details they dredged up show the defenders as practically leaderless. Although Governor Nadau Du Treil was in the vicinity, he appears not to have exercised command—but "se retira au reduit"—and to have let the conduct of the battle devolve upon company officers who took a lieutenant's-eye view of things and led small bodies back and forth to real or imagined danger points. Thus developed a scene of steadily increasing confusion on the French side. The best troops in the world, under such conditions, could not have stopped the intelligently-led redcoats. And the French colonials were not the best troops in the world. As for their leadership, there is no evidence that Nadau Du Treil exercised real control of troop actions in any part of the whole campaign.[27]

That night the British slept at Ste. Marie. On the next morning (21 April) the column moved into that fat valley, the Capesterre, which Clavering called "the richest and most beautiful part of this or any other country in the West Indies." The wealth and social structure of the neighborhood were revealed by the surrender of 870 Negroes (21 April), the property of one man.[28] The nut had been cracked and the meat was there for the picking. In eight days the troops under Clavering, aided by a frigate and a bomb ketch, had performed eight military operations on a coast

27. *Ibid.*; "Guadeloupe/Jugement du Gouverneur de cette isle/Nadau Dutreil," 1759, Archives nationales, Marine et colonies, B⁴ 92.
28. Clavering to Barrington, 24 April 1759, *Gentleman's Magazine*, 29 (1759), 274.

line about thirteen miles long. One of these operations could be dignified by the term battle (Arnoville). Not once had the British been checked for more than an hour or so. Although the French still had eight or nine hundred men under arms, all resistance appeared to be disorganized. Certainly the civilians knew when they were beaten. On 21 April Dubourg de Clainvilliers and another inhabitant, deputed, they said, by the principal residents of the island, met Clavering in the Capesterre, accompanied by their lawyer bearing a white flag. It now appears that they went to the British without the consent of Nadau Du Treil, but that he saw them depart with their white flag and made no effort to stop them. The next day Clavering took them to Petit Bourg, where Barrington now made his headquarters.[29]

2. *Armistice and capitulation*

That it was the civilians who chose to treat with the invaders was significant. Governor Du Treil saw all of his entrenchments and redoubts forced or abandoned, his mountain refugees cut off from Dutch supplies, and his militia dispirited. So, partly against his wishes, he gave in to the importunities of the civilians who saw their wealth blowing away in the smoke of fires set by Crump's earth-scorchers. Privately, the British command was delighted by the request to negotiate, for it was not at all certain they could storm the Dos d'Âne before the hurricane season was upon them. Consider the unpleasant prospect of a summer campaign in the tropics: if half of their force had been laid up by sickness during the healthful part of the year, what would the sickly season bring? But the French, on their side, were not so sure they could hold the Dos d'Âne; at least Dubourg de Clainvilliers doubted it in private correspondence, although he

---

29. *Ibid.;* "Guadeloupe/Jugement du Gouverneur de cette isle/Nadau Dutreil," 1759, Archives nationales, Marine et colonies, B[4] 92. Du Treil refused to co-operate with the negotiators although he received a petition signed by eighty civilians. In Clainvilliers' narrative (*ibid.*, C[8] A 62) it is asserted that Du Treil claimed he was unwilling to be a party to such negotiations without the advice of Beauharnois. When Clainvilliers and Duqueray left to seek the British, they and Nadau preserved the polite fiction that they were going on a reconnaissance mission, which gave the governor an opportunity, later, to say he had opposed the whole business at all times.

never admitted it to the British negotiators. The Guadeloupe defenders, it is clear, feared they could expect little help from outside. Clainvilliers probably expressed the civilian mood correctly when he said "the danger was evident . . . the women, the children, the slaves, and all of the resources of the island were exposed to the pillage and the fury of the soldier." He further emphasized the increasing difficulty of maintaining discipline among the slaves, and thought that he and his fellow civilians had a much better understanding of the waning of morale among the troops than did the governor. The letter which Moore had intercepted earlier, and which led him to believe no attempt at relief would be made, had been from Beauharnois to Du Treil, and said he could send no relief since he had sent all of the arms he could spare and Bompar "found himself unequal" to try the British squadron in combat. And the British were better equipped to besiege the Dos d'Âne than before, for they had captured fifty guns. The mountain stronghold was the last refuge of the inhabitants. There was still an organized militia force at Trois Rivières, but this, presumably, could be broken in the same way as the other lowland detachments had been shattered.[30]

On 1 May two capitulations were made to Barrington, one by the inhabitants, the other by the governor and the military. There were twenty-two articles of capitulation agreed to by Barrington and Moore, on the one side, and Du Treil, De Clainvilliers, and another inhabitant, acting for the islanders, on the other. These are summarized briefly as follows.

(1) The residents were to march past the British troops, and then to surrender all military materials, posts, and powers.

(2) The inhabitants of neighboring islands were to go to their homes, excepting those of Marie Galante who were to go to Martinique. (This, because Marie Galante was next on Barrington's schedule of conquests.) All such persons were to be allowed to take their personal property with them.

---

30. Beatson, *Memoirs*, II, 257; Clainvilliers' narrative, Archives nationales, Marine et colonies, C⁸ A 62. The complete story, down to the last detail, of the negotiations was written by Clainvilliers, who peppered his account with animadversions on Du Treil's conduct. The whole is an interesting psychological document, expressive of the state of the defenders' minds and spirits.

(3) Religion was to remain as it was, except that all ecclesiastical correspondence was to pass through the hands of the governor.

(4) Military service was not to be required of any of the inhabitants who would swear to abide by the terms of the capitulation.

(5) The political government was to remain as it was except that it would be in the name of His Majesty George II.

(6) All property rights were secured.

(7) The usual imposts and duties would be continued unless the island were later ceded to Great Britain.

(8) All prisoners were to be exchanged.

(9) Free Negroes who had been taken prisoners were not to be enslaved. (As Pares said, this was an honorable self-denying ordinance whereby the British lost much possible booty.)

(10) English fugitives from justice who had been residing in the island were to be free to leave.

(11) If the inhabitants chose to migrate from the island after the postwar settlement, they were to be free to do so, but could sell their property only to the British.

(12) Any preference given to Guadeloupe, in a possible exchange of islands at the peace table, would depend entirely upon the wishes of His Britannic Majesty. (The inhabitants had asked for such preference.)

(13) The children of the inhabitants might be educated in France if the parents so chose.

(14) The property of absent owners was to be safeguarded.

(15) Wives of men absent from the island were to be permitted to leave, with their effects.

(16) The produce of the island could be exported to Great Britain.

(17) Troops were not to be quartered upon the inhabitants, but barracks were to be built. The Negro labor employed in such construction would be paid for.

(18) All inhabitants were to be given one month's time in which to decide whether to sign the articles or to leave the island.

(19) Any persons without property (*e.g.*, privateersmen) were

free to go to Martinique. But debtors must settle their scores first.

(20) Inhabitants were free to emancipate their Negroes, but such freedmen must leave the island.

(21) The inhabitants were to have the commercial privileges of the British, except where charters or navigation laws conflicted.

(22) The capitulation applied equally to the inhabitants of Grand Terre and Basse Terre.[31]

The governor's military capitulation was signed only by the three officers concerned, Barrington, Moore, and Du Treil. Its seventeen provisions are summarized here:

(1) The governor, his staff, his officers, and the regular troops, were to march out with the honors of war; two brass cannon—for which four rounds each were to be allowed—and their arms and baggage were to be retained by them. The British were to take over the posts at Trois Rivières at eight o'clock in the morning of 2 May, and all magazines and revenue papers were to be delivered to officers appointed for that purpose.

(2) The French governmental and military personnel mentioned above were to be sent in comfort to Martinique.

(3) The commissary-general and the officers of the admiralty were also to go to Martinique.

(4) All men going to Martinique were permitted to take their wives and children.

(5) Officers were to be allowed to take servants to the number allowed for the members of the military establishment by the king of France.[32]

(6) The land titles of absentees were guaranteed.

(7) A vessel would be provided for all of the ladies of the officers.

(8) The Martinique volunteers under the lieutenant-governor of that island were to be allowed one ship, and to take all the property they had brought with them.

---

31. *Gentleman's Magazine*, 29 (1759), 276-277; Pares, *War and Trade*, 257.
32. The number of servants allowed by the French military regulations seems surprisingly large. For example, the commissary-general was allowed twenty-four. The number was scaled down to ensigns, who had the privilege of keeping six servants each.

(9) The same privileges were to be extended to the volunteers from the island of Dominica.

(10) All prisoners were to be exchanged.

(11) The promise made by the French government of Guadeloupe to free any slaves who fought in defense of the island was to be kept (at the colony's expense), but such freedmen were to leave the island.

(12) Any privateersmen desiring to go to Martinique were to be allowed one vessel for the purpose.[33]

(13) All persons who were to go to Martinique were to have a reasonable time to gather their effects.

(14) A hospital ship was to be provided for those of the sick and wounded who could be moved. Those who could not safely be moved were to be cared for by the British at the expense of the French Crown.

(15) British fugitives in the island must leave.

(16) All of these provisions were to apply to the forces on Grand Terre, except that, unlike the regular troops at Basse Terre, they were not to be allowed to keep two brass cannon.[34]

(17) The ships for those going to Martinique would be gathered on 2 May.[35]

These terms were pleasing to the inhabitants, because the governors of Martinique and Guadeloupe, in order to stoke the furnaces of patriotism, had foretold that the British would drive them all from the islands.[36] The governors may have had good commercial instincts, for there was a feeling among a certain class of British enterpriser that such would be the correct policy to pursue. Witness Newcastle's letter to Philip Yorke, Earl of Hardwicke on the subject: "Lord Anson told me there were letters in town from some American proprietors, who are not satisfied with the capitulation, as the island, upon their total submission

---

33. At this point the published text mis-numbered the articles, repeating the title "XII." I have not followed this error.

34. This deprivation of a military honor was probably a mild slap on the wrist for not surrendering earlier.

35. *Gentleman's Magazine*, 29 (1759), 275-276.

36. Pares, *War and Trade*, 186, citing Du Treil to Massiac, 25 December 1758, Archives nationales, Marine et colonies, C⁷ A 17; Beauharnois to Du Treil, 8 February 1759, C⁸ A 62.

GUADELOUPE: CAPESTERRE   *143*

is left as it was, with regard to the inhabitants and their effects; whereas they wished to have it destroy'd, their Negroes taken, and the whole demolished. But it is always a good thing to have in hand."³⁷ Hardwicke pointed out in a brief note written on the next day that such men only wanted to kill competition in the sugar industry. This view seems reasonable, when one reflects that by thus limiting the number of sugar cane fields the price of sugar would rise, while, by taking the Negroes, the cost of labor would decline. But, except for the British sugar makers, most Britons were satisfied with the surrender. As Newcastle observed—and as I think Pitt intended—it was "a good thing to have in hand."

3. *Beauharnois achieves an anticlimax*

The wild waves, as usual, were saying nothing, but if they had told Moore what they knew, they would have saved him a great loss of face. For while Barrington was dispersing colonial resistance on land, Bompar was ultimately to join with Beauharnois to get to sea with some kind of force to be used against the British. He had brought with him from France four seventy-fours, three sixty-fours, a fifty, and three frigates, and added a seventy-four and a frigate at Martinique. He had been there since 8 March, and had found the island in "disarray" and reported that its food supply was short, its people frightened and revealing symptoms of incipient anarchy. After six weeks of work on his inadequate squadron, concurrent with an earnest campaign to enlist volunteers, and an influx of provisions from St. Eustatius, he put to sea, convoying Beauharnois with a force of at most six hundred men—mixed French regulars, Swiss, free mulattoes, white volunteers, and slaves. With this force they reached up the windward side of Martinique and of Dominica, thus nullifying Moore's poorly-prepared plan of interference with him. Entirely unperceived by his stronger opponent, he safely put the eighteen small privately owned transports under cover of two frigates into the roadstead off the blackened ruins of Ste. Anne on 27 April. Beau-

---

37. Newcastle to Hardwicke, 14 June 1759, Newcastle Papers, folio 58, Add. MSS. 32892, British Museum (Transcripts in the Library of Congress).

harnois disembarked, prepared to strike some kind of blow for his unworthy king. The evasion of Moore's squadron was well done, but French knowledge of affairs on Guadeloupe was limited. The capitulation articles had already been written, and the documents were in process of signing. Beauharnois set off to find Beaulés, the commandant of Grand Terre.

When found, at three in the morning, the discouraged commandant had just received the articles of capitulation and refused to offer any more resistance to the invader. He gave as reason that the people were tired of fighting. Those who were present—and a number of inhabitants had been gathered to discuss capitulation—agreed unanimously. (It would probably be more accurate, if more awkward and less charitable, to say they were tired of being fought—they had not done much themselves.) Beauharnois, therefore, "bien etonné," finally went on board on 29 April, two days before the last signatures were affixed to the capitulations. He apparently did not try to communicate with Du Treil. The latter, it was said, ignored the presence of his compatriots because he was on bad terms with Bompar![38] If true, the cause would probably be an old grudge dating from the time when Bompar was his peer and neighbor as governor of Martinique.

Barrington's informants exaggerated the strength Bompar and Beauharnois had been prepared to throw into the island, but the report he received of this episode probably made him entirely happy with the terms of the surrender. He wrote to Pitt that the articles had just been signed when a messenger arrived at the French camp with the news that troops had been landed from Martinique. The figures of this reinforcement accepted by Barrington were: six hundred regulars, two thousand buccaneers, two thousand stand of spare arms for the inhabitants, and also heavy guns and mortars.

---

38. Richard Waddington, *La guerre de Sept ans*, III, 357-358. The details are in Bompar, "Mémoire justificatif," Archives nationales, Marine et colonies, B^4 91, and Bompar to Berryer, 20 March, 22 April 1759, *ibid*. Peguireau de Thumisseau, who commanded the volunteers of Martinique in this expedition, wrote a vivid account to the Minister, 17 May 1759, of the psychological collapse of Grand Terre: Archives de la Guerre, Corresp. suppt. A 429. Dr. Thomas P. Neill, of Saint Louis University, tells me that in working on the subject of the French physiocrats he has learned that Le Mercier de la Rivière, who came out to Martinique as intendant, in 1759, gave as gloomy a report of the spirit of the French colonials as Bompar did in his several letters above.

If this force had come an hour sooner, he continued, it would have made the conquest "very difficult, if not impossible." He reported that when Beauharnois learned of the capitulation he sailed away with five hundred stolen Negroes, originally engaged by him on Grand Terre to serve as porters. Barrington intended to send a flag to demand their return.[39] It ought to be added that this story of the stolen slaves is nowhere else confirmed.

Where the figure of two thousand buccaneers came from is impossible to say. Certainly the crews of the eighteen small transports would not add up to that total. Moore scoffed at it, and I am inclined to agree with him. Perhaps the volunteers from Martinique were unemployed privateersmen, who might be regarded as buccaneers by aggrieved British traders. Their numbers could be as easily magnified as the numbers of the defenders of Martinique. A postscript to this notice of numbers is the report that from thirty to fifty of the Swiss soldiery deserted during their one night ashore.[40] This would be almost fifty percent of their number, and may argue that, despite the presence of the Swiss, the British might have continued their triumphant series of engagements even if the inhabitants under Beaulés had supported Bompar and Beauharnois.

The reader will recall that these happenings on the island were unknown to Moore. On 30 April a rumor reached him to the effect than an enemy squadron was prowling somewhere south of Grand Terre. A ship was sent to look. The news was confirmed by a merchant brigantine out of Barbados, although not with complete accuracy, on 2 May, three days *after* the French had withdrawn from Grand Terre. In the inaccurate form that Moore received the news this second time, Bompar had been seen on 1 May east of Marie Galante, rolling along to Grand Terre. Thus Moore's information was misdated, and was actually at least four

---

39. Barrington to Pitt, 9 May 1759, Pitt, *Correspondence*, II, 104-105. But see note 26 *supra*. British sources regarded this as Bompar's expedition; actually the impetus came from Beauharnois. Bompar's part was only to deliver the troops. Whether he attempted any further naval action was left entirely to his discretion. Bompar to Berryer, 22 April 1759, Archives nationales, Marine et colonies, B⁴ 91, and, Bompar's secret order of 19 April 1759, *ibid*.

40. Beatson, *Memoirs*, II, 258; Gardiner, *The West Indies*, 69. The desertion is not confirmed by any French source.

days old, possibly five. Bompar dropped his hooks in Fort Royale Bay, his home base at Martinique, by 6 May, a fact to be borne in mind when considering Moore's ineffectual efforts to come up to his enemy.[41]

There are three sources of knowledge of Moore's chase of Bompar; one is Moore's dispatch, which may be presumed to put Moore in a not unfavorable light, another is Moore's factual, impersonal, and not very informative journal, and the third is Captain Gardiner's account, bitterly hostile to Moore. From these accounts the chronology of futility is easily established.

In the afternoon of 2 May Moore signalled to prepare to sail and again at night to weigh and steer out of the bay. With his lumbering squareriggers he was going to attempt to make easting against the trade wind! In the morning of the 3rd he was fifteen miles west of Marie Galante. The following dawn revealed Marie Galante to be only twelve miles east. During that day they did not gain a yard over the bottom although they tacked all day (however, they *did* receive a copy of the Guadeloupe capitulation). At day break of the 5th Marie Galante was still twelve miles to the east of them. By the end of the 6th they had made good another three miles. If this progress were maintained they could beat to Ste. Anne in another week. In the last fifty-seven hours they had made six miles to the east.

During the night of the 6th and 7th the *Griffin* rejoined the squadron (having been posted to the leeward of Martinique) and reported that Bompar was safe in Fort Royale Bay.[42] At seven in the morning of the 7th Moore threw out the signal for all cruisers to come in; an hour later he hoisted his flag and bore away for Prince Rupert Bay.[43] At noon he ordered the *Rippon, Bristol, Emerald,* and *Griffin* to chase four sail to the south. They

---

41. Gardiner, *The West Indies*, 69, 74. Beauharnois returned in his own transports on, or before, 5 May.—Bompar, "Mémoire justificatif," Archives nationales, Marine et colonies, B⁴ 91. Cf. Moore, "Journal," Admiralty 50/22 for the chronology.

42. Moore, "Journal," Admiralty 50/22. Unfortunately no contemporary seems to have raised the question why the captain commanding the *Griffin* did not see Bompar leave Martinique in the first instance.

43. Moore to Pitt, 9 May 1759, Pitt, *Correspondence*, II, 105-106; Gardiner, *The West Indies*, 70, 72-74; Moore, "Journal," Admiralty 50/22.

steered after the strangers all afternoon only to discover they were British ships carrying Frenchmen to Martinique according to the terms of the capitulations. The commodore and the rest of the squadron came to an anchor in Prince Rupert Bay that night. Gardiner said the Dominicans amused themselves with a saying that "the *English* went on one Side of the Island, and the *French* on the other, for fear they should meet."[44]

44. Gardiner, *The West Indies*, 73-74.

VIII.

Consolidation

1. *Loose ends*

The job was not completely finished when the capitulations were signed. There were voluminous reports and inventories to be made. Putting the terms of the capitulations into effect provided much work. And there were other things.

On 30 April a complete casualty table of the commissioned officers was drawn up.[1] It showed that eleven officers had been

[1] It was published in *Gentleman's Magazine*, 29 (1759), 292, and is reproduced here (names omitted).

REGIMENT	Killed	Died	Wounded	Total
Third	1	3	1	5
Fourth	2	3	2	7
Sixty-first	1	1	1	3
Sixty-third	3	2	2	7
Sixty-fourth	0	6	3	9
Sixty-fifth	1	3	3	7
Thirty-eighth	1	1	3	5
Forty-second	2	2	5	9
Total	11	21	20	52

No such table of enlisted men appears to exist, but their casualties may be estimated. This writer's record of officers and men casualties for the period of the whole campaign, as taken from various sources, shows the following: killed—nine officers and a hundred men, wounded—fifteen officers and 238 men. In the officer record above the figures are somewhat larger, probably due to the fact that some casualties occurred which, by reason of the triviality of the engagements in which they happened, did not get into the various diaries and records. Increasing my totals of enlisted casualties to the same extent as the official tables increased my totals of officer casualties, approximately twenty-five percent, gives the following estimate of the total casualties.

	Officers	Men	Total
Killed	11	125	136
Wounded	20	298	318
Total	31	423	454

Assuming that the total force numbered about five thousand, that is almost a

killed, twenty had been wounded, and twenty-one had "died"—
of disease, no doubt. It will be observed that deaths from disease
were almost twice the number of deaths in action. These officers,
the greater part of them, were the game cockerels of the great
houses of the United Kingdom; of them Benét might have written,

>   . . . they went to war with an air; as if they went
>   to a ball.²

The military action was almost finished. But disease continued
its grisly war all the remaining days of the British occupation.

The French régime was shortly liquidated. The ceremonial
marching out with the brass cannon, and the surrender of Trois
Rivières, took place as scheduled. The wife of the lieutenant-
governor-general of all the French West Indies and all of the other
officers' ladies were sent off in a vessel as promised. It was the
convoy carrying the governor and his officers which was chased
by Moore's ships on 7 May. All terms of the surrender seem to
have been carried out with propriety.³

Barrington summarized the military situation of the first week
of May in a dispatch he sent home in care of Clavering. Lieutenant Colonel Crump was appointed governor of Guadeloupe,
a post he accepted reluctantly, taking it only because he hoped
it might improve his chances of military advancement (he had
served as acting brigadier general since Haldane went to Jamaica).
Men were at work repairing Fort Louis and fortifying the Isle
des Cochons in the harbor, just off Fort Louis, for Barrington
hoped to make that point strong enough to defend itself against
any but a decidedly superior squadron of the enemy. He said
he would leave a sufficient force in garrison and return home with
the remainder—if any—and with his officers. Along with the

---

ten percent casualty rate. When it is recalled what a large number of men were
ill at all times, it would indicate an even higher casualty rate for men in actual
combat.

With regard to deaths from disease among enlisted men up to 30 April it is
impossible to give a total with any pretense to accuracy. Assuming the presence
of three to four hundred officers, and the death of men in the same ratio (an
arbitrary assumption), their total would be between 250 and 350, which might
establish a total of all casualties for the force up to 30 April of between seven
and eight hundred, about fifteen percent.

2. Stephen Vincent Benét, *John Brown's Body* (New York, 1928), 74.
3. Gardiner, *The West Indies*, 61-64, 73-74.

military consolidation and reconstruction, Barrington encouraged and aided the rebuilding of towns and sugar houses; this work, he thought, would in the long run increase the royal revenue.[4]

There was another offensive operation to be undertaken, the reduction of Marie Galante. Barrington intended to try it as soon as Moore sailed back to Guadeloupe. Occupation of Marie Galante would help to render Guadeloupe secure. It promised to be difficult, and he had nothing but hearsay intelligence of the place; but he was confident of the result of an attack, inasmuch as he had done rather well on Guadeloupe under much the same conditions.[5]

He reported that the inhabitants of Guadeloupe had behaved well and that they seemed satisfied to be under His Majesty's government. He had spent a great deal of money to hire and arm small vessels, but excused the expenditure on the ground that Moore had been unable to help him very much. Money had also been laid out for Negroes in Barbados, for the pay of the island volunteers, for three months' provisions for six thousand men (purchased in Antigua), and for the maintenance of hospitals in Guadeloupe and elsewhere. But the sum was not great and it represented unavoidable expense. Although he had not yet inspected all posts, he thought the island would require a garrison of 2500 men. A return of neither the artillery nor the stores had yet been received. In closing he said that Clavering could speak of the future needs of the place.[6]

This news went home to Pitt in the *Woolwich* with Clavering, who left the island on 11 May. Armiger returned to England in the same ship.

This capitulation must have been an excellent one to have pleased both sides so much. Gardiner was quite carried away by it. As he put it: "Fortune at last declared in their Favour, and Conquest became the Recompence of Virtue."[7] On the French

---

4. Barrington to Pitt, 9 May 1759 (the second letter on this date), Pitt, *Correspondence*, II, 102-104. French administrators had planned to make Pointe-à-Pitre a principal port, a project realized during the British occupation, 1759-1763. Maurice Satineau, *Histoire de la Guadeloupe sous l'ancien régime, 1635-1789* (Paris, 1928), 209.

5. Pitt, *Correspondence*, II, 102-104.   6. *Ibid*.

7. Gardiner, *The West Indies*, 91.

side, a brief illumination of an aspect of Barrington's character, which is otherwise unknown, was Gardiner's statement that within ten days of signing the articles Barrington became quite popular with the islanders.[8] At home in London, the staff poetaster of the *Gentleman's Magazine* expressed the campaign with real feeling (and, perhaps, synthetic art), in his praise of the year 1759:

> 'Tis done! unclouded sets the radiant year,
> To heroes, bards, and statesmen ever dear:
> A year, *Sylvanus,* which each future age
> Shall wond'ring view in thy historic page;

After celebrating other victories of that year he arrived at the subject of the conquest of the island of Guadeloupe:

> Then, cross th' *Atlantic* flood, through Western groves,
> By lapse of murm'ring streams, VICTORIA roves;
> In citron-shades ambrosial odours breathes,
> And decks *Britannia's* chiefs with plantane wreaths.[9]

The men who lived and died in the stench which followed every eighteenth-century army in the field probably did not recognize themselves in the "citron-shades" and "ambrosial odours," but it is true enough that the future ages have wondered at the historic page of 1759, the year when the great Pitt's influence finally made itself felt in a large number of important places.

In the midst of the capitulation discussions Barrington had received instructions from Pitt to take a sheltered harbor at St. Lucia as a precaution against being caught in the islands during the hurricane season with no safe anchorage. This was more than two months after the seizure of Fort Louis located on a spacious bay, but can be understood when one remembers the time which elapsed while dispatches were being carried to and from the field. Moore and Hopson sent news of the bombardment and occupation of Basse Terre on 30 January. Pitt learned

8. *Ibid.,* 75.
9. *Gentleman's Magazine,* 29 (1759), iv.

of it early in March. In the middle of the month he replied with the instructions to take a hurricane-proof harbor. These instructions were received by Barrington on 17 April. Thus an exchange of information or instructions, from London to the West Indies, involved about three months' time.

Although St. Lucia was by treaty a "neutral island," it had been occupied by the French in October, 1755, after British reprisals had begun, but before the declaration of war. The commodore then commanding on the station had replied to this occupation by ordering all French ships in British West Indian waters detained.[10]

Pitt's orders were detailed. Hopson (he did not know of that officer's death) should take Guadeloupe and keep it with an adequate garrison; next, in cooperation with Moore, he should take St. Lucia to acquire a hurricane season anchorage, because such a harbor was essential to continued annoyance of the French. Hopson should keep all of his troops except the Highlanders who had originally been intended for service in North America under Amherst's command. Pitt recommended "hutting" the men because of the climate. Hopson could get fresh provisions from the captured French islands, or from the Dutch ports south of Guadeloupe. The provisions for four months, which had been mentioned in a letter of 30 November 1758, sailed from Ireland on 21 March, after having been detained there by contrary winds. The letter closed with instructions to communicate its contents to the naval commander.[11]

Barrington and Moore consulted, decided, and chewed their quills preparatory to replying. Barrington pointed out that the King had not heard of the acquisition of Fort Louis with its excellent harbor at the time he made his wishes known,[12] and that the troops in Guadeloupe were all busy—and successfully so. The capture of St. Lucia's positions would require a very large force because it was defended by two strong forts on high hills, which

---

10. See Chapter I, note 8.
11. Pitt to Hopson, 9 March 1759, Pitt, *Correspondence*, II, 56-59.
12. Pitt always expressed his instructions in a form prefaced by "the king wishes," "the king directs," "the king hopes," or some such phrase. This is common ministerial practice.

could not be reached by the ships' batteries. This circumstance would oblige a regular attack, and the forts would also require permanent garrisons, once they were taken. On his part, Commodore Moore did not consider the place a safe hurricane anchorage.[13] The General concluded by indicating that Brigadier Clavering, bearing the dispatch, could explain the St. Lucia situation very well.[14]

Moore's companion dispatch was briefer. He agreed with Barrington's statement of the tactical problems an attack on St. Lucia would pose and he added that the forts were in good condition to withstand a siege. As for the immediate future of the expedition, he intended to cooperate with Barrington in making a descent upon Marie Galante.[15]

Sir Julian Corbett, in criticizing Moore, said that Sir Francis Drake had originated a principle which would have saved the commodore the embarrassment he suffered by Bompar's safe landing and safe departure from Ste. Anne. When your enemy is gathering a fleet for a task you know not, Drake is supposed to have said, the best thing to do is to assemble your fleet at a point to windward of his departure place. Thus you will always be ready to strike him as soon as he comes to sea, and you need not worry about defending a multitude of places, any one of which might be the objective of the enemy force.

This is sound naval sense. But Sir Julian reads it into Pitt's mind as the motive for the instructions to take St. Lucia as a place from which to annoy the French—it being to windward of Bompar's probable West Indian base. He said Pitt ordered it as soon as he heard of the evacuation of the British army from Martinique, and probably for the reason Drake is said to have given. This distorts the facts to fit Corbett's theory. Pitt said he wanted a harbor (a) for a base during the hurricane season, (b) as a place from which to annoy the French. As soon as he heard of the availability of the Petit Cul-de-Sac of Guadeloupe, the body of water on which Fort Louis was situated, he immediately lost in-

---

13. Strangely enough, this opinion did not occur in Moore's letter on the same subject.
14. Barrington to Pitt, 9 May 1759, Pitt, *Correspondence*, II, 101-102.
15. Moore to Pitt, 9 May 1759, *ibid.*, II, 105-106.

terest in St. Lucia, which would hardly have been the case if St. Lucia seemed of any great strategical importance beyond offering security to the squadron during the coming hurricane season.[16]

Pitt's reply to his West Indian commanders showed an understanding of their situation. He confirmed Barrington in command, and commended his actions. With what might be described as his calm urgency he added that the general, by the time the letter had reached him, would have put the forts in condition to be defended, and would have sent men to North America in as large numbers as his discretion permitted. He told Barrington he might return to England with any men not needed for these two services. Barrington's requests to the governors of the Leeward Islands and Barbados were warmly approved, and he was advised to keep the men of those islands in Guadeloupe if he could, because light troops were useful in wooded country, and these particular light troops were acclimated. Pitt closed his communication by remarking that Barrington must doubtless have judged it unnecessary to take St. Lucia, since the end of such a conquest had already been accomplished.[17] It is this last statement which is rather hard on Corbett's opinion of Pitt's motives for desiring at this juncture to take St. Lucia. After all, the island was still to windward of the French base in Martinique, and there was still a French naval force in Martinique.

2. *Consolidation and departure*

On 9 May Barrington summoned Petite Terre, the Saintes, Désirade, and Marie Galante to surrender on the same terms Guadeloupe had accepted. All but Marie Galante did so; Marie Galante prepared to resist. Five days later the *Berwick, Bristol, Ludlow Castle,* and two bomb ketches, accompanied by transports, put to sea. The commodore remained at anchor with his foretopsail shaking[18]—perhaps to deceive the French into thinking the whole squadron would soon be on its way. Marie Galante's garrison forthwith hauled down the golden lilies of France and

16. Pitt to Moore, 20 May 1759, *ibid.,* II, 111-112.
17. Pitt to Barrington, 20 May 1759, *ibid.,* II, 112-114.
18. The shaking foretopsail was the usual signal to the squadron to weigh anchor.

the men of the expeditionary force rejoined the main body on 19 May. Within four days a detachment commanded by Major Ball of the Sixty-fourth was disposed on the island as a garrison.[19]

On 27 May Barrington informed his co-commander that he intended to send part of his troops to England at the end of June or early in July. During the next two weeks he toured the outposts and quarters in the conquered island, and also supervised the erection of a battery on the Isle des Cochons, using ten twenty-four pounders kindly given to him for the purpose by Moore from one of the ships.[20]

In preparation for the contemplated return to England, Moore made appropriate naval dispositions. Deciding not to maintain a base at Fort Louis (to which place he had come to help Barrington negotiate the capitulations), he ordered the squadron from Prince Rupert Bay to Basse Terre Roads. On 31 May the total of ships of the line under his command was increased to fifteen by the addition of the *Nassau,* 70, and the *Raisonnable,* 70, the latter a captured French ship. To facilitate the exercise of command he divided the squadron into two divisions, he himself taking command over the Red, and Captain Hughes over the White. At three in the afternoon of 3 June he signalled to weigh anchor and all ships left in the respective divisions, except the two newcomers that remained behind to complete their watering. The ships joined in Basse Terre Roads on 4 June, at eight o'clock in the morning. The *Nassau* and the *Raisonnable* appeared there two days later.[21] Transports from Grand Terre were dropping their anchors in the roadstead daily during the second week of June. The *Roebuck* came into the roads on 12 June and sailed the same day for English Harbour, Antigua, to clean her bottom before convoying transports to England.[22] She had probably been in the tropics a long time and therefore needed cleaning. She

19. Gardiner, *The West Indies,* 74-76.
20. *Ibid.,* 76, 79; Moore to Pitt, 25 July 1759, Pitt, *Correspondence,* II, 142-143.
21. The *Nassau* had smallpox on board, and her inclusion in the squadron, as though she were a healthy ship, irritated Gardiner, who thought the men were being unnecessarily exposed.
22. Gardiner, *The West Indies,* 76, 77, 80, 81.

had been a part of Moore's little fleet when Hughes' convoy arrived from England, bringing the army.

During these weeks Moore had lost contact with Bompar and was unsure of the location of his enemy. On 15 June he sent Jekyll in the *Rippon* to look into Grenada. She sailed at noon and arrived off the island early in the morning of 17 June. There Bompar was seen, close in under the land, with seven ships of the line. Venturing as close as possible for the next half hour, Jekyll wore ship at half-past eight, cracked on all sail, and beat to quarters. The press of sail unfortunately caused her to spring her main topgallant mast. One Frenchman loosed his topsails at nine o'clock, but none pursued the *Rippon,* probably because they feared she was bait for a trap just beyond the horizon. Jekyll's ship returned to Basse Terre Roads shortly after day break of 20 June. Her men were disappointed that Moore did not stir to attack Bompar. He did, however, send the *Ludlow Castle* scampering down the trade wind to Jamaica with an express for the admiral commanding there "who was barely equal to the Force under Mons. *Du Bompar.*"[23]

The *Rippon's* five day voyage showed her to be a fine product of the naval architect's art. She sailed 233 sea miles in forty-four and a half hours, which was an average for straight sailing of better than five knots—this after eight months at sea, six of them in tropical waters where weed grows at a great rate. She was probably the smartest ship on the station. Moore used her whenever a job came up requiring a frigate's speed and a ship's armament. His true frigates were not much faster, if any, than this heavy gunned ship of the line. On her return passage from Grenada she averaged better than three knots, in foul weather, with

---

23. *Ibid.,* 74, 81-83, 84. Vice Admiral Thomas Cotes commanded a permanent force at Jamaica which was about the strength of the squadron normally stationed in the Leeward Islands. The British had little to fear from the French. Bompar reported that all of the French West Indies were in disorder and insubordinate. He feared for the lot. He also declared that he had difficulty in securing supplies, and fretted over the approach of the hurricane season. He continually expressed a hope of reenforcement. In short his mood was entirely defensive. Bompar to Berryer, 22 May 1759, Archives nationales, Marine et colonies, B[4] 91.

CONSOLIDATION   157

her main topgallant mast sprung and her fore topgallant sail blown out.[24]

In his next report to Pitt, Moore said that Bompar was still lurking in the islands, for which reason Moore had determined to keep his force together as long as it was safe to do so. Therefore he would send only one convoy with the "sugars," which would sail from St. Christopher, if possible, on 25 July, with such force as would insure its safety.[25]

On 23 June the troops for North America sailed under convoy of the *Rye*. These included the drafts from three English regiments, the Third, Sixty-first, and Sixty-fourth, which totalled 693 men (exclusive of officers, commissioned and noncommissioned), while the whole of the Scottish soldiery was also sent, numbering 507 privates. Thus Amherst received 1200 private soldiers from Barrington.[26] But Wolfe's great decision at Quebec had been reached before these toughened and experienced troops arrived in that quarter of the world.[27]

When the America-bound men boarded their transports, Barrington went up the gangway of the *Roebuck*, which was to convoy forty transports of troops to England. Clavering had reached England on 13 June, and Pitt had hustled him off to Kensington to gladden the old King. Crump was left with the Fourth, Sixty-third, and Sixty-fifth regiments in garrison. They had been brought up to full strength by drafts likewise from the Third, Sixty-first, and Sixty-fourth—the three regiments which had already given a man-transfusion to the force intended for America. Now these

24. Gardiner, *The West Indies*, 74, 81-83, 84.
25. Moore to Pitt, 24 June 1759, Pitt, *Correspondence*, II, 135-136.
26. "A return of the draughts sent to N. Amer. Guadeloupe 25th June 1759." signed "Robert. Skene Adjt Genl. Copy." War Office 1/5. Endorsed: "M. G. Amherst, 10th August 1759." (Transcript in the Library of Congress.) Skene's table follows (adapted):

Drafted from Regiments	Privates
Third	271
Sixty-first	201
Sixty-fourth	221
Total draft	693
Forty-second (the whole battalion)	507
Total to North America	1200

27. Pares, *War and Trade*, 278.

twice-drafted regiments were going home, each with less than twenty percent of its theoretical wartime strength.

At five in the morning of 25 June the *Roebuck* signalled to the transports to loose their moorings. At nine o'clock the signal to weigh was made. An hour later guns began to boom as Moore and Governor Melville (of the citadel) saluted the departing major general. The homeward passage of these transports was uneventful. On 5 August Hardwicke wrote to Newcastle that Barrington was home from the islands with five or six hundred men, "the debris" of three regiments and their officers. The *Roebuck* was the only war ship which had returned by that date.[28]

How closely trade followed the flag was revealed by a note in the August issue of the *Gentleman's Magazine* that on the 18th of that month the first sugars from Guadeloupe reached the English market, less than a fortnight behind the conqueror of the island.

Three weeks after arriving home Barrington submitted a recommendation for a military establishment at Guadeloupe, which would provide a full government for the island group at a cost to His Majesty's government of almost five thousand pounds yearly.

Place	£.	s.
	(per diem)	
Guadeloupe		
1 governor	3	
1 lieutenant governor		10
2 majors of brigade, each 10s.	1	
1 judge advocate		10
1 secretary		10
1 surgeon		10
2 mates, each 5s.		10
1 commissary of provisions, self and clerks	1	10

28. Woods to Newcastle, 13 June 1759, folio 38, Newcastle Papers, Add. MSS. 32892, British Museum; Hardwicke to Newcastle, 5 August 1759, folios 491-492, Newcastle Papers, Add. MSS. 32893; Gardiner, *The West Indies*, 86. (Transcripts of the above Newcastle Papers are in the Library of Congress.)

Fort Royale (citadel at Basse Terre)
- 1 governor — 1
- 1 fort major — 5
- 1 fort adjutant — 4
- 1 barrack master — 5
- 1 commissary of provisions — 10
- 1 port sergeant — 1

Fort George (i.e., Fort Louis)
- 1 governor — 15
- 1 fort adjutant — 5
- 1 barrack master and store keeper — 6
- 1 port sergeant — 1

Marie Galante
- 1 commandant — 15

Grand Terre
- 1 commandant — 15

Per diem	13	2
Per annum	4781	10

This sum would, of course, be in addition to the cost of materials and troops. The stipends of the administrators might be expressed in 1955's purchasing power as from twenty to twenty-five thousand pounds sterling, or from eighty to one hundred thousand United States dollars. This does not seem excessive for the military occupation of the richest sugar island in the world. Whether this or some other plan for organizing the government was adopted is not to be found in the records,[29] but it is an interesting example of an intelligent man's plan for the military government of a conquered land.

On 27 June Moore's squadron took its departure for Antigua. Merchantmen were gathered at Antigua and Barbados, and convoyed from there to St. Christopher. On 26 August Captain Hughes sailed for England, convoying the "trade." The fleet of more than two hundred West Indiamen and the major part of

---

29. Barrington to Martin, 28 August 1759, Treasury 1, Bundle 390, folios 104-105. Transcripts in the Library of Congress.

the naval squadron which had served under Moore against Martinique and Guadeloupe arrived off Spithead on 5 October after a rather rough passage.[30]

The only "military" event out of the ordinary which occurred in Guadeloupe after Barrington left happened when Crump sent a lieutenant in disguise to meet a Dutchman and several other alleged malcontents in Martinique. These conspirators had offered to present the forts of Martinique to the British if Moore and Crump would make a military diversion. All those concerned in the attempt at espionage were detected and hanged, including the lieutenant.[31]

Moore was ultimately relieved from his duty on the Leeward Islands station by Sir James Douglas, who sailed from England in the *Dublin* on 10 March 1760. The commodore arrived in the Downs from Antigua late in June, 1760. Early in the same month Lieutenant Colonel Campbell Dalrymple of the Third Dragoons was appointed governor, *vice* Crump who had died of some tropical pest. He arrived in Guadeloupe in September, and took over from Lieutenant Governor Melville who had served as governor after Crump's death.[32] Thus by the end of the next year after the capitulations of 1759, only a few miserable soldiers and sailors of the original force which had come against it were left in the island. A few officers also remained, but not many, although the correspondence of the governors is full of requests that Pitt require the presence of the officers with their men, instead of flashing their uniforms and drawing their pay in London or the more salubrious pump rooms of Bath.

As for the unfortunate Bompar, he got safely into Brest with his ships on 18 November 1759 in the absence of the hawk-eyed Hawke, who was unable to maintain his blockade of that port during a bit of foul weather. The *Gentleman's Magazine* heard an easily credited rumor that "this squadron is said to have been

---

30. On convoying merchantmen, see Appendix, Topic 21.
31. Crump to Pitt, 26 December 1759, Colonial Office 110/1.
32. *Gentleman's Magazine*, 30 (1760), 151, 294; Secret instructions to Dalrymple, 10 September 1760, Colonial Office, 5/215.

CONSOLIDATION   161

richly laden with private property from Guadeloupe and Martinico."[33]

The French government probably did not give up hope of some successful naval action against the British in West India. After Minorca was secured, a French squadron, otherwise perpetually immobilized in Toulon, was released for service elsewhere. The defeat of a French force by Vice Admiral Edward Boscawen at Lagos in 1759 may have prevented a movement against Guadeloupe. This fleet was said to have been intended for Brest in order to join Hubert de Brienne, Admiral le comte de Conflans in attempting an invasion of the British isles, but it seems to have been also, at one time or other, intended to be used in the West Indies.[34]

3. "*The Recompence of Virtue*"

Some idea of contemporary opinion on the value of the services of individuals who participated in the campaign can be seen in a brief account of the kudos gathered by a few of them, although it may serve just as well to indicate the strength of the political "pull" possessed by each at court.

In May 1759 Melville was promoted lieutenant colonel of the Thirty-eighth—the regiment perpetually in garrison in the Leeward Islands. He was appointed lieutenant governor of Guadeloupe in July.[35]

Clavering was appointed aide-de-camp to a grateful king, with rank as a colonel of foot troops, in June 1759.[36]

Armiger and Barrington were gazetted major generals. Barrington was given Hopson's regiment, the Fortieth.[37]

Major Teesdale, who apparently acted as lieutenant colonel of

33. *Gentleman's Magazine*, 29 (1759), 548. Actually most of the private property came from San Domingo where Bompar, required by his orders to call there, was smothered under requests that he carry home ten times as much as his ships could load with safety. For each planter accommodated he appears to have made nine enemies who denounced him to the court at Versailles, among them the Marquise de Ségur.—Bompar, "Mémoire justificatif," Archives nationales, Marine et colonies, B⁴ 91.
34. This point was canvassed by Pares, *War and Trade*, 184n.-185n., citing all the relevant French documents.
35. *Gentleman's Magazine*, 29 (1759), 294.
36. *Ibid.*
37. *Ibid.*, 294, 443.

the Sixty-first after Barlow relieved Crump in the Fourth Regiment (thus freeing Crump to lead a brigade) was promoted lieutenant colonel in the Sixty-ninth Regiment, in September, 1760.

Lieutenant Archibald Campbell, who made the survey used by Thomas Jefferies for the best contemporary map of Guadeloupe, was made a captain, March 1760.[38]

Peter Parker was moved into the *Buckingham* (a larger ship than his first) in May 1759, in which he returned to Britain in the following year.[39]

38. *Ibid.*, 30 (1760), 155.
39. J. K. Laughton, "Sir Peter Parker," *Dictionary of National Biography*.

IX.

The Campaign as a Work of Art

1. *The British exercise of command*

In considering the control of the British armed forces by the politically responsible officers in London, two facts stand out. The first is the difficulty of communication with commanders in the field; the second is the unification of control through Pitt's personal direction of the war as a whole.

An example of the difficulties of distance, and the results of the difficulties, is best to be found in the consideration of the dates of reports and instructions, from which it can be seen that it took about four months to get an answer to a letter to the prime minister. This meant the campaign was practically completed when the field commanders received orders based upon dispatches sent at its beginning. As a result, Barrington and Moore were forced to make their own decisions within a very broad framework of intelligently drafted initial instructions. The commodore and the major general had to make up their own minds. All things considered, they did well.[1]

Nevertheless Pitt accomplished a unity of control which could be envied by modern political leaders who do not always do so well despite the great improvements which have taken place in the

---

1. The following table shows the slowness of the exchange of communications between Whitehall and the field.

From Guadeloupe		From London	
Sent	Arrived	Sent	Arrived
30 January	6 March	9 March	17 April
6 March	6 May	20 May	ca. 25 July
9 May	12 June		

field of military and naval communications. He did not carry on the war through his war and navy offices, nor through a chief of staff and a chief of naval operations. He issued orders personally, in his own name. The war office and the admiralty seem to have been administrative offices, concerned with supply and maintenance and with little else. This technique of Pitt's, plus the urgent tone of every order,[2] provided a satisfactory solution of the problem which always bothers the directors of world wars—the coordination of land and sea forces. Moore and his opposite number in the army were always explicitly instructed to reveal their orders and instructions to each other. There is a constant record that each did so, faithfully, and their cooperation was excellent at all times, even when they made requests of each other which might have seemed unreasonable to lesser men. This sort of cooperation has not always been found in the story of the relations of army and navy officers. It seems to have been done so well because Pitt, a great and forceful man, was great and forceful in his orders. The Pitt correspondence should be required reading for every civilian who has authority over his country's arms.

The army command, when in Hopson's hands, was exercised at best with hypercaution, at worst with indolence. This is not to charge Hopson with lack of zeal, because he was undoubtedly very ill during the last month of his life. But every act of his, and the boredom found between the lines of contemporary accounts, showed a caution which went beyond prudence. When Barrington came into the command, all this changed. He was faced with a decidedly unpleasant situation. After the protracted inactivity the sick list was appallingly long. Subtracting the total of men who must be left in garrison in Basse Terre's citadel from the total of men able to carry their arms, left Barrington with but 1500 soldiers who could be used in the field. And the sickly season, which promised terrible loss of life,[3] came closer with each sunset. He decided to attack. His war of detachments dispersed the militia who could not afford to sit in the Dos d'Âne while Bar-

---

2. Probably the recent execution of Byng, for not doing everything he could have done, had its effect on the zeal of commanding officers.

3. From May to December, 1759, nearly eight hundred officers and men of the garrison died of disease. Fortescue, *History of the British Army*, II, 357.

rington's men ravaged their plantations. Their Negroes, too, were very "portable" plunder, since they would carry themselves where they were told to go. When Barrington got to Grand Terre desertions from the militia increased.[4] The nature of community life facilitated Barrington's work also. The cultivated lands of the eastern slope of Basse Terre lie in valleys, and for ease of communication with other valleys the planters settled in small villages at the mouths of the valleys, along the sea coast. Rather stupidly, it now seems, each such village was defended by its own small militia force, which meant that Barrington could attack each element in turn at his leisure—a dispersion of defense of which he took intelligent advantage.

Some persons might think he should have defeated instead of treated, that in a few more days he could have imposed terms, willy-nilly, rather than negotiate. In the first place this would have been contrary to the spirit of eighteenth-century warfare which had as its chief object the conciliation rather than the annihilation of the enemy. In the second place, Barrington had reasons of expediency for the generous terms he gave. He could not grant a truce and then await the arrival of more experienced negotiators to represent the British, because such a course would give the enemy time to recover from his panic and to realize that Barrington's position was not tenable for long. The most that the invading forces could do—if the war were to be prolonged—was to destroy property and withdraw from the island. Lastly, "Mr. Moore" was absent, and there was no one but the unskilled diplomatist Barrington to make the terms.[5]

The character of a commander is sometimes revealed by the amount of credit he gives to subordinates. Barrington was generous, especially to Clavering and Crump. And he paid constant tribute to the capabilities of the naval officers with whom he came in contact.[6] Sir John Fortescue characterized him very well. These were his achievements: the army was weakened by sickness, worn by defensive warfare of the most harassing kind, disheartened by a

4. Pares, *War and Trade*, 250-251.
5. Barrington to Pitt, 9 May 1759 (second letter on that date), Pitt, *Correspondence*, II, 100-101.
6. *Ibid.*, II, 102-104.

consciousness of working to no purpose. With this blunt knife he cut off the island and destroyed its supplies at a time when the fleet could no longer support him. In his many small battles he always showed forethought in planning and skill in execution. He defeated his enemy in every engagement although the enemy never fought except in strong positions which were protected by artillery.[7] To which it may be added that the enemy was fighting on his own soil in defense of his own home.

The critic of this campaign has a considerably larger task when he comes to review the naval side. For Moore was explicitly and publicly charged with many defects and defections. His sharpest critics were one of his own officers, Captain Gardiner, and the civilians of the islands. The more important charges against him are seven in number, of which two are very grave. The latter are: first, that Bompar's successful landing at Sainte Anne was due to Moore's negligence, and, second, that he could and ought to have sailed against Bompar when the latter was discovered at Grenada. The lesser charges are as follows: (1) He underestimated French strength. (2) He did not protect commerce. (3) He exerted unnecessary force in his operations. (4) He did not take proper care of one of his ships, the *Rippon*. (5) He neglected the refreshment of his men and did not take suitable hygienic precautions to protect them.

To consider each one of these charges is to review the exercise of the naval command, since they survey all important aspects of the leadership required by this force.[8]

First and most important of the charges against him was that his negligence permitted the unopposed landing at Sainte Anne by Bompar. Moore first heard of Bompar's approach about 11 March, when the troops were being ferried to Fort Louis from Basse Terre.[9] As has been shown, on receipt of this news Moore went to Prince Rupert Bay. Many persons have been dissatisfied

---

7. Fortescue, *History of the British Army*, II, 356-357.
8. Before undertaking this sifting of charges, a parallel examination of the conditions under which the British and French naval establishments carried out their West Indian duties might serve to give the reader a background against which the accusations will appear in proper perspective. See Appendix, Topic 22.
9. Corbett, *England in the Seven Years' War*, I, 382-383.

with this solution. The local civilians asserted that he should have gone to Fort Royale Bay, forcing Bompar either to engage a superior force or to withdraw to the sheltered careenage, which would leave the anchorage to the British.[10] Physically it was entirely feasible to blockade Bompar but Moore ruled it out on the ground that it was inexpedient. He felt too keenly his grave responsibility to Barrington's invaders and he was unwilling to go so far away from them. Whether he could or should have tried to bring Bompar to an action will be left for later consideration. Nevertheless, his position at Prince Rupert Bay seems poorly chosen. It offered little more than rest and refreshment of sea weary crews. The commodore was in the situation of a man trying to checkmate a king with a king on an otherwise empty board. But to criticize him in this fashion is to assume that he wanted a fight with Bompar—that remains to be demonstrated.

What was the reason Moore failed to keep Bompar at a distance from Guadeloupe? The answer is simple but almost incredible. It occurred to no one that Bompar would not head up the leeward side of Dominica with Basse Terre or Fort Louis as his goal but would appear out of the horizon to windward of Guadeloupe. So Moore got to windward of what he guessed would be Bompar's objective. He was so sure that he had covered Basse Terre that he expressed the opinion Bompar would have to attack him to do anything constructive. The intercepted letter had said Bompar had no intention of attacking Moore. The commodore—having convinced himself that such an attack was essential to the French success—deduced that Bompar would do nothing. Then Bompar landed at Sainte Anne. The facts point to one evident conclusion: Moore was complacent and his mind did not explore every possibility offered by the situation. His actions can be understood but not excused.

10. *Ibid.*, I, 385. Since one's opinion of Moore's conduct depends so much on one's opinion of the best place to assemble the British squadron at that moment, it may be inserted, just for the record, that in March Moore praised the anchorage at Fort Louis without reservation. Moore to Admiralty, 6 March 1759. In April he spoke of Prince Rupert Bay as follows: "It is the most convenient Place for watching their Motions, giving Assistance to the Army & protecting our Leeward Islands." Moore to Admiralty, 11 April 1759. Both letters in Admiralty 1/307.

What should he have done? It seems the only other courses of action open to him were to go directly to the enemy fleet at Fort Royale or to stay with Barrington at Fort Louis. To go to Fort Royale meant to ask for a fight. If he did not want a fight, as he probably did not, he could only stay with Barrington, for none of the other islands of the group offered a suitable anchorage to windward of the field commander. Of course, had he stayed in the bay off Fort Louis he might have been surprised—just as he was in Prince Rupert Bay—but he would have been only about six miles from the landing point of an inferior force.

Having been surprised as he was, why was he unable to catch up to Bompar? The answer is not difficult to find. In five days of beating against the almost constant east wind he gained little. As he told Pitt, the "almost constant Lee Currents" made it "very difficult for Ships that sail so heavy as some of our's, to get to windward."[11] Gardiner insinuated that one cause of the failure to catch Bompar was indolence;[12] but this view is not supported by a reading of Moore's journal which was written before he knew he would need a defense.[13] The existence of lee currents is a verifiable fact. The West India pilot has the answer: "The equatorial current runs to the westward between the Windward islands. It varies much in velocity, but is strongest between Trinidad and Grenada, where it has an average velocity of 1½ to 2 knots ... sometimes accelerated to 3 knots."[14] And on a chart one can find this inscription: "In the Dominica, Guadeloupe, and Antigua passages a gentle westerly current sets into the Caribbean; the velocity being least in the northern passages."[15] Consequently it can be said with an approach to certainty that Moore's heavy

---

11. Moore to Pitt, 9 May 1759, Pitt, *Correspondence*, II, 106; Moore, "Journal," Admiralty 50/22. Moore added that unless he had sufficient strength to divide his squadron it would always be the enemy's choice to avoid or to fight a general action. This of course would only hold true of a fleet which was obliged to secure the communications of a land force, and is a revealing commentary on a basic difficulty confronting the responsible naval officer of a combined operation.

12. Gardiner, *The West Indies*, 72, 73.

13. Moore, "Journal," Admiralty 50/22.

14. U. S. Navy Department, *Lesser Antilles and the Coast of Venezuela* (*Sailing Directions for the West Indies*, II), II, 50.

15. U. S. Navy Department, Hydrographic Office, No. 2318, *The West India Islands, Hispaniola to Saint Lucia*, 17th edn.

ships could not have caught Bompar, no matter what the commodore did, by starting from Prince Rupert Bay, since the leeway of the fleet would be about equal to their speed to the east. Thus they would be almost standing still as long as the trade wind blew from east to west as it did nearly all the time. There is no slower point of sailing than to attempt to beat to windward against a current.

The question whether Moore could and should have sailed against Bompar when the *Rippon* located him at Grenada is identical with the question whether he should have tried to fight Bompar at Martinique. It is obvious that he did not feel called upon to fight Bompar unless Barrington's soldiers were threatened by the French squadron. The offensive in this campaign seems to have been the army's job, once the navy put it ashore. The fleet's task was to put the army in possession of a "beach head" and then to cover the operations by taking up a position where the ships could attack any enemy naval force which attempted to interfere.

Considering only the safety of the King's ships, Moore had the advantage over Bompar. If the British were so battered they could not recross the Atlantic, or could not prevent being blown to leeward, they could always take shelter in Jamaica. The French had no such forlorn hope. But to run to Jamaica meant to leave Barrington and to leave the islands to Bompar, or, if he too were disabled, to the first comer from Europe. Both Moore and Bompar, in Pares' judgment, refused to fight because to lose a single sea battle was to lose all of the islands. Thus a war of maneuver risked much less than a fire-away-Flannigan fight. An error of maneuver might be righted; a disabled squadron could lose the campaign in an hour.[16]

In recapitulating the major charges against Moore, and his defense, it would appear that the commodore used bad judgment in selecting Prince Rupert Bay as a base from which to cover the operations of Barrington's battalions, and was guilty of a commander's cardinal sin: allowing himself to be surprised. But Moore's situation did not call on him to engage Bompar in combat unless the latter threatened Barrington. Again, the commodore,

16. Pares, *War and Trade*, 275, 275n.

it was alleged, gave less protection to the commerce of the British islands than he could have given. Since we have seen how Bompar kept Moore pretty well occupied, this count of the indictment could be quashed immediately, because the fleet's job in connection with the expedition was not the protection of commerce. A study of the matter, however, is of value because it reveals the condition of the islands during war time. These charges came from civilians and went so far as to request disciplinary action against the commodore.

Gardiner, with evident pleasure, synopsized the civilian complaints. The French and the British watched each other for eleven weeks, during which the ship-hungry French privateers were free to practice their precarious trade. This they did, taking eighty or ninety vessels which they carried into Martinique. Greatly exercised over these losses, the British planters took the position that the commodore could have anchored in Fort Royale Bay and have served two ends: the privateers would have been locked out and the French men-of-war would have been locked in. Roaming privateers would then have been taken by British cruisers, since only St. Pierre or Grenada would have been open to them. Either of these two places could have been blockaded by a single frigate. At Fort Royale Bompar could either fight a superior force or retire into the careenage.[17]

The figures for ship losses which were given—eighty or ninety vessels—are impossible to check. The *Gentleman's Magazine* published an unsystematic record of ships lost to privateers as an irregular feature. For the year 1759 it listed only captures made during the months of January, April, and July. It will be noted that those were the months in which Moore was most constantly engaged in the projects of the campaign. The figures for those three months are: total of all ships taken by enemy privateers, sixty-seven; of prizes carried into Martinique and Guadeloupe, twenty-one. If this was a constant figure, and the rate of capture continued all the year around, the total number of prizes taken into these French islands in fifty-two weeks would be from eighty to ninety, which is the figure given by Gardiner for the short

17. Gardiner, *The West Indies*, 46.

period of eleven weeks. But during the hurricane season the take would probably be less. Furthermore, the number of prizes carried into Martinique and Guadeloupe during April was only five, for four of the weeks during which Moore was in Prince Rupert Bay. If captures continued at that rate for the whole of the eleven-week period, the total would be little more than a dozen, not eighty or ninety. To show how these things grow, Laughton observed that the number of prizes charged to Moore's inactivity was from 175 to 180![18] Since privateers worked alone or in small groups the problem of counting all of the prizes would very likely be insoluble; some of the captures might be unknown to the owners for months.

Not all of the animadversions can be taken as made in good faith. Underneath much of this righteous wrath one comes upon the enlightening fact that the civilians who complained against Moore had a monetary interest in getting rid of him. There were a number of illegal ways in which these people could get rich during the war and Moore did his best to keep them poor but honest.

Moore incurred commercial enmity when in 1759 he attempted to detect the principals who were the organizers and chief profit-takers from a brisk but illegal trade in slaves between Barbados and St. Vincent.[19] Moreover the French had been taking over the "neutral islands" and all through the war the inhabitants of these undeveloped places had gratefully dined on imported Barbadian foodstuffs. To stop this profitable and unpatriotic trading with the enemy, the commodore had sent one of his captains ashore in Barbados to testify against two "illicit business-as-usual" men who had been seized on the request of the collector of customs. Barbados answered this display of zeal for the law in her own way. The visiting captain was jailed. Moore thereupon wrote, "I shall continue to use my endeavours to stop these dangerous and traitorous proceedings, in which I am afraid too many of the people

18. Barham, *Letters and Papers of Charles, Lord Barham*, J. K. Laughton. ed.. I, 22n.
19. Pares, *War and Trade*, 198.

at Barbados are concerned."[20] Not only Barbadians but many other colonials were also willing to turn a dishonest dollar. The naval commander at Jamaica estimated that over two hundred northern ships had loaded at Monte Cristi in 1759.[21] Moore's interference so heated the passions of the traders of Barbados that he was burned in effigy. That his interest in suppressing traffic with the enemy was the cause of this display of his unpopularity was asserted by the commodore and confirmed by Governor Pinfold.[22]

One reason why so many privateers swarmed in those seas was the arrangement for the exchange of prisoners by masters of ships bent upon trade with the enemy. A contemporary letter writer said that, according to cartel, prisoners were exchanged on the spot, that some of them were nine and ten times in the same jail but returned to sea in swift privateers before the wallowing ships which had taken them reached open water again.[23]

The commodore, himself, denied that conditions that faced him in line of duty were abnormal. "Tho' it is concern to me," he wrote, "that it was not in my power to force the French squadron to an action, yet it was some satisfaction that my constant attention prevented them doing the least harm to the trade,[24] or our islands, where a few hours might have caused great destruction, had I not constantly kept the squadron under my command in a situation and readiness for their immediate protection."[25] In short, Bompar was the enemy, not the privateers.

While Pitt received complaints against Moore, he "would not even appear to give up a deserving sailor to colonial faction."[26] For example, the council and merchants of Barbados wrote to their London agent, Joseph Pickering, to take some action against the

---

20. Moore to Pitt, 20 October 1759, Colonial Office 110/1; Crump to Pitt, 26 December 1759, *ibid.*
21. Pittman, *The Development of the British West Indies*, 317. By "northern ships" would be meant ships from the British colonies of North America. Pitt once said that illegal trade with the enemy had lengthened this war two years.
22. Pares, *War and Trade*, 300n., citing Moore to Admiralty, 13 December 1759, 26 December 1760, Admiralty 1/307.
23. Middleton to Pringle, 4 December 1759, Barham, *Letters and Papers*, I, 8-17.
24. That is, the great annual convoy from the West Indies to the British Isles.
25. Moore to Pitt, 25 July 1759, Colonial Office 110/1.
26. Pares, *War and Trade*, 300.

interfering naval officer.²⁷ Pitt replied that the council and merchants could, if they wished, prefer formal charges by means of an address to the King or to the lords of the Admiralty, but these must be supported by oral testimony in order that the accused be given an opportunity to examine the witnesses against him.²⁸ As this testimony would be taken in London, the whole project would be quite expensive for the complainants.

The remaining accusations against the commodore can be treated very briefly.

It was said that he exerted unnecessary force at Basse Terre in burning the town, for he could have landed north of it since it was undefended on the land side.²⁹ Against this assertion can be balanced the statement of the chief engineer that Basse Terre was impregnable (yet Moore put it in possession of the army) and the commodore's concern that the town had been burned by accident—an expression of regret which was written before the charge of unnecessary force had been made publicly.

The question of whether the *Rippon* was unnecessarily exposed has been treated in the narrative of the fighting. As to the mortality on the ships, Gardiner thought part of the death toll from disease was caused by the commodore's neglect. He cited an instance when some convalescent Marines who had sickened during the passage from England were ordered on shipboard upon discovery they could walk about the town at Barbados. His position was that if the men had been suitably refreshed at Barbados, fewer of them would have died later and that deserters who remained in Barbados could easily be found.

Pares, who has studied the problem of manning the fleet in the West Indies, affirmed that any navy man who could walk was commonly kept on board because privateers and merchantmen, who were short handed, sometimes paid as much for one voyage as enlisted men got for a year's service in the fleet.³⁰ Veteran

27. Barham, *Letters and Papers*, I, 20-23.
28. Pickering to the Barbadian committee, 21 November 1759, Barham, *Letters and Papers*, I, 23-26.
29. William Laird Clowes and others, *The Royal Navy* (Boston and London, 1897-1903), III, 202.
30. Pares, "The Manning of the Navy in the West Indies, 1702-1763," Royal Historical Society, *Transactions*, 4th ser., 20 (1937), 31-60.

Marines would be very valuable to privateersmen. The personnel policy of the royal navy at that time seems cruel and inhumane to us now, but Moore did not make naval policy. If the campaign had failed because of preventable desertions, the commodore might have been shot on his own quarterdeck by a squad of his own Marines.

Considering the insular campaign of 1759 as a whole, it is plain that Moore did an excellent job, except where he exercised faulty judgment in choosing Prince Rupert Bay as a base from which to ward off blows by Bompar. And such errors were to be expected when men learned the warrior's trade by apprenticeship, rather than by a scientific, many-sided formal education. Perhaps Moore could have done with a little less experience, a little more study of hydrography and meteorology.

2. *The defense of the islands*

The human defenses of Guadeloupe—as has no doubt been decided by the reader—were not of a high quality. It is not that the inhabitants of Guadeloupe were uniquely craven; for, given command of the sea, a French army might have done as well on a British island. The fault lay in the structure of island society, which had an enervating effect upon the militia. All of the West Indies were vulnerable. A raiding party could carry away Negroes, fire the canes and the sugar works, and depart in a fortnight, destroying more wealth in that period than could be destroyed in a similar time anywhere else in the civilized world outside the metropolitan areas of continental Europe. Most of the planters carried but little insurance, and the white population was very small because agriculture was organized and carried on in latifundia. Where an agrarian society is dominated by a few great planters the militia tends to consist of many officers and few men. As J. E. B. Stuart once said of a Virginia unit in the 1860's: "They are pretty good officers now, and after a while they will make excellent soldiers too. They only need reducing to the ranks." Another factor was absenteeism, which also deprived the islands of potential military strength, for absentee landlords could not influence or supervise the Negroes.

Interisland cooperation was rare because the enemy was not often out in force unless he had command of the sea and the channels between islands. The islands would usually spare more men for offensive actions than for defense of an invaded neighbor. When Hopson and Moore left Martinique for Guadeloupe, Beauharnois could send only a few score men to Du Treil. Antigua sent many more to aid the British regulars. The simplest explanation is this: the men just would not go. And even those who went were of low quality. Further, the gentry seem to have dispensed themselves and their Negroes from such service. The men were not well trained and, as for the planters, they hired others to do their guard duty for them. Thus, when they rolled out of their luxury to answer an alarm they—unlike Stuart's Virginians—were soft and unprepared. These men, who should have been the natural soldiers, were said to have been less useful than the peasantry, because the peasants at least were used to hard living.[31] Certainly, the sugar islands meet the description of ill-faring lands—where wealth accumulates and men decay.

Therefore the British went up against an ill-prepared defense force which consisted of regular troops in a minute quantity (and low quality), slaves who were promised their freedom but who had more spirit than skill, and fat militia who were used to low thinking and high living. There were also privateersmen, of whom less said the better, since they pursued a scorched-earth policy of their own devising, burning and looting so freely they were thought to have been more destructive than the British invaders.[32] The "regular troops" were French Marines, not seagoing soldiers who might be presumed in good physical condition, if alive, but colonial garrison troops administered by the French navy, and subject to all the defects of French garrison troops mentioned in a previous chapter. And there were only 150 of them on Guadeloupe. The total of the island's defenders, counting a few volunteers from Martinique and Dominica, might be as much as three thousand; that is the most generous and charitable estimate pos-

31. Pares, *War and Trade*, 232-240.
32. Pares, *War and Trade*, 251-252, citing La Vassor de la Touche to Berryer, 20 November 1761, Archives nationales, Marine et colonies, C^8 A 63.

sible. And that is how an island population of some thirty thousand could be outnumbered by an invading army of five thousand.

The manner in which this force of colonials was beaten has been shown. A great commander might have done more with them. On several occasions opportunities to do something constructive for the defense were overlooked or neglected. The heart of the matter was the maldistribution of the forces of the colonials, who placed small units at many points instead of holding a few larger bodies in the hills for sudden raids on the British. As a matter of fact, even small constantly moving parties in the hills would have been more dangerous to the invaders than the many petty garrisons that sat in trenches and let the British choose the times and places of attacks.

In the hearings conducted to determine responsibility for the failure of the defense of Guadeloupe there was endless testimony concerning who abandoned what redoubt at what time and on what authority, who ordered the guns to be spiked, and so on. Gradually from this mass of petty, bickering detail emerged a sketch of an excitable, timorous, moody governor, never sure of himself—which would indicate that the man who actually lost Guadeloupe was the man who commissioned Nadau Du Treil to be governor. But the hearings never canvassed underlying principles, never criticized the structure of the militia corps, and never studied the inevitable effect of defending by the use of small detachments in scattered positions, which were successively knocked off by Barrington and Clavering as one knocks targets off a shelf in a shooting gallery.

Badly organized as their defense was, some may think the punishment of the defeated French officers was extremely rigorous. Du Treil, for his feeble opposition, was degraded and condemned to life imprisonment (from which he was released, without restoration of rank, before 1780). Lacour-Gayet, always a hard loser, said the Governor deserved it.[33] Waddington put Du Treil's case less bitterly. If there had been more understanding between the French high commanders, and if Beauharnois had expended

---

33. Georges Lacour-Gayet, *Marine militaire*, 392.

THE CAMPAIGN AS A WORK OF ART 177

more energy, Waddington thought the island might have been saved, because the British were becoming desperate.[34] (Barrington's dispatches supported this thesis of British desperation.) Nevertheless, Du Treil always bore the responsibility for the loss.[35] In his favor it should be said that there was a kernel of sense in his "do nothing" campaign. The climate was his best ally, and his inoffensive strategy gave him time to organize his amorphous militia while the British were falling sick in great numbers. All of the British officers agreed that his post in the Dos d'Âne was very strong, with a trench or a cannon wherever it could do any good.

Lacour-Gayet scolded each of the French leaders. He said Beauharnois only decided to help Guadeloupe after three months of the campaign, although the island was but a few hours distant. Bompar's squadron, he declared, wasted six weeks at anchor, and to Bompar's campaign he applied the adjective "stérile."[36] Waddington added that Beauharnois, who was not at all distinguished by the events of 1759, threw the blame on Du Treil and Du Treil's subordinates, Poterie and Beaulés. These latter two men may have been culpable but not to the same degree as the governor. Nevertheless a court-martial condemned all three, for laxity and incapacity, to be cashiered, degraded, and imprisoned for life—or, as the French more grimly puts it, "à perpétuité."[37] Of course Beauharnois' status was much higher, since the invaders had tried to take his island and had failed. He would hardly be the one to reveal that geography and the enthusiasm of a quasi-leaderless militia, not the governor, repulsed the British from Martinique,[38]

34. Waddington, La guerre de sept ans, III, 358.
35. "Guadeloupe/Jugement du Gouverneur de cette isle/Nadau Dutreil," 1759, Archives nationales, Marine et colonies, B⁴ 92.
36. Lacour-Gayet, Marine militaire, 392-393.
37. "Guadeloupe/Jugement de Gouverneur de cette isle/Nadau Dutreil," 1759, and, Du Treil to the King, 2 January 1780, both in Archives nationales, Marine et colonies, B⁴ 92. Du Treil was back in Guadeloupe by 1780, although without rank or pension. A native of the West Indies, self educated, he claimed to have entered the service of Louis XIV as a cadet in 1706. (As for the successful defenders of Martinique, the French government scattered royal swords, crosses of St. Louis, and promotions among them. Malo, 12.)
38. Although Martinique has gone through twenty wars, it has remained almost continuously in possession of the French.

and British officers did not testify in enemy military courts. Poterie was governor of the citadel at Basse Terre Roads, and his sin was his disorderly evacuation of that strong point while still capable of defense. As to his authority for leaving the fort, the question of whether Du Treil's aide gave the wrong order to Poterie should be susceptible of proof, but the "trial" by deposition, without cross examination, and with much hearsay included, confused the story to the point where the writer can only say he inclines toward thinking that Du Treil authorized the withdrawal but one could also produce strong evidence that he did not. As for the disorder of the evacuation, the defenders probably could not have managed any maneuver in orderly fashion. The water being undrinkable, it would have been correct for them to retire, even though sober. To which anti-Poterie witnesses said other water was available from uncontaminated (but not clearly described) sources. The reader can take it or leave it. There was *one* fact unanimously agreed upon by the deponents and by British witnesses: the guns were spiked—which indicates some order in the withdrawal.

The question of French naval activity during these months also demands some scrutiny. At Versailles, in 1760, Bompar produced a written justification of his conduct, listing allegations and invidious questions raised against him, and replied to each, here much condensed. (1) He left France too late. *Reply:* He was ready to go when his orders came, but it took a month for the port authorities to fit and man his ships. (2) Why did he not convoy the seven ships carrying supplies for the squadron? *Reply:* He was not ordered to do so, nor would it have been appropriate to his mission to act as a convoy. (3) Having arrived at Martinique on 8 March, he dallied until 23 April before moving to help Guadeloupe. *Reply:* His orders contemplated offensive action against the British West Indies, and assumed that he could draw aid from the French islands, but he found on his arrival, to his surprise, that the French islands were disordered and on the defensive. Knowing his force inferior to that of the British, and that word would have reached France of the state of the islands, he expected that four vessels, then idle, would be sent to reinforce him. He therefore decided not to risk exposing all the islands to conquest as a possible result of sending his inferior force to battle on the eve of expected reenforcement. If he lost there was no place where he could refit. He thought of an attack on Barbados, but his captains unanimously disagreed. So he waited for the expected help, and meanwhile sent aid in men and arms to Guadeloupe. By his presence he freed the Dutch from a blockade and food came in from St. Eustatius to the rationless French islands. When Beauharnois proposed an expedition to Guadeloupe he agreed. (4) He had not attacked Barrington's transports lying off Fort Louis (Point à Pitre). *Reply:* It was impractical because of the direction of the wind, and because they lay under well-tended shore batteries. (5) His departure from Martinique was a flight. *Reply:* His orders required him to visit Grenada to meet his supply ships, and also to deliver men to San Domingo.

Nadau Du Treil was the only one to examine the conduct of Beauharnois, and that was in 1780, as an old man, when he said that Beauharnois could not have done better if he had tried to lose Guadeloupe; that he gave no real help, ignored requests for assistance, supported the insubordinate, harbored deserters, concealed the true state of affairs from Bompar, talked the Grand Terreurs out of further resistance (on 27 April), exceeded his authority in trying Du Treil, denied admission of protests against the personnel of the court (all being Du Treil's declared enemies), and thereby was able successfully to predict the outcome of the "jugement." These are the recriminations of an aged man; of their weight the reader may judge. His best points were not so emphatic as his denunciations of persecutors. Among them was the suggestion that if guilty as charged his punishment was too light, that his career in public service since 1706 had been otherwise blameless, that the French lost many other stronger places in the Seven Years' War.[39]

39. "Guadeloupe/Jugement du Gouverneur de cette isle/Nadau Dutreil," 1759, Archives nationales, Marine et colonies, B⁴ 92; Bompar, "Mémoire justificatif," *ibid.*, B⁴ 91.

Du Treil was detained by the British when they took Martinique in 1762, sent by them to London, from where (before the end of the war) he passed to Amsterdam, and thence to Paris. Expecting a review and reversal of his case as decided in Martinique, he was disappointed. After a short while in the Bas-

Mention has been made that the climate was Du Treil's best assistant. How true that was can be easily demonstrated. One would expect the officers to take better care of themselves than the men took of themselves, yet they had a very high mortality rate. Governor Haldane died at Jamaica in July, 1759, six months after his arrival. General Hopson's death has been previously noted. Haldane's successor, Rear Admiral Charles Holmes, died in Jamaica after a year's tenure. Brigadier Crump died as governor of Guadeloupe, nine months after Barrington left. When generals and admirals died at this rate the cost of disease among the men can readily be imagined, and Barrington was no doubt correct in saying the British would have had to leave shortly if the inhabitants had not surrendered when they did.

A return of the strength of the Sixty-third Regiment for 3 March 1759 has survived.[40] It follows.

Fit for duty:	Commissioned officers	34
	Warrant officers	5
	Non-commissioned officers	35
	Musicians	18
	Men	435
Sick present:		260
Sick absent:		110
Deceased since last return (3 February)		27

This regiment, then, two months after reaching the island had been weakened by loss or disability of approximately forty percent of its full personnel. Loss from combat had so far been negligible.

In spite of the improvements of the past two centuries in hygiene and sanitation, the contemporary condition of life in Gaudeloupe as described in the *West India Pilot* is impressively stated. The facts are quoted without comment. Of Pointe à Pitre, which is near the site of Fort Louis, "The sanitation of the town is poor." Of Basse Terre, "Water should be boiled before using." Of the

---

tille he was confined in a fortress.—Nadau Du Treil to the King, 2 January 1780, *ibid.*, B⁴ 92.

40. H. C. Wylly, *The Manchester Regiment*, I, 14.

island as a whole, "Guadeloupe is considered unhealthful; fever and sickness prevail."[41]

3. *Significance*

When the capitulation became known in London, the reaction was immediate and enthusiastic among those in power who knew (or thought they knew) the island's true worth. Newcastle bubbled over. A single letter he wrote to the Admiralty contained these phrases: "great good news . . . I want something to revive my spirits, and this has done it . . . must be great in its consequences . . . hope will refresh our stocks . . . great affair."[42] Hardwicke, who knew more about most things than Newcastle did, said, "It certainly is a great stroke."[43] To another correspondent Newcastle commented: "I hear the city is greatly pleased," and added that the King was happy.[44] Barrington's brother, the Secretary at War, wrote, "The king . . . was pleased to express his intire [*sic*] approbation of Colonel Barrington's conduct in the most gracious manner."[45] Pitt, whose opinion mattered more than the opinions of the rest, was quoted as saying that "Louisbourgh [*sic*] & Guadeloupe, are the best plenipos at a Congress."[46]

The French reaction was perhaps best shown by the punishment of Du Treil, Poterie, and Beaulés. A spy on Newcastle's payroll wrote from Paris: "I have never seen any publick affairs that wounded M. Bellisle so much as the loss of Guardeloupe [*sic*]. I was with him very soon after he received the news of it; and I found by his discourse, that he, as well as the other ministers had flattered themselves, the climate, sickness & the number of the inhabitants with the safe arrival of M. Bompart [*sic*] at Martinico, would have obliged the English to quit that

---

41. U. S. Navy Department, *Lesser Antilles and the Coast of Venezuela*, II, 159, 162, 49.
42. Newcastle to Admiralty, 13 June 1759, folio 36, Newcastle Papers, Add. MSS. 32892, British Museum (Transcripts in the Library of Congress).
43. Hardwicke to Newcastle, 15 June 1759, f. 88, *ibid*.
44. Newcastle to Devonshire, 14 June 1759, f. 55, *ibid*.
45. Viscount Barrington to Newcastle, 9 June 1759, f. 510, Newcastle Papers, Add. MSS. 32891, British Museum (Transcripts in the Library of Congress).
46. Newcastle to Stone, 1 August 1759, f. 403-407, Newcastle Papers, Add. MSS. 32893, *ibid*.

island [Guadeloupe]." He thought the French would try to retake the island and that they had no fear of losing Martinique which was so well defended now it would require eight thousand troops to reduce it.[47] The same spy had substantially the same opinions a month later.

Bompar, who knew the West Indies well, wrote to Berryer that the rest of the French islands were now badly disposed toward the Paris government. Dominica, by virtue of its neutrality, was selling provisions to the British garrison in Guadeloupe and doing quite well out of it and the Martinique inhabitants were thinking silent but dark thoughts when they compared their own economic straits with the new prosperity of Guadeloupe. Sugar was moving slowly in the once rapid stream of French West Indian commerce.[48]

The most immediate gain to the British by the capture of Guadeloupe accrued to the merchant marine, in part because of increased carrying trade but also, and perhaps more important, from the destruction of a nest which hatched out able and advantageously placed privateers. Désirade was the chief landfall for British ships trading to Nevis, St. Kitts, Antigua, Jamaica, and the Spanish Main. Near Désirade they were easily cut out by privateers from Guadeloupe, who carried them into Basse Terre Roads and sold them under the guns of the citadel.[49]

Gardiner, no business man, looked at the wealth of the island and saw it good, unlike some business men who saw it only as competition. "The Attention of the Public in *England* on this Expedition being totally swallowed up in the Idea of *Martinico*, the Conquest of *Guadelupe* [*sic*]," he affirmed, "became little considered by the Generality of the People there." They thought of it as a satellite of Martinique, but they were wrong. Guadeloupe was strong, productive, and beautiful; "like a Queen, it sits enthroned amongst the lesser Islands, in Power to convey Relief or

---

47. Intelligence to Newcastle, 1 July 1759, f. 339-341, Newcastle Papers, Add. MSS. 32892, British Museum. The reference is to Charles, Duc de Belle-Isle, Secretary for War, 1757-1760.

48. Bompar to Berryer, 22 May 1759, Archives nationales, Marine et colonies, B⁴ 91.

49. Gardiner, *The West Indies*, 79-80.

THE CAMPAIGN AS A WORK OF ART   183

Destruction to all the Colonies around." Its soil was rich, and Grand Terre was so fertile that some landholders got six cane harvests without replanting. The best fields of Martinique got seven harvests, but they were few. Most *"Martinico* Sugars"—as they were known in the trade—had come ultimately from Guadeloupe, being shipped to Europe via Martinique. The island probably produced more sugar than all the other sugar islands put together.[50]

This prodigious sugar production was just what the British West Indian nabobs feared. In London it became an open question whether to keep the place or not. Many Englishmen expected to clear the islanders off and to settle Englishmen there—if it were to be kept at all. A movement to this end did not get under way—but only because of the provisional nature of the conquest and the fact that the terms of the capitulation forbade it.[51]

Early in 1762 Étienne François, duc de Choiseul's peace proposals were forwarded to London. The reader will bear in mind that Pitt was no longer in office to receive them. The terms were as follows: (1) France would persuade Spain to settle her questions in a way satisfactory to Britain. (2) Prizes were to be adjusted by the British admiralty. (3) The British were to destroy their Honduran forts. (4) The Newfoundland fisheries were to remain as they were. (5) More than the island of St. Pierre was to be provided as an *abri* for the fishermen of the Newfoundland waters, but no such *abri* was to be fortified. (6) The retention of conquered Canada by the British was accepted. (7) France was to get one slaving station on the African coast. (8) Britain was to settle the question of India as she wished. (9) Minorca would be restored to the British. (10) Territory on the continent of Europe which belonged to Britain and her allies was to be evacuated by the French. (11) Martinique, Guadeloupe, and Marie Galante were to be restored to France. (12) The neutral islands were to be divided equitably.

The British disliked giving up the French West Indies, but John Stuart, Earl of Bute, finally prepared to settle for the neu-

50. *Ibid.*, 79-80.   51. Pares, *War and Trade*, 186.

tral islands and Grenada, and for an admission that the Mississippi River was the western boundary of British North America south of Canada (whereby he thought to gather in New Orleans). Choiseul, for his part, said he must have St. Lucia, Cape Breton Island, and what history students now designate as West Florida. In the end he got the islands conquered by Barrington and Moore, plus Martinique, and the British got, except St. Lucia, the rest of the disputed Indies.[52] But before the final settlement, came the famous Canada-Guadeloupe controversy, so much better known than the acquisition of Guadeloupe,[53] an issue, however, that does not come within the range of this study.

The outcome of that controversy should be of great interest to Americans, in that it weakened British naval power in the next war, and French sea power contributed to the success of the Americans in their war for independence. As Edward Channing put it, when France entered the Revolutionary War in 1778, the British realized the impolicy of restoring Cuba, Martinique, Guadeloupe, and St. Lucia to the Spanish and the French. The Lesser Antilles lie in a long curve. Since the wind usually blows from the east or southeast, these islands were maritime outposts of the mainland colonies and the economically more important islands to leeward. The British held the southern end of the curve: St. Vincent, Grenada, Tobago, and Trinidad. Barbados, still farther to windward, made an excellent base. But the lack of posts toward the northern end of the curve weakened British sea power to a great extent.[54] Supposing that British strength at sea had been increased to the extent that good Antillean bases might imply, could the French during the war for American independence have put the Americans in possession of urgently needed war materials? If the balance of strength in the West Indies had been in favor of Britain, could a French naval force have used the West Indies as a stepping stone in a campaign which ended when Charles, Lord Cornwallis, was bottled up in Yorktown?

52. Corbett, *England in the Seven Years' War*, II, 331-333, 339-340, 382.
53. The latest and the best of many accounts of the controversy are in Pares, *War and Trade*, and Gipson, *The British Empire before the American Revolution*, VIII.
54. Channing, *History of the United States*, III, 288.

THE CAMPAIGN AS A WORK OF ART

Perhaps Barrington's victory, if used for purposes of long range strategy, could have been exploited by naval men in such a way as to affect the outcome of the war for American independence.

This is a summary of the insular campaign of 1759. To gain a prize to be traded for Minorca, Pitt sent an amphibious force against Martinique in 1759. Failing here, the commanders attacked Guadeloupe. Opposed there more by the climate than the inhabitants, victory was gained in a three months' campaign. At a moment when the British commander, General John Barrington, was toying with thoughts that he might have to withdraw, the inhabitants took the lead in surrendering to him. The capitulation was luckily arranged before a tardy French naval force eluded a badly posted British squadron and landed unwelcome reinforcements for the defeated and dispirited inhabitants. In that sense the attack on the island was an afterthought, the conquest an accident.

Credit for the victory belongs chiefly to Major General John Barrington, for his vigorous use of a decaying army which had been rotting in the feeble grasp of his predecessor. Supporting Barrington was Commodore John Moore, a good tactician but not so good a strategist, whose error of judgment in stationing his squadron might well have delivered his co-commander into the hands of a French relief force if the enemy had been more spirited and energetic.

The reduction of Guadeloupe was, on the one hand, a blow to the French privateers of the West Indies, and on the other hand allowed the island to be traded for recognition of the Mississippi River as the western boundary of the thirteen British colonies of North America—although it might have been wise to keep it as a naval base in the northern part of the Antillean curve.

From the French point of view the resistance of the defenders of the island was little more than a series of blunders. A later French critic of the campaign said that the history of naval activities in the Antilles was much like French naval history with regard to Canada. In each case it was intended to send some squadrons, but the government ended by sending some ships, which arrived too late.[55] That is to say, "too little and too late."

55. Lacour-Gayet, *Marine militaire*, 389-390.

Appendix

1. THE RAID, THE ECCENTRIC ATTACK, AND THE INVASION

Sir Julian Corbett gave a useful classification of the kinds of attacks in his *England in the Seven Years' War* (London, 1907), I, 206-209. He classified them as of three kinds, the defensive diversion or raid, the eccentric attack, and the true invasion.

The raid is an operation which aims to contain or attract an opposing force greater than the force sent against the enemy. The smaller the force sent, within reason, the more likely it is to achieve this aim, for, as Clausewitz said, fifty thousand men can defend a province against fifty thousand, but one thousand can not defend the same province against a thousand. The raid should be used only as a measure of defense.

The eccentric attack is a raid so large as to lose defensive character because with its size it risks the loss of rapidity, secrecy, and surprise which are essential to the success of a raid. Thus its objects are necessarily fewer than the many possible objectives of a true raid. It should be used only for acquiring a definite place and holding it as a permanent diversion and annoyance. Being truly offensive this operation must rely more on intrinsic strength than on surprise.

The true invasion is an action so large and strong as to be an undisguised strategical offensive.

The attacks on the French islands of Martinique and Guadeloupe seem each to have the character of an eccentric attack.

2. THE RANK OF COMMODORE

The title "commodore" was used in referring to a general officer in command of a detached squadron, if the officer were not

APPENDIX   187

an admiral. A commodore ranked with a brigadier general. It was and is also a courtesy title applied to the senior captain of several ships cruising together. William Falconer, *The Mariner's New and Complete Naval Dictionary* (London, 1804). In war time the United States Navy has issued commissions of the rank of commodore.

3. EIGHTEENTH-CENTURY MILITARY DRAFTS

The eighteenth-century "draft" of soldiers should not be confused with twentieth-century conscription. A draft was a levy upon an organized military unit to fill the gaps in another unit. With regimental spirit sometimes stronger than national patriotism the draft was often bitterly resented by those drafted. Commanding officers usually disposed of their hard cases, incorrigibles, and what an adjutant might lump together as "the sick, lame, and lazy."

4. THE ORGANIZATION OF THE ARTILLERY

The army was considered to have but one regiment of artillery, stationed at Woolwich Arsenal, and every artillery unit serving in the field, anywhere in the world, was regarded as a detachment from that regiment. The detachments were usually organized as companies under captains or "firemasters." The presence of a major would imply the presence of at least two companies or, as we call them, "batteries." The ranks in the artillery can be learned from Barrington's casualty list of 2 March 1759.

> Captain or Firemaster
> Lieutenant Fireworker
> Gunner
> Mattross

For the artillerymen, the *New English Dictionary* gave: "Fireworker . . . 1. One who has to do with fireworks or explosives in war; *spec.* an artillery officer under the firemaster." According to the same source a mattross was a soldier next in rank below a gunner, acting as assistant or mate. Today he would be a "private." The casualty list from which above ranks were taken is in Barrington to Pitt, 2 March 1759, Colonial Office 110/1.

As a matter of interest it may be noted that for three centuries after their introduction to warfare, artillerymen were civilian contractors and employes. The British artillery did not "assume a military appearance" until the War of the Austrian Succession, 1744-1748, and the artillery drivers were not soldiers before 1793. Cf. Charles Francis Atkinson, "Artillery," *Encyclopaedia Britannica,* 11th edn., for an excellent account of the history of this arm.

5. THE BRITISH REGIMENTS WHICH SERVED IN MARTINIQUE AND GUADELOUPE

The regiments are referred to by so many names in the sources that a reference list may be useful. The following gives regimental number, name or names, owner (in 1759), officer commanding during the insular campaign, and the brigade of which the regiment formed a part.

Third. Old Buffs, East Kent, Howard's. Lt. Col. Cyrus Trapaud, ranking locally as a brigadier general. First Brigade.

Fourth. Royal Lancashire, Duroure's. Lt. Col. Byam Crump. Second Brigade.

Thirty-eighth. South Staffordshire, Ross's. Major Robert Melville. Not brigaded.

Forty-second. Royal Highlanders, Black Watch, Murray's. Brevet Major —— Anstruther. Not brigaded.

Sixty-first. Formerly the second battalion of the *Third.* Elliott's. Lt. Col. John Barlow. Third Brigade.

Sixty-third. Manchester, Watson's. Lt. Col. Peter Debrissay. First Brigade.

Sixty-fourth. North Staffordshire, Barrington's. Major Thomas Ball. Second Brigade.

Sixty-fifth. York and Lancaster, Armiger's. Brigadier General and Colonel Robert Armiger, assisted by Lt. Col. John Salt.

The shortage of colonels in the line is explained by the fact that colonels were almost always general officers whose colonelcies were their chief sources of income, because generals were paid per diem and only during actual campaigning. For example, Hopson's regiment was at the moment serving on the continent of Europe under a lieutenant colonel. During the War for American

APPENDIX   189

Independence the Congress of the United States found it necessary to establish the rank of lieutenant colonel commandant as the rank of a regimental commander, in order to facilitate prisoner exchanges. American regimental commanders were made full colonels in the 1790's.

British regiments were also popularly known by soldiers' nicknames which rarely got into print, and some of which were unprintable. See Kipling's fiction for examples of such (printable) regimental esoterica.

6. EIGHTEENTH- AND TWENTIETH-CENTURY STRENGTHS COMPARED

Just as we habitually translate eighteenth-century currency into modern purchasing power by multiplying by a fixed number, nowadays 3 or 4, so we can translate eighteenth-century military strength into modern units. Thinking along this line, I have tentatively decided that where we send divisions, they sent brigades. Thus where they sent three brigades and two independent detachments, we might well send three divisions plus two spare combat teams. Their total manpower in the campaign of 1759 was less than six thousand men. We would probably use fifty or sixty thousand for the same sort of job, including Marine Corps, Air Force, and all useful arms and branches of the Army. Hopson's modern counterpart would be a corps commander.

7. RANKS IN THE INFANTRY REGIMENTS

Infantry ranks can be learned from a casualty list of 2 March 1759. The "service and headquarters" category is modern terminology.

Line	*Service and Headquarters*
Colonel	Chaplain
Lieutenant Colonel	Adjutant
Major	Quartermaster
Captain	Surgeon
Supernumerary Captain	Surgeon's Mate
Lieutenant	
Ensign	
Sergeant	

Drummer
Rank and File

The casualty list from which the above is taken is in Barrington to Pitt, 2 March 1759, Colonial Office 110/1.

8. THE FRIGATE

A frigate was "a light nimble vessel built for the purpose of sailing swiftly. These vessels mount from twenty to forty-four guns, and make excellent cruisers." Falconer, *The Mariner's... Dictionary*. The true frigate of thirty guns had only recently been introduced. Moore apparently regarded his old two-decked forty-four-gun frigates as no longer worthy of the name. Beatson always called them simply "men of war." Cf. Corbett, *England in the Seven Years' War*, I, 377n. The new frigates were long, slim, and fast, with one bank of guns. The best remembered pages of American wooden-wall naval history were written by frigates, e.g., the *Constitution*.

9. BOMB KETCHES AND NAVAL BOMBING

Bomb ketches were sturdy little fore-and-aft vessels built with heavier frames and beams than usual for such small craft, and mounting one or more mortars each of which could throw a bomb on a high parabolic line for a distance of two or three miles. They were intended for use against shore installations. The bombs were "shells" of iron, spherical in shape, packed with powder. The wall of the shell opposite the fuse was given an extra thickness in order that the bomb would not fall to earth with the fuse on the downward side. The fuses were made of a mixture of wax and gunpowder, and were cut by the gunners so that the bombs would explode at the approximate moment of contact with the ground. At least that was the theory of fuse-cutting. "The Star Spangled Banner," which celebrates the successful defense of a shore installation, Fort McHenry, against naval attack, bears contemporary witness to the fact that bombs frequently burst in the air.

APPENDIX   191

10. THE NUMBER OF MEN IN THE NAVAL FORCE

The number of men in Moore's fleet cannot be determined merely by adding up the figures given with the list of ships. It must be borne in mind that the complements of ships as given in the sources were rarely, if ever, complete at any given moment, being limited by casualties, disease, desertion, and the difficulty of "enlistment." Naval life was on the whole unattractive to eighteenth-century seamen, and without the method of recruiting called "impressment" the Royal Navy could hardly have been kept at sea. In time of war the competition of the merchant service for men was particularly keen, since the navy paid its officers and men on a pay base fixed by Parliament in 1700. Merchants sometimes paid as much for a single hazardous voyage as the navy paid for a year of service. Privateering also absorbed capable seamen, who might hope by one engagement or a few lucky strokes to win enough prize money to set themselves up ashore, or at least to remain on the beach in idleness for months if they did not intend to swallow the anchor. Navy food was certainly bad at times, surgeons and physicians were uncertain on the subject of antiscorbutics, family life was practically reserved to commissioned officers, pay was often deliberately kept in arrears to discourage desertions, and punishments were harsh.

The following casual news note for the year 1758 well illustrates the difficulty of obtaining men for the service. "Thursday 22. Was the hottest press for seamen on the *Thames* that has been known since the war began, no regard being paid to protections, and upwards of 800 swept away. The crew of the Prince of *Wales,* a letter of marque ship, stood to arms, and saved themselves by their resolution." *Gentleman's Magazine,* 28 (1758), 289.

11. THE WEEKLY RATIONS OF THE SOLDIER

The weekly ration for each soldier on the West India expedition of 1759, computed from the table in the text, was approximately as follows: bread 4½ pounds; beef and pork, each, about 3/5 of a "piece"; peas, 1 1/3 pints; "grotts," a little less than a pint; oatmeal, the same; "oil," about ½ pint; vinegar, about 1/3 of a pint. These figures are subject to correction because the peas, "grotts," oatmeal, "oil," and vinegar may well have been reserved to the sick and wounded. The weight of a "piece" of beef or pork might be five or ten pounds, which would allow six to twelve pounds of meat weekly, per man. "Grotts" is or are not defined, but the *New English Dictionary* has "Groats. 1. Hulled, or hulled and crushed grain of various kinds, chiefly oats, but also wheat, barley and maize." This is probably identical with "grits"—a staple of diet in the southern part of the United States to this day.

Some commodities are conspicuous by their absence from the ration: coffee, tea, sugar, alcohol, tobacco. Four of these were obtainable in the West Indies, but tea would not be easily had there. Today, who would expect to find British troops very far from a container of boiling water at 4:00 P.M.?

12. THE OFFICER'S GORGET

The earliest form of the gorget was a kind of breast plate for protection of the throat and neck. By the eighteenth century it was only a relic, like the vermiform appendix, and had become a pendant ornament worn at the base of the throat by officers as a part of the uniform. Charles Willson Peale's portrait of George Washington, at Washington and Lee University, shows the gorget prominently, and the gorget itself worn by Washington may be seen in the museum of the Massachusetts Historical Society.

13. THE GRENADIERS

The largest men in each regiment in the army were organized as a separate company called the grenadiers. They were distinguishable by their mitre-like hats, whereas the other troops wore the tricorne hats. They fought in the place of honor on the right of the line and, unlike the rest of the troops, were trained in extended order combat. In the 1770's the other extreme was reached: the organization of the smallest men of each regiment as a company of light infantry, trained as skirmishers, who fought on the left flank. Light infantry, generally more agile and thought contemporaneously to be more intelligent, might have been better than grenadiers for skirmishing with the guerilla bands which infested the north shore of Fort Royale Bay early in 1759.

APPENDIX

14. Warping a Ship

To warp a ship is to pull it from one place to another by means of a cable made fast to some object off the ship and secured to a capstan on board. The capstan is then manned and as it turns the line is "wound up" like thread on a spool and the ship moves in the direction of the fixed point to which the cable is fastened. If the outboard end of the cable is made fast to an anchor the operation is properly called "kedging." It is a rather dangerous operation in close quarters for, if the line parts, the ship has little steerageway and is liable to drift foul of some projection before it can be gotten under way.

15. West Indian Fortifications

West Indian forts were nearly always erected in a hurry because the inhabitants disliked to spend the money until Mars was removing his hat and coat in the vestibule. The temporary forts were built by Negro laborers, theoretically under *corvées* apportioned and commandeered by the governors. The French commandants were sometimes hampered in their engineering efforts by shortages of food for the laborers, although such shortages were often artificial, created by uncooperative planters. Ordinarily the labor was not paid for, but Beauharnois at Martinique in the face of landlord apathy had to hire labor for his forts. The service was especially unpopular at harvest time, or in parts distant from the workers' home plantations. Most planters objected to having their slaves mixed with others, since they thought it bad for discipline. The frequent money commutation of *corvées* was of little assistance, because the revenues were just as hard to collect. Pares, *War and Trade,* 240-243.

16. The Carcass

The carcass was kin to a shell, but was incendiary rather than explosive, and was used to cause fires and as a flare to guide night artillery fire. It was frequently packed with charged pistol barrels of various lengths which fired from time to time, thus causing them to be approached cautiously, at best, by would-be extinguishers. The carcass used by the Royal Navy was probably loaded with a mixture of wax, sulphur, nitre, and gun powder, and therefore could not be extinguished by the use of water. See Falconer, *The Mariner's New and Complete Naval Dictionary* (3d edn., 1804).

17. NAVAL HYGIENE

The Royal Navy had a very bad reputation for hygiene in the eighteenth century, and Moore's need of men was no doubt real. The subject of naval ill health was one that called forth "letters to the editor." Such a letter was written by Thomas Reynolds, who said he was a former surgeon, to the editor of the *Gentleman's Magazine*, 28 (1758), 61, 105, 157, 207.

To preserve the seamen's health he advocated four reforms for the navy. (1) Impressed men were worked in the clothing in which they were taken until their pay had accumulated to a point where they could get clothing from the purser, because the officers feared they would desert with new clothing if allowed to get it on credit. Therefore green hands lived in clothing which was often wet, and always dirty (and, we may add, lousy). He suggested that each seaman be immediately issued four shirts and two each of all other articles of clothing. Officers should frequently inspect the men's clothing and should punish those who literally lost their shirts by gambling, or who sold their clothes for drink. Further, he thought the clothing should be of better quality than that provided at the time, since it frequently went to pieces in a few days. (2) The navy made no particular provision for milder fare for the sick. Such food, if it was to be had, was paid for out of the officers' pockets. To feed the sick the navy should carry live meat, and soup stock. (3) Sick men's berths should be ventilated, or, better, they should all be kept together. As it was, no one place was provided for sick men unless, as frequently true, they were given the pump dale berths, which were the berths under the troughs which carried water over the side from the chain pumps and which were the most dangerous berths in which they could be placed. He advocated that the sick should be put together in the gun room. Being scattered over the ship, they were not seen by the surgeons as frequently as they otherwise could have been. Further, their messmates used the "sitting

APPENDIX   195

up with a sick friend" excuse to absent themselves from duty, get candles and have parties in their own berths. (4) Surgeons should be encouraged to keep case histories and disseminate them in published journals.

18. MISSING STAYS

To stay a vessel is to tack her so that the wind from being on one side of the ship is brought to blow on the other side, by turning her head from one side to the other. When a vessel is attempting this maneuver but fails to come to the other tack and hangs helplessly with her bow pointing directly into the wind she is said to have "missed stays," as did the *Falcon* on 17 April 1759. In such a position the ship may make sternway, i.e., drift "backwards," for some distance before she can be maneuvered so that her sails again feel the force of the wind and drive her forward. When a small sailboat misses stays you simply poke the boom out to one side with an oar or any pole available, push the tiller to the opposite side, and she spins about like a top and all is well. In a vessel as large as the *Falcon*, a foresail would be put to one side, the tiller (the long handle which controls the rudder) would be put to the other side, and, if there were time and room enough, she would eventually come about. The *Falcon* must have drifted on to a bar or reef while moving backwards, lacking time and room for the maneuver.

To use a rather strained analogy, which may make the matter clearer to landsmen and motor boatmen, a weather vane spends most of its existence "in stays," pointing directly into the wind. On sailing craft the job is to balance the wind resistance ahead of and behind the axis so that the ship does *not* act as a weathervane. There are many good manuals which introduce beginners to the art and science of sailing. The writings of any of the following may be profitably consulted on these matters, H. A. Calahan, W. F. Crosby, E. F. Knight, and Peter Heaton.

19. INFANTRY TACTICS

Space does not permit an extensive examination of eighteenth-century infantry tactics but some clarification of the subject is possible in a few words. The controlling limit was the fact that the musket was not accurate at a range of more than about fifty yards. This helps to account for the fewness of the casualties suffered in such warfare, but woe to the mass of men who got within range!—the musket shot balls which ran twelve to the pound and knocked men down as though they had been struck by pile drivers. Regular forces fought in close formations and moved in a manner quite similar to modern close-order drill which all civilians have seen on occasions of military displays and pageantry, if only in the news reels or on television. The use of infantry was analogous to the modern use of state troops against mobs of rioters, with this difference, that the enemy was not usually a mob. It was the object of infantry commanders to turn the more or less disciplined enemy forces into a mob by the shocking-power of a volley delivered at close range, followed by a bayonet charge. Once the regular formation of the enemy was smashed by casualties or, more likely, by fear, the opposing force was nothing but a mob and was unable to put up any systematic resistance. Then, like policemen in formation, the attacking force moved forward to "break it up" and "keep moving." Because the arms of the soldier were relatively poor, the aim of the commanders was the total disorganization and, if possible, the capture of the enemy, rather than his annihilation by fire power.

To achieve the above effects the troops marched toward the enemy in rank, at sixty steps to the minute, with bands, fifes, and drums sounding. It is often recorded that they halted under fire to "dress right, DRESS," in order to preserve their formation on which the effectiveness of their volley fire depended. All firing was done at command, "by the numbers." Of course, infiltration with accurate, rapidly firing weapons made these tactics obsolete.

20. To Spike a Gun

To spike a gun was to drive a large nail or spike into the vent, which was the hole through which the powder was touched off. The gun could not be used again until the spike was drilled out, which, in the field, could not always be done easily or speedily. This tactic was used only when it was impossible to use the cannon, either for lack of equipment, or, in the case of an army's

APPENDIX

own guns, when a hasty retreat was planned which would not admit of retiring the guns with the troops.

21. CONVOYING MERCHANTMEN

In convoying merchantmen, the ships of the line sailed ahead in a circular formation, the circle enclosing the trade. The following diagram explains the formation.

```
                              c
                              f
                           s xxx s
Legend:                  s xxxxxxx s
                       s xxxxxxxxxxxxx s
c—cruiser(s)         s xxxxxxxxxxxxxxx s
s—ship of the line   s xxxxxxxxxxxxxxx s
                     s xxxxxxxxxxxxxxx s
f—flagship             s xxxxxxxxxxxxx s
                          s xxxxxxxx s
x—merchantman             s  xxxx  s
b—bomb ketch               s  b  s
                              b b
                               s
```

The diagram is not made to scale. The course of the ships would be in the direction of a line drawn through the cruiser from the flagship. The most frequent danger to such a convoy in those ante-steam and ante-submarine days was the attack of one or more trim privateers, which in most cases would be faster and more maneuverable than the wallowing high-walled ships of the line. In the above formation they would have to go through the line of heavy ships, cut out a rich sugar ship, and then take her back through the line of protectors. To get out would be much more difficult than to get in. The ships most distant from the flagship would be more easily taken than those in the van. This was probably the reason why the fleeter bombs were posted astern of the "trade." The frigates were needed ahead as "cruisers" to run down to strange craft ahead in order to identify them before the fleet came into the immediate vicinity of the strangers. The formation is from an illustration in Gardiner, *The West Indies*. Gardiner's account of this passage is on pp. 86-90.

22. CONDITIONS OF WEST INDIAN NAVAL SERVICE

Provisions: The British were chiefly provisioned by local contractors, who secured most of the supplies from North America. The French brought their own rations from France.

Personnel: The crews who sailed and fought in the ships under the Union Jack were relatively smaller than the French, but since some ships were permanently on the station many of the seamen were acclimated. Their enemies had to expect a good deal of sickness on arrival from France.

Blockade efficiency: The British, because of their flexible system of supply, could maintain an effective blockade of the French in any one locality, but, because of their precarious food supply, the French could not return the disfavor.

Maintenance: British vessels were not efficiently repaired, nor were they often cleaned, but the French came from home bases with good equipment and clean bottoms. As a result they often outsailed the British ships. However the British could quickly be made seaworthy, after a fashion, if disabled in action; the French had almost no local repair facilities.

Hurricanes: Since the British were always to be found in the islands they were frequently exposed to hurricanes. On the other hand, their enemies were rarely in those waters during the summer and fall seasons.

Effects of policy: The British station system was a permanent dispersal system. The Channel fleets and Gibraltar were the real defenses of the West Indies. The flotillas on the out stations were too weak to defend them against a strong force, and, in any crisis, needed re-enforcement from Britain. The French kept the British guessing as to their objectives by their annual assembly of ships and frequent redistributions of forces.

For greater detail see Pares, *War and Trade,* 279-288.

Bibliographical Note

With a few exceptions the materials used as sources fall into two categories, the memoirs of witnesses and executive documents. Without exception the memoirs are those of army or navy officers. The executive documents consist of letters and orders written by the elder Pitt, in Colonial Office 5/215, 1757-1763, most of which with the replies thereto have been edited for publication by Gertrude Selwyn Kimball, *Correspondence of William Pitt, When Secretary of State* (2 vols., New York, 1906); there are also the reports of Generals Hopson and Barrington and Commodore Moore in Colonial Office 110/1, 1758-1761. These Colonial Office papers have been transcribed for the Library of Congress. Related executive documents will be found in Admiralty Secretary, In Letters, Admiralty 1/306, 1/307, and Admiralty Secretary, Out Letters, Secret Orders and Letters, 1745-1761, Admiralty 2/1331, all preserved in the Public Record Office, London. British memoirs are in Loudoun Papers, Letters and Enclosures from Walter Pringle, Huntington Library, San Marino, California, and in the Newcastle Papers, Additional MSS. 32887, 32891, 32893, British Museum, London. Commodore Moore's laconic "Journal" is in Admiralty 50/22, Admirals' and Captains' Journals, Public Record Office. Related materials of lesser importance are in Treasury 1, Bundle 390, and War Office 1/5, copies of both being in the Library of Congress.

Except for one document in Archives de la Guerre (Corresp. Suppt. A429) of which a copy is in the Library of Congress, almost all of the French sources are concentrated in the Archives nationales, Marine et colonies (B⁴ 91, B⁴ 92, C⁸ A 62) because in the French government the Ministry of Marine administered colonial affairs. This includes the vast collection of depositions taken in 1760 during hearings in Martinique, seeking to determine responsibility for the fall of Guadeloupe, the merit of which is commented on in my preface. Other documents are there also, most of them arranged and selected so as to achieve an effect in the mind of the reader.

The most valuable British printed sources, in addition to the writings of Pitt mentioned above, are Richard Gardiner, *Account of the Expedition against Martinico, with the Reduction of Guadeloupe etc.*, of which this writer used the third edition, Birmingham, 1762, and Robert Beatson, *Naval and Military Memoirs, 1727-1783* (6 vols., London, 1804), which appears to lean on Gardiner for chronology. The *Gentleman's Magazine*, vols. 28-31, gives a valuable tapestry of the contemporary British scene with occasional scraps of directly useful information. One French document has been printed by Henri Malo, "L'échec des Anglais a la Martinique en 1759," *Feuilles d'Histoire*, 8(1912) 1-12, a rather free rendering of an anonymous document in Marine et colonies, C⁸ A 62. An English translation of this document appeared in the *South-Carolina Gazette*, 26 May 1759.

Useful secondary materials are notable for the brevity of their treatment of this campaign. The best (and it is very good) is Richard Pares, *War and Trade in the West Indies, 1739-1763* (Oxford, 1936). Very readable but occasionally careless is Sir Julian Corbett, *England in the Seven Years' War* (2 vols., London, 1907). For understandable reasons, French historians have slighted the subject. The best French account is in volume III of Richard Waddington, *La guerre de sept ans* (5 vols., Paris, 1899-1914), volume III of William Laird Clowes, *The Royal Navy* (7 vols., London, 1897-1903), and volume II of Sir John Fortescue, *History of the British Army* (13 vols., London, 1899-1930), have helpful but brief accounts. Lawrence Henry Gipson's monumental history, *The British Empire before the American Revolution*, has an excellent summary in Volume VIII.

BIBLIOGRAPHICAL NOTE

Certain reference works are indispensable for this study in addition to the usual encyclopaedias and biographical dictionaries. William Falconer, *The Mariner's New and Complete Naval Dictionary,* many editions, is the necessary guide to eighteenth-century sea faring. Volume II of the United States Department of the Navy, Hydrographic Office, *Sailing Directions for the West Indies,* many editions, is of greatest utility as are the same office's many charts of the islands and their anchorages. For the geography of the place the best is the production of the Société d'Éditions Géographiques, Maritimes et Coloniales, directed by G. Grandidier, *Antilles Françaises,* which is carte 37 of their *Atlas des Colonies Françaises* (Paris, 1934), containing the only good topographical map of Guadeloupe.

Index

Abbeville, 32
Admiralty, 74, 173, 181; preparations for expedition, 26, 28, 29, 31; policy for Leeward Islands, 35; learns of arrival at Martinique, 43n
Africa, 6, 7, 8, 183; near war, 12; attack planned, 17
Aix-la-Chapelle, Treaty of, 11, 16n, 19
Albany Congress, 10
Alexander, Charles, 33
Amazon frigate, 26, 66
America, 3, 10, 13
American Independence, War for, 132
Amétiste ship, 116
Amherst, General Jeffrey, 20-1, 32, 157, 157n
Anglo-Dutch Treaties, 132
Anson, George, Admiral Lord, 17, 20, 74, 90, 142-3
Anson ship, 30
Antigua (island), 66, 99n, 160; governor, 36; recruits from, 37, 115-6, 123, 129, 136, 154, 175; supplies, 73n, 96, 108, 150; invalids sent to, 90, 91, 99, 107, 110; squadron base, 114; has full information of Bompar, 116n; *Rippon* at, 118; Bompar's arrival proclaimed, 119; squadron sails to, 159; trade with, 182
Antigua *Gazette*, 37n
Antigua Passage, 168
Armiger, General Robert, 47; his commands, 22, 23; jealousy of, 23-4; in Council, 105-7; returns home, 150; promoted, 161
Army. *See* name of army, as Austrian Army
Arnoville, 127, 127n, 130, 137
Artillery, Royal Regiment of, detachment serves, 22; in action of 17 Jan., 49-50; how landed, 52n; casualties through Feb., 109n; organization of, 187; how guns spiked, 196-7
Austrian Army, 13

Baie la Mahault, 127, 128, 132
Ball, Major Thomas, 22, 104, 155
Barbados (island), 23n, 91, 145; and neutral islands, 12; movement from Britain to, 20, 34, 35; operation staged at, 25, 28, 37, 38, 46n, 150, 173-4; recruits and supplies from, 21, 99, 108, 109, 110; sugar industry at, 74, 159; militia, 124; illegal trade of, 171-3; Beauharnois contemplates attacking, 179; naval value, 184
Barbados sloop, 26
Barlow, Lieutenant Colonel John, 22, 123, 136, 162
Barnes, John, 99
Barrington, General John, 25, 37, 91n, 109, 112, 126, 160, 179, 180, 184, 187; Pitt's choice, 19; deputes regimental command, 22; Armiger jealous of, 24; recommends landing at Negro Point, 46; land Council sends to Moore, 53, 55; not consulted at St. Pierre, 62; thinks of sending sick to North America, 91; energy of, 93; urges attack on Grand Terre, 96, 102; reopens evacuation question, 101n; succeeds to chief command, 102, 105-7; protests order to send 42nd Regiment away, 107-8; optimism of, 108; second report to Pitt, 108-9; reembarks, 111-2; force guarded by Moore, 114, 167, 168, 169; reaction to Bompar's arrival, 115-6; situation at Grand Terre, 120-2; responsibility for holding Ft. Louis, 123; planning, 123-4, 127-8; death, 128n; ill, 129; headquarters at Petit Bourg, 138; receives capitulations, 139-43; on Beau-

harnois landing, 144-5; summary of events to Pitt, 149-50; popularity, 151; on taking St. Lucia, 152-3; confirmed in command, 154; return home, 155, 157-8; sends troops to Amherst, 157, 157n; promoted, 161; responsibility of, 163, 164; critique of exercise of command, 164-6; tactics, 176; desperate, 177; praised by King George, 181; author of the victory, 185
Barrington, William, 2d Viscount, 23, 102n, 112n, 181
Basse Terre Citadel, 93; described, 76-7; garrison drunk, 82, 83n; surrendered or abandoned, 85-6; mined, 87, 87n, 91n; strength of, 89, 115, 122; governor named, 98; governor killed, 126; British garrison, 105, 109, 164
Basse Terre city, 73, 99-100, 167; reduction and occupation of, 76-86, 88, 93, 151, 173; egress from, 88; casualties at, 89; distance to Dos D'Âne, 92; *Lancaster* arrives, 100; troops reembarked, 111; troops ferried from, 166; unsafe water supply, 180
Basse Terre Island, 114, 120, 135; described, 70-3, 165; half conquered, 127; capitulation, 141, 142
Basse Terre Roads, 73, 123-4, 127, 156; squadron steers for, 65; reconnaissance of, 75; squadron returns to, 104; distance to St. Eustatius, 134; unguarded, 116; ship rendezvous, 155; privateer base, 182
Battalions. *See* Regiments
Bayne, Commander William, 66n, 112
Bayonet, 103, 103n-4n
Beatson, Practitioner Robert, engineer officer, 22; late arrival, 36; early career, 61n; on prizes, 63, 69; on Light Infantry, 93; on weather, 128
Beauharnois, François, Marquis de, 138; knowledge of British intentions, 40n; claims damage to British vessel, 43n; neglect by, 50-1, 51n, 69; ships his property, 57n; low spirits, 58-9; satirized, 59; aid to Guadeloupe, 75, 75n, 175, 176-7; letter to Treil intercepted, 139; lands at Grand Terre, 143-7, 179; culpability, 177-8, 177n, 179; and Martinique landlords, 193
Beaulés, Lieutenant Joseph de, loses Ft. Louis, 102-4; unwilling to fight, 144; outlook for, 145; culpability, 177; sentenced, 181
Beckford, Alderman William, 15n, 16, 16n, 90
Bell-Isle, Charles, Duc de, 181, 182n
Bellona frigate, 43, 43n, 57n

Ben Nevis, 72
Bermuda, 35
Bernis, François Cardinal, 32
Berryer, 182
Berwick ship, ordered to West Indies, 25; departure, 34; action at Basse Terre, 78, 79, 82; reconnaissance of coast, 102-3; loses lieutenant, 104; sails against Marie Galante, 154-5
Black Watch. *See* Regiment—42nd
Bligh, General Thomas, 17, 30
Boats. *See* Landing craft
Bomb ketches, 190
Bombs, 190
Bompar, General and Chef d'Escadre Maximin de, 157, 174; brings force to West Indies, 113, 116-7, 126; spies on British, 118n; lands on Grand Terre, 119-20, 136n, 143-7, 153, 166-70; dependent on Dutch supplies, 134; unequal to British fleet, 139; relations with Treil, 144; to Grenada, 156; on poor state of French islands, 156n, 182; returns home, 160-1; visits San Domingo, 161n; criticized, 177, 178-9; not up to expectations, 181-2
Bonetta bomb, 102-3
Boscawen, Admiral Edward, 66n, 161
Boscawen, General George, 23, 23n, 24
Braddock, General Edward, 13, 51, 57, 67
Brest, 160, 161
Bridgetown, Barbados, 34
Brigades, 22-23
Brilliant ship, 91-2
Bristol ship, 43; on Leeward Islands Station, 26; used for sounding, 39, 41-2; at Negro Point, 44-5; off Basse Terre Citadel, 76, 78, 82, 82n, 84, 85; given to Parker, 100; blockades St. Eustatius, 118, 134-5; chases British ships, 146; sails against Marie Galante, 154
British Army, 18, 18n
British East India Company, 8
British Honduras, 183
British West Indies, 6; smuggling, 7; Army in, 18; defenses, 124; Bompar ignores, 178-9
Buckingham ship, Tyrrel commands, 78, 99; joins squadron, 88; given to Leslie, 100; covers Basse Terre garrison, 111, 116, 126; given to Parker, 162
Burford ship, ordered to West Indies, 25; Gambier commands, 52n; off Basse Terre Citadel, 78, 79, 81, 82
Burgoyne, General John, 51, 52n
Burnett, Captain Thomas, 26, 62, 85
Burt, William Mathew, 33, 84-85, 88-89, 99

INDEX
205

Bute, John Stuart, Earl of, 183
Byng, Admiral John, 13, 66, 67; Moore on court martial of, 19; trial on board St. George, 26; effect of execution, 164n

Cambridge ship, 52, 53, 54, 62; commanded by Moore, 20; flagship, 26, 35, 60, 100; blown to leeward, 59; at Basse Terre Citadel, 78, 79, 81
Campbell, Lieutenant Archibald, 162
Campbell, Captain Colin, 56, 56n
Campbell, Major ———, 23n
Canada, 183, 184, 185; endangered, 9-10; Pitt on, 16; Newcastle on, 17; Amherst to invade, 21; trade compared with Guadeloupe's, 73
Cape Breton Island, 9, 73, 184
Capesterre, 127, 128, 137-8
Carcass, 84, 193
Caribbean Sea, 7, 168
Carlisle Bay, 28, 34, 35
Carronade, 66n
Cas Navires Bay, 45-9, 50, 52
Catamarans, 52n, 101
Catholics, 98, 102n
Channing, Edward, 184
Charles II, King of England, 11
Charleston, S. C., 100n
Chaundy, Lieutenant ———, 80-81
Cherbourg, 17, 30, 32
Choiseul, Etienne François, Duc de, 183-4
Clainvilliers, Dubourg de, 138-43
Clavering, Lieutenant Colonel John, commands Second Brigade, 23; recommends landing at Negro Point, 46; parley with Treil, 95; reconnoiters south coast, 102, 105; signs Council articles, 107; career, 128n; leads unsuccessful surprise, 128-9; leads final drive for Capesterre, 129-32; reports supplies at Baie la Mahault, 135; strengthens Petit Bourg, 136; storms Ste. Marie, 136-7; takes dispatches home, 149, 150, 153, 157; *aide-de-camp* to King George II, 161; praised by Barrington, 165; tactics, 176
Clarke, Captain Edward, 26
Cleaveland, Major Samuel, 22, 29-30, 89, 99
Cleiland, Captain ———, 95
Clevland, John, Secretary of the Admiralty, 17
Clive, General Robert, 13, 14
Closterseven. *See* Kloster Seven
Cochons, Isles des, 103, 149, 155
Cohorn, 98, 98n
Coin, Rivière du, 127n, 129-130
Commodore, 20n, 186-7

Conflans, Hubert de Brienne, Admiral le Comte de, 161
Constitution ship, 190
Convoy formation, 197
Cornwallis, Charles, Lord, 184
Cotes, Admiral Thomas, 156n
Crown Point, 13
Crump, Lieutenant Colonel Byam, 56; commands 4th Regiment, 22; commands 2nd Brigade, 23; action of 17 Jan., 49, 50; on Guadeloupe revenues, 74, 74n; leads raid, 96; leads attack on Ste. Anne and St. François, 123, 125; leads unsuccessful surprise, 128-9; in final drive for Capesterre, 129-32; on supplies at Baie la Mahault, 135; destroys property, 138; Governor of Guadeloupe, 149, 157; promotes espionage, 160; dies, 160, 180; a Brigadier, 162; praised by Barrington, 165
Cuba, 184
Cumberland, William Augustus, Duke of, 13, 24n
Cunningham, Captain ———, Deputy Quartermaster General, 21-22, 43, 75
Cunninghame, Lieutenant Colonel William, Engineer Officer, 22; surveys *Diamond*, 30; late arrival at Barbados, 36; reconnaissance of Fort Royale Bay, 43; on difficulties at Martinique, 51-52; reconnaissance of Basse Terre Roads, 75; reports on Basse Terre Citadel, 76; on strength of Basse Terre Citadel, 89, 108, 109, 173; deprecates Ft. Louis, 122-3; repairs Basse Terre Citadel, 126
Cust, Lieutenant General Edward, 58

Dalrymple, Lieutenant Colonel Campbell, 160
Danish West Indies, 74, 135
Deacon, Commander Sabine, 25
Debrissay, Lieutenant Colonel Peter, 116, 122; commands 63rd Regiment, 22; action of 17 Jan., 49; action of 3 Feb., 97-8; Governor of Basse Terre Citadel, 98, 108; sally, 111; killed, 126
Désirade (island), 70, 154, 182
Devonshire ship, 20
Diamond Rock, 40, 42
Diamond ship, 20, 30
Dolphin ship, 27
Dominica (island), 120, 143, 167; a neutral island, 12; loyal to France, 16n; altitudes, 72; squadron near, 75, 76; volunteers from, 77, 142; description, 118; satires on naval operations, 147; illegal trade of, 182
Dominica Passage, 168

Dos D'Âne (Guadeloupe), 93n, 107, 111, 138, 164; inhabitants withdraw to, 77, 101-2, 101n; fortified, 88, 91, 177; description, 92; decision not to assault, 106-7; garrison pinned, 122; prospects of siege, 139
Douglas, Sir James, 160
Drafts, 20n, 187
Drake, Sir Francis, 153-4
Dublin ship, 160
Duqueray, ——, 138, 138n
Du Treil, Nadau. *See* Treil, Nadau Du
Ducharmey, Mme. ——, 94, 96-7, 100, 102, 108
Duquesne, Fort, 13, 14

East Kent Regiment. *See* Regiment—3rd
Eccentric attack, 14, 186
Emerald frigate, 119, 146
"Encirclement," 9
England, 26, 28, 35, 91, 109
English Channel, 32, 34, 198
English Harbour, Antigua, 90, 117

Falcon bomb, 25, 29, 119, 195
Flanders, 17, 40n, 65n
Florissant ship, 43-44, 99n
Forbes, General John, 13
Fort de France (city). *See* Fort Royale (city).
Fort Royale Bay, 40n, 42-3, 99n, 192; Bompar in, 114, 146; Moore leaves open, 167, 168, 170-1
Fort Royale Citadel, Guadeloupe. *See* Basse Terre Citadel
Fort Royale (city) 93; expedition approaches, 39; description, 39n; decision to attack, 42; defenses, 42, 51-2, 53-4, 58-9; and St. Pierre, 60, 61; British operations criticized, 66, 67-8
Fortifications, 193
France, 178; rivalry with Great Britain, 3-13; military state in 1758, 16; inclined toward peace, 17; blockaded, 73; few supplies exported, 91, 197; colonists educated in, 140
Frankland, Captain Thomas, 16n
Frederick, King of Prussia, 13
French Army, 13, 141, 141n
French Navy, 26, 197-8
French West Indies, 6, 18, 26, 31; illegal trade, 6-7; windward islands taken, 15; rivals of Jamaica, 16n; precarious state, 73-4, 156, 178-9; restored to France, 183
Frigate, 101n, 190

Galion, Rivière, 97, 106

Gambier, James, Admiral Lord, 52n
Gambier, Captain James, commands *Burford*, 25; early career, 52n; council with Hopson, 52-3; fires on *Panther*, 79; supervises landing, 85; parley with Treil, 95
Gardiner, Captain Richard, animadversions against Moore, 23n, 67-69, 76, 104; on passage to islands, 34-5; career and personality of, 39n-40n; on attack at Negro Point, 44-5, 44n-5n; action of 17 Jan., 50; on St. Pierre attack, 61, 62-5; on health at English Harbour, 90; on Prince Rupert Bay, 115; on blockade of St. Eustatius, 133, 133n, 134-5
Gayton, Captain Clark, 25, 81n-2n
Gentleman's Magazine, 151, 158
George, Fort. *See* Louis, Fort
George II, King of England, 28, 140, 173; chooses land commander, 19; "impatient," 29; "still impatient," 31; report from Tyrrel, 90; pleased by victory, 181
Gibraltar, 18, 102n, 198
Goree, 14, 104
Gorget, 192
Goyave, 127, 128-9, 135, 136
Gozier, 123, 124-5, 124n
Granada bomb, 26, 131
Grand cul-de-sac, 70
Grand Terre, 113, 114, 145; Marines attack, 23n, 102-4; description, 70-3; decision to invade, 105-7; defense, 123n, 125; casualties, 125-6; conquered, 127, 128, 141, 142, 179; transports from, 155; desertions, 165; fertility, 183
Great Britain, rivalry with France, 3-13; financial burdens, 17; garrison of, 18; island produce to, 140
Grenada (island), 168, 184; visited by *Emerald*, 119; Bompar at, 156, 166, 169, 179; privateering, 170
Grenadiers, 47, 47n, 48, 49; action of 3 Feb., 97-8; described, 192
Griffin frigate, 26, 119, 146, 146n
Guadeloupe (island), 14, 26, 31n, 40n, 52n, 65n, 66n, 90, 93, 114, 119, 120, 122, 128n, 140, 160, 168, 178, 179, 181-2; in diplomacy, 15, 181, 183; Horace Walpole on, 17; French knowledge of British intentions, 32; attack proposed, 65, 68, 186; news of first success at, 66; small aid from Martinique to, 67; description and maps, 70-75, 162; squadron arrives, 75-6; defense of, 77, 92-3, 123n, 174-81, 185; health in, 90-1, 110, 110n, 180-1; governor characterized, 92;

split by fall of Ft. Louis, 104; cost of living, 112; progress of operation as of March, 127; blockade of, 133-5; Marie Galante (island) necessary for security of, 150; British garrison of, 154, 157, 158-9; sugar to England, 158; private property shipped out, 160-1; privateering, 170-1; value, 182, 184; summary of war in, 185

Haiti, 135
Haldane, Lieutenant Colonel George, commands 2nd Brigade, 22; Governor-designate of Jamaica, 23; suspects espionage, 33; on landing site, Martinique, 46-8 on action of 17 Jan., 49; on enemy fire, 51; opinion of attack at Martinique, 52; not consulted at St. Pierre, 64; reference to militia as "Indians," 67; on disorder at Basse Terre, 86; "proceedings" sent to Pitt, 88; on prospects at Guadeloupe, 94; in Council of War, 105-7; departs for Jamaica, 119, 122, 149; dies, 180
Hampshire ship, 27
Hanover, Kingdom of, 13
Hardwicke, Philip Yorke, Earl of, 142-3, 158, 181
Harman, Captain William, commands *Berwick*, 25; departure, 34; council with Hopson, 52-3; leads naval attack at Ft. Louis, 103; Pitt's approbation of, 104; blockades Guadeloupe, 134
Hastings, Warren, 128n
Havana, 14
Hawke, Admiral Edward, 20, 160
Henry and John ship, 29, 30, 31, 32
Holmes, Admiral Charles, 180
Hood, Captain Samuel, Viscount, 43n, 57n
Hopson, General Peregrine Thomas, 47, 107, 108, 161, 175; chosen by King George II, 19; embarkation activity of, 20-2, 24-5, 28-34; staging in islands, 36-38; orders reconnaissance of Fort Royale Bay, 43; on Negro Point landing, 46; operations at Martinique, 48-53; embarkation at Martinique, 55-9; off St. Pierre, 62, 64-5; Walpole on, 66-7; reconnoiters Basse Terre city, 76; with Moore during bombardment, 78; landing at Basse Terre, 83; sends dispatches, 88, 96, 112, 151; letter to Governor of Guadeloupe, 89; decline and death, 90, 93, 98-102, 105, 180; headquarters, 94; manifesto of, 98; seeks recruits, 99; critique of his command, 136n, 164
Hospital ships, 38, 88
Houelbourg, 127
Howe, Richard, Earl, 17, 30
Hudson's Bay Company, 8
Hughes, Captain Robert, 27, 100; convoy commander, 20; takes 800 Marines, 23n; receives orders, 28; departure difficulties, 28-34; squadron straggles, 36, 156; made Commodore, 155; convoys sugars to Britain, 159

Illness, before arrival in islands, 32-3, 34; surgeons engaged, 36; at Barbados, 38; health conditions of Guadeloupe, 72; in forces at Guadeloupe, 90-1, 91n; sick to Antigua, 99; increasing, 108-9, 110; deaths after victory, 164n; health conditions of West Indies, 180-1; naval hygiene indicted, 194-5; effect on navies, 198
Impressment, 191
India, 6, 14, 18, 183
Infantry, 189-90, 192, 195-6
Infernal bomb, 26
Innes, Captain Peter, 89
Invasion, defined, 186
Isabella and Mary ship, 30

Jacobite Rebellion (1745), 33
Jamaica (island), 33; as market, 7; governor's income, 7n; Spanish trade of, 12; Beckford's interest in, 16n; Governor Haldane, 22-3, 149; not visited by fleet, 35; Governor Trelawney, 41n; productivity compared with Guadeloupe's, 73; dock yards, 117; militia, 124; naval defenses, 156, 156n; shelter for fleet, 169; health conditions, 180; trade of, 182
Jeffries, Thomas, 162
Jekyll, Captain Edward, 50; commands *Rippon*, 25; attacks Negro Point, 43; engaged at St. Pierre, 62-5; in action, Basse Terre Roads, 79-84; seeks Bompar, 156
Juno ship, 27

Keppel, Captain Augustus, 19, 104
King George's War, 11
King William's War, 10
Kingfisher bomb, 25, 29
Kloster Seven, Convention of, 13, 24n

Lancaster ship, 30, 31n, 100
Landing craft, training in, 36; described, 36n; use at Martinique, 46, 46n; at Guadeloupe, 60, 83. *See also* Catamarans

Langrage shot, 100, 100n
Le Cras, Captain Edward, 25, 75
Leeward Islands, 90, 99n; war starts in, 16n; British garrison, 18; Moore commands naval station, 20; governor to assist Hopson, 21; British ships on station, 26, 36; sugar production, 74; privateering, 75; recruits from, 99; new commodore, 160
Leslie, Lieutenant George, 89
Leslie, Captain Lachlin, commands *Bristol*, 26; sounds Fort Royale Bay, 39; attacks Negro Point, 43-5; commands *Buckingham*, 100; temporary commodore, 104
Lesser Antilles, 70, 72, 73, 184
Lezarde, Rivière, 131, 131n
Ligonier, John, Viscount, 24, 24n
London, 20, 36, 66, 152, 163, 170, 179n, 181, 183
London ship, 36n
Loudoun, John Campbell, Earl of, 57-8, 88
Louis XV, King of France, 16n, 32
Louis, Fort (Guadeloupe), 72, 123, 123n, 134, 155, 167, 179, 180; captured, 23n, 102-4, 124n, 125, 151; Barrington resolves to hold, 106, 107, 115; troops ferried to, 111-3, 166; value of, 114, 120, 122, 152, 167n, 168; twin sallies from, 125; reinforces Basse Terre Citadel, 126; repaired, 149
Louisbourg, captured, 13-4; Pitt's evaluation of, 15-7, 181; Hopson governor of, 19; Gambier at, 52n
Louisiana, 9, 10
Ludlow Castle frigate, convoys 42nd Regiment, 26; arrives in islands, 37; silences battery, 100; blockades St. Eustatius, 134, 134n; sails against Marie Galante, 154; to Jamaica, 156
Lynn, Captain Thomas, 64
Lyon ship, 40-1, 43; ordered to islands, 25; Trelawney commands, 40n; blown to leeward, 44, 53; action in Basse Terre Roads, 78-81; helps to land Artillery, 101

McHenry, Fort, 190
McKaarg, Captain John, 56n
Mackenzie, Captain George, 25
Mackenzie, Commander James, 26
Magloire, Rev. Roger, S. J., 95n, 107n
Man, Captain Robert, 30, 100
Manchester Regiment. *See* Regiment—63rd
Manila, 14
Marie Galante (island), 70, 145, 146; to be attacked, 139, 150, 153; surrenders, 154-5; restored to France, 183
Marines. *British:* in fleet, 23; Gardiner in, 40n; attack Negro Point, 44-5, 44n; proposed to assist soldiers, 53; losses aboard *Rippon*, 84; ashore at Basse Terre City, 85; take Ft. Louis, 103-4; augmented by soldiers, 115; no shore leave, 173. *French:* defend Guadeloupe, 77; low quality, 175
Martinique, 16n, 34n, 39, 40n, 46, 52n, 89, 107, 114, 136n, 139, 146, 160, 169, 175, 179, 179n, 181-2, 184; Pitt's view of, 14-7; to be attacked from Barbados, 20; aided by Dutch, 26, 99n, 133; forewarned, 32, 36, 37; attacked, 38-42, 47-51, 59n, 185; description and map, 39n, 41; defense, 57-9, 67, 67n, 69, 143, 154, 160-1, 177-8, 177n, 193; relation to St. Pierre, 60; aid to Guadeloupe, 67, 77, 91-2, 126, 141, 145; in campaign of 1762, 68; relation to Guadeloupe economy, 73; military value compared with Guadeloupe, 74; privateering, 75, 170-1; prisoner exchange, 98; Bompar and, 113, 116, 144; travelers from Guadeloupe, 147; espionage in, 160; fertility of, 183; restored to France, 183; attack "eccentric," 186
Mediterranean Sea, 13, 15, 52n
Melville, Major Robert, commands detachment of 38th, 22; joins expedition, 37n, 65-6; career, 65n-6n; alleged Light Infantry command, 93; versus Mme. Ducharmey, 93-4, 96-7, 100, 108; wounded, 109n; governor of Citadel, 126, 158; rewarded, 160, 161
Mermaid ship, 82n
Minorca (island), taken by French, 13; Pitt's evaluation of, 14-5, 17, 183, 185; capture frees French fleet, 161
Mississippi River, 9, 15, 184, 185
Monte Cristi, 172
Montserrat (island), 90n, 93, 123
Moore, Henry, D.D., 19
Moore, Commodore John, 28, 37n, 59, 76, 89, 100, 117, 150, 155, 158, 175, 184; chosen naval commander, 19; career, 20, 20n, 26, 35n; staging activities, 20, 21, 25, 35, 36, 38n; quality of "Journal," 23n; accused of misuse of Marines, 23n; and Anglo-French illegal trade, 26; and Martinique operation, 40-1, 42-3, 45-6, 52-5; at St. Pierre, 61-5; proposes attack on Guadeloupe, 65; critique of command in Martinique, 66-9; blockading activities, 75n, 91, 101, 101n,

126, 134, 135, 139; operations off Basse Terre Citadel, 78, 81n-2n, 83, 84-5; letter to Governor of Guadeloupe, 89; on health of fleet, 91; dispatches, 96, 151, 157; manifesto, 98; refuses to evacuate dependents, 101-2, 101n; takes Ft. Louis, 102-4, 113, 125; to Dominica on Bompar's arrival, 113-6, 118, 122; evaded by Beauharnois and Bompar, 119-20, 121, 143-4, 145-7; agrees to capitulations, 139-43, 165; on St. Lucia question, 152-3; convoys sugar fleet, 155-6, 159-60; relieved, 160; responsibilities of, 163-4; critique of command, 166-74, 185

Morne Rouge, 78, 81n
Morne Tartenson, 50-1, 51n, 58
Moule, Le, 70
Moyston, General John, 19n
Muskets, 49

Nassau ship, 155, 155n
Naval stores, 27
Navy. *See* Royal Navy
Negro, Fort. *See* Negro Point
Negro Point, value of, 42; action at, 43-8; garrison moves, 50; limit of naval approach, 52
Negroes, with British Army, 37, 38, 52, 90, 128, 136n, 150; of Guadeloupe, 72-3; in militia, 77, 175; captured by British, 89, 99, 165; assist French, 91-2; fight for Mme. Ducharmey, 96-7; free Negroes confirmed in freedom, 98; help to land artillery, 101; fear of uprisings, 124; disposition of in Capitulations, 140-1; desire to confiscate, 143; allegedly stolen by Beauharnois, 145; unsupervised, 174; slave trading station, 183
Nelson, Admiral Horatio, 100n
Neptune ship, 27
Netherlands West Indies, 26, 59, 74, 92, 128, 132. *See also* St. Eustatius
Neutral islands, 12; taken by British, 15-6; and Treaty of Aix-la-Chapelle, 16n; population, 118; divided at peace, 183
Nevis (island), 93, 182
New England, 7, 9, 27, 70
New Orleans, 184
New Port, 32
Newcastle, Thomas Pelham Holles, Duke of, 158; political function, 13-4; and 1759 campaign, 15n; knowledge of French thought, 16; deprecates raids into France, 17; asked to promote J. Barrington, 112; journal from Haldane, 122; on capitulations, 142-3, 181

Newfoundland, 8, 183
Niagara, Fort, 13
Norfolk ship, 25, 34, 59, 78-9, 81
North America, 6, 52n, 91; illegal trade with, 6-7, 172; territorial rivalry, 11-2, 16; British Army in, 18, 21; 42nd Regiment to, 32, 107; suffers from Guadeloupe privateers, 74; troops sent to, 157, 157n; supplies from, 197
North Atlantic Ocean, 17
North Staffordshire Regiment. *See* Regiment—64th
Nova Scotia, 19, 117

Ohio River, 10, 12
Oswego, Fort, 10, 13
Old Buffs. *See* Regiment—3rd

Pacotilles, 117
Panther ship, 34, 34n; ordered to islands, 25; newly built, 26; action at Cas Navires Bay, 43; action at St. Pierre, 61-3; action at Basse Terre Roads, 78-9, 81-3, 85; off Ft. Louis, 103
Paris, 12, 43n, 179, 182
Parker, Captain Peter, 26, 100, 100n, 162
Parliament, 4, 6, 14
Patrickson, Robert, 99
Pelée, Mont, 61
Pelican bomb, 29
Petit Bourg, surprise attempted, 127-9; advance toward, 130-2; anchorage at, 131n; British headquarters, 135, 138; strengthened, 136
Petit cul-de-sac, 70, 153-4
Petite Terre (island), 70, 154
Pickering, Joseph, 172
"Picquets," 105, 105n-6n
Pigeon Island, 42, 43, 113
Pilots, 53-5
Pinfold, Governor Charles, 36, 38, 172
Pitt, Fort, 13
Pitt, William, 13, 23, 27, 46, 47, 84, 98, 99n, 100, 102n, 104, 105, 108, 112, 119, 127, 144, 152-3, 157; joins cabinet, 14; plan for 1758-1759, 14-5, 17, 185; knowledge of French thought, 16; relations with Beckford, 16n, 90; strengthens army, 18; choice for land commander, 19; quiets Armiger, 24; prods commanders in Britain, 28-34; Guadeloupe suits purposes of, 74-5; to send supplies, 100; orders 42nd Regiment to America, 107-8; on value of St. Lucia, 151; takes Clavering to King George, 157; unifies command, 163-4; communications of, 163n; supports Moore in trouble, 172-3; on utility of the victory, 181

Plymouth, 32, 40n; as port of embarkation, 20, 23n, 28, 29
"Point Peter," 72
Pointe à Pitre, 72, 150, 179, 180
Pompadour, Jeanne, Marquise de, 32
Pool Bar, 29, 30
Portsmouth, 96; assembly of troops at, 20; as port of embarkation, 28-31; new landing craft at, 36n
Portugal, 3
Poterie, Le Roy de la, 86, 87n, 177-8, 181
Prince Rupert's Bay (Dominica), Moore moves to, 114, 116-8, 166; distance to St. Eustatius, 134; British return to, 146-7; squadron leaves, 155; poor choice for vantage point, 167, 167n, 168, 169, 171, 174
Prince William ship, 27
Pringle, Walter, 88
Privateers, French, 15, 70, 74, 75, 170-1; unemployed men, 37; British take Danes and Dutch merchants, 74; prisoner exchange, 172; danger of reduced, 182, 185; convoy protection against, 197
Providence ship, 30
Protestants, 98
Prussia, 13

Quebec, 14, 157
Queen Anne's War, 10-1
Quiberon, 14

Raid, defined, 186
Raisonnable ship, 155
Randell, James, 30
Rations, 27, 109n, 191-2
Regiment:
 Coldstream Guards, 128n
 2nd Guards, 23
 3rd Dragoons, 160
 3rd Guards, 22
 3rd, ordered to Plymouth, 20; commander and brigade, 22; near Basse Terre Citadel, 87, 94, 105, 105n; casualties through February, 109n; casualties, officers, 148; draft from, 157, 157n
 4th, ordered to Plymouth, 20; commander and brigade, 22; casualties at Martinique, 56; near Basse Terre Citadel, 94; casualties through February, 109n; action of 25 March, 123; at Battle of Rivière du Coin, 129-30; casualties, officers, 148n; garrisons Guadeloupe, 157; Barlow made commander, 162
 12th, 40n
 25th, 65n
 (Regiment:)
 38th, 93; condition of, 18; detachment to serve with expedition, 20-1; Melville commands detachment, 22, 23; leaves Antigua, 37n; Melville promoted Major, 65n; joins main force, 65-6; high casualty rate, 108, 109n; casualties, officers, 148n; Melville made commanding officer, 161
 40th, 161
 42nd, sent to West Indies, 25-6, 32, 38; action at Martinique, 47-50; at Basse Terre, 85, 88, 94; at Ft. Louis, 102-4; ordered to North America, 107; casualties through February, 56, 89, 96-7, 108, 109n; action of 25 March, 123; casualties, officers, 148n; at Battle of Rivière du Coin, 129-30; sent to North America, 152, 157, 157n
 61st, ordered to Plymouth, 20; commander and brigade, 22-3; transport stranded, 30-1; garrisons Basse Terre Citadel, 86, 94, 98; Grenadiers, in action of 3 Feb., 97-8; casualties through February, 109n; takes Gozier, 124; casualties, officers, 148n; draft from, 157, 157n; Teesdale commands, 161-2
 63rd, ordered to Plymouth, 20; commander and brigade, 22; completed by drafts, 23n; action at Martinique, 49-50; casualties through February, 89, 109n; near Basse Terre, 94; action of 1 Feb., 96; Grenadiers, action of 3 Feb., 97-8; garrison of Citadel, 98, 111; completed by drafts, 109; men killed accidentally, 126; casualties, officers, 148n; garrisons Guadeloupe, 157; strength report, 180
 64th, Barrington's, 19; ordered to Plymouth, 20; commander and brigade, 22; near Basse Terre, 94; garrisons Ft. Louis, 104; casualties, 109n; casualties, officers, 148n; occupies Marie Galante Island, 155; drafts from, 157, 157n
 65th, ordered to Plymouth, 20; commander and brigade, 22-3; near Basse Terre Citadel, 94; casualties through February, 96-7, 109n; casualties, officers, 148n; garrisons Guadeloupe, 157
 69th, 162
 100th, 56n
Regiments, list of new, 18n; full data published, 37n; all landed at Basse Terre, 85; casualties through February,

INDEX

108n-9n; casualty totals, 148-9, 148n-9n; fully identified, 188
Renown frigate, 25, 103, 119
Reynolds, Thomas, 194-5
Rhode Island, 8
Rippon ship, 40-1, 43, 50, 133; ordered to West Indies, 25; newly built, 26; use of at Martinique, 44-5, 55, 62-5; in action of Basse Terre Roads, 79-81, 81n, 83-4; convoys the sick, 90; helps to land artillery, 101; used as "cruiser," 101n; at Antigua, 117-8; chases British ships, 146; voyage to Grenada, 156-7, 169; Moore charged with neglect of, 68-9, 69n, 166, 173
Rivière, Le Mercier de la, 144n
Robinson, Commander Mark, 25-6
Roebuck frigate, 40-1; action at Martinique, 43, 64; action of Basse Terre Roads, 82, 84-5; sent against Ft. Louis, 103; to English Harbour, 155; convoys troops to America, 157-8
Royal Highlanders. See Regiment—42nd
Royal Lancashire Regiment. See Regiment—4th
Royal Navy, manpower, 18, 191; state and condition in 1758, 25; use of incendiaries, 193-4; bad hygienic practices, 194-5; circumstances of West Indian service, 197-8
Russian Army, 13
Rycaut, Colonel ———, 23, 23n, 85, 103
Rye frigate, 26, 88, 157

St. Christopher (island), 123, 157, 159, 182
Ste. Anne, Guadeloupe, taken, 123, 124n, 124-5; Bompar at, 153, 166, 167
Ste. Anne's Bay, Martinique, 42
Ste. Marie, Guadeloupe, 127, 128-9, 136-7, 136n
Saintes (islands), 70, 76, 119, 154
St. Eustatius (island), trade with French, 57, 77, 143; Tyrrell attacks convoy from, 99n; blockade of, 101, 113, 114n, 134-5, 134n, 135n, 179; described, 132-3
St. François, 123, 124n, 125
St. George ship, ordered to West Indies, 25, 26; flagship, 59; at Basse Terre, 76, 78-9, 81-2, 81n-2n, 84; covers garrison, 111; called away from garrison, 116, 126
St. Helen Roads, 29
St. John's, Antigua, 90, 117
St. Lawrence River, 9, 15
St. Lucia (island), 39, 40; a neutral island, 12; loyal to France, 16n; taken by Samuel Barrington, 102n; population, 118; Pitt orders attack, 151-2; taken by French, 152; stakes of diplomacy, 184
St. Pierre, 40n, 60-1, 78, 82n, 183; deliberations on question of attack, 33, 42, 59, 64-5, 66; description, 60-1; Rippon's attack, 68, 68n; prizes available at, 69; privateering, 170
St. Vincent, 12, 171, 184
Saxon Army, 13
Ségur, Marquise de, 161n
Seven Years' War, 13, 14, 20
Ships. See names of individual ships
Shuldham, Captain Molyneaux, 34; prisoner at Martinique, 15n; commands Panther, 25; early career, 34n; council with Hopson, 52-3; sounds St. Pierre Roads, 61; supervises landing, 85; parley with Treil, 95; reinforces squadron off Ft. Louis, 103
Skene, Captain Robert, 21-2, 157n
Soufrière, 72, 73
South-Carolina Gazette, 54n
South Staffordshire Regiment. See Regiment—38th
Spain, 3, 10, 11
Spanish Main, 182
Spanish Town, 41n
Speedwell sloop, 52n
Spithead, 28-9, 31, 43n, 160
Spy sloop, 66, 90, 100, 112
Stays, missing, 195
Stuart, Charles, the Young Pretender, 33
Stuart, J. E. B., 174, 175
Sugar industry, 5-7; Guadeloupe production, 73, 74; Guadeloupe sugar arrives on English market, 158; wealth of French, 182-3
Swedish Army, 13
Swiss soldiery, 113, 143, 145

Tathan, Reverend John, 21
Teesdale, Major Charles, 86, 87, 124-5, 161-2
Thomas, Governor George, on French intelligence, 36; recruiting efforts, 99; 109, 110; reports Tyrrell's action, 99n; sends laborers, 107; reports on trade of St. Eustatius, 133
Thumisseau, Peguireau de, 144n
Tobago (island), 12, 184
Trapaud, Lieutenant Colonel Cyrus, 22, 47, 105-7
Transports, 26, 29
Treil, Nadau Du, 139; orders cease fire at Morne Rouge, 81n; trial of, 83n; responsibility of abandoning citadel, 86, 87n; letters from Moore and Hopson, 89; characterized, 92; alleged

proposal to abandon lowlands, 93n; receives flag of truce, 94-5; occasions popular murmuring, 95n; requests evacuation of women and children, 101-2, 101n; on bad terms with his people, 123n; frees officers seized under flag, 132n; critique of leadership, 137-8, 138n, 176-8, 177n, 179, 179n-80n, 181; no cooperation with Beauharnois or Bompar, 144, 175; capitulations, 139-43
Trelawney, General Henry, 40n
Trelawney, Captain Sir William, 25, 40-1n, 43, 53, 79
Tribe, Benjamin, 21
Trinidad (island), 168, 184
Trois Rivières, 127; counter-desertion force, 123n; still French, 139; surrendered, 141, 149
Trollope, Major John, 96, 126
Trunnions, 45n
Tyrrell, Captain Richard, commands *Buckingham,* 78; joins fleet, 88; sent home, 89-90, 100; local hero, 99; action of 3 Nov. 1758, 99

Unicorn ship, 27
United States Navy, 187
Utrecht, Treaty of, 8, 11
Uvedale, Commander Samuel, 26

Vaillant ship, 116-7
Versailles, 161n, 178
Vestal frigate, 43n, 57n
Virgin Islands. *See* Danish West Indies
Virginia, 7, 9, 12, 174-5

Walpole, Robert, 13
War of Jenkins' Ear, 11

War of the Austrian Succession, 11, 188
War of the League of Augsburg, 10
War of the Spanish Succession, 8, 10
Warping and kedging, described, 193
Warwick ship, 15n, 34n
Washington, George, 12, 192
Water supply, limited, 38n; shortage on Martinique, 52, 53; Antigua, 73n; purchased for sick, 90; shipped in from Montserrat, 90n
Weazel sloop, 96, 100
West Florida, 184
West India Pilot, cited, 168, 180-1
West Indies, 19, 22, 23n, 25, 33, 108; rivalry in, 6; campaign of 1759, its purpose, 14; French privateers of, 15; disease in, 90. *See also* French, British, Danish, Netherlands West Indies; Neutral Islands
Whitehall, 112, 119, 163n
William ship, 27
William and Mary yacht, 20
William Henry, Fort, 13
Winchester ship, 40-1; ordered to islands, 25, 30, 31n; to attack at Cas Navires Bay, 43; at Basse Terre Roads, 75, 78; helps to land artillery, 101
Wolfe, General James, 157
Woolwich Arsenal, 22, 187
Woolwich frigate, 40-1, 78; on Leeward Islands Station, 26; at Cas Navires Bay, 43; flagship, 85; sent against Ft. Louis, 103; guards transports, 116; in attack on Arnoville, 129; carries news of victory, 150

York and Lancaster Regiment. *See* Regiment—65th
Yorktown, 184

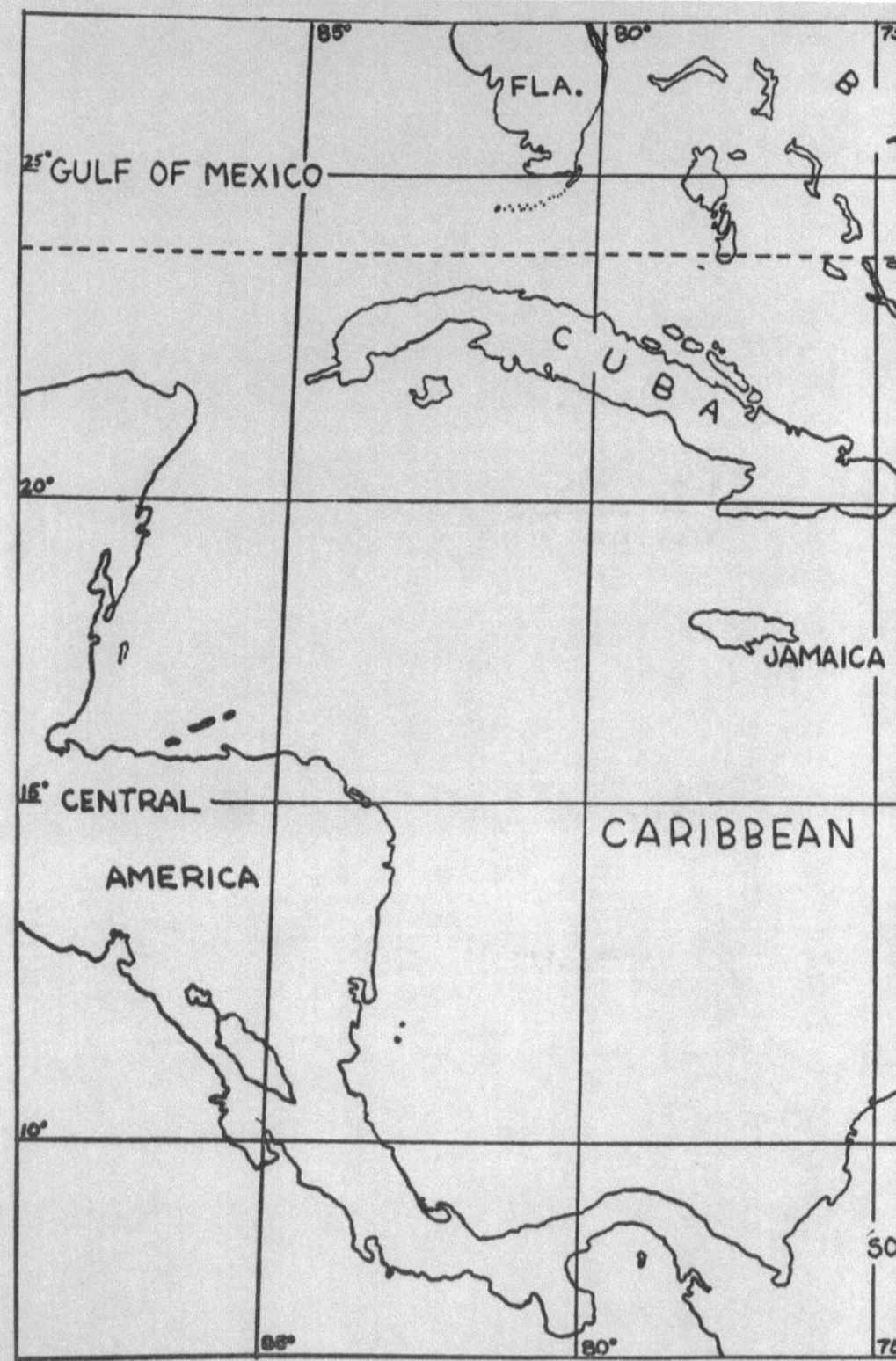

www.ingramcontent.com/pod-product-compliance
Lightning Source LLC
Chambersburg PA
CBHW021403290426
44108CB00010B/368